BARBARA CELARENT

Dialectica est tentativa, quia tentare proprium est ex principiis extraneis procedere. Secundum quod est utens recedit a modo scientiae. Oportet media multiplicari ad conclusionis manifestationem, ut in syllogismis dialecticis accidit.

ST THOMAS AQUINAS

BARBARA CELARENT

A Description of
Scholastic Dialectic

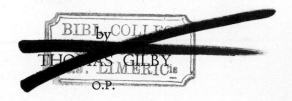

by

THOMAS GILBY

O.P.

LONGMANS GREEN AND CO
LONDON • NEW YORK • TORONTO

LONGMANS, GREEN AND CO LTD
6 & 7 CLIFFORD STREET LONDON WI
ALSO AT MELBOURNE AND CAPE TOWN

LONGMANS, GREEN AND CO INC
55 FIFTH AVENUE NEW YORK 3

LONGMANS, GREEN AND CO
215 VICTORIA STREET TORONTO I

ORIENT LONGMANS LTD
BOMBAY CALCUTTA MADRAS

First published . . . 1949

Printed in England
SPOTTISWOODE, BALLANTYNE & CO. LTD.
London & Colchester

To

ELIZABETH GULLY

CONTENTS

Introduction

INTRODUCTION

THESE pages were worked up in the Mediterranean between action stations in H.M.S. *Renown*, from rough notes all pulpy and partly indecipherable from the seas shipped when she was holed fighting but continuing to chase her two opposite numbers, *Scharnhorst* and *Gneisenau*, in the Arctic Circle. In attempting this picture of the thomist dialectic it was not altogether a disadvantage that there was nothing else but a miniature *Summa Theologica* to consult and no fair certainty of ever going to press. What is lacking in the apparatus may perhaps be made up in other ways, for while an elementary scholastic manual was not intended, neither was a scientific monograph on logical analysis, but rather a description of a habit of mind and method. Logic and dialectic are now overlapping terms; yet the original bent of the former is to pure form, while the latter mingles with the variety and sensibility of existing nature.[1] I thought, too, that a swing and a breeze from outside might be welcome where the conventional demeanour is rather stiff and the atmosphere often close. Some of this ease may remain despite the scholastic interpolations that have since been run in. Service language itself turns phrases with the ponderousness of the periwig period schoolmen, ordering the scheduled personnel to remove their dentures before submersion, not divers to take out their false teeth before going under. Technicalities can scarcely be avoided, and

> *English* cut on *Greek* and *Latin*,
> Like Fustian heretofore on Sattin.

Even so, the final version is not for the advanced student but for the general reader who would like to wander along an old, and perhaps beaten, track, and is prepared to take some dull bits in his stride. These notes on the route, based on the geography of the logic but meditating on the conditions of the dialectic, are offered

---

[1] Corresponding to the Aristotelean distinction between the apodictic logic of demonstration and the discourse on probabilities and suggestiveness. *Cf.* Commentary, VII *Metaphysics*, lect. 7. IV, lect. 4.

to those who can chuckle at the description of thomism in the *Concise Oxford Dictionary*—'theological doctrine of Thomas Aquinas (d. 1274) who maintained predestination and efficacious grace and denied the immaculate conception.' Some may be inclined to shape their thoughts to the classical discipline of the Christian West, and they may have an inkling that the doctrines are not confined to the Latin culture or the medieval centuries. They may already have caught a glimpse of a general design offering violence to none of the details of experience—nothing human strange to me, a claim that could not be urged without extravagance for some ideologies. Yet perhaps they have been baffled by the tangle of strange terms, and have felt like an explorer hacking his way through the Matto Grosso without chart, compass, or sight of the sky. These reflections, then, are for those who are discouraged by the entanglements of philosophy, but are suspicious of short cuts.

Tristram Shandy praised St Thomas for having so good a mechanical head, both for tying and untying the knots of school divinity; and so he had, yet with it a fundamental simplicity of thought. His sweep may engage the encyclopedist, his depth the mystic, his finesse the logical critic, nevertheless, as Mr Lewis Mumford observes, 'in no derogatory sense, one may call him a master of platitude, provided one adds that in medieval culture some of the platitudes of Greece and Rome came forth from their ancient graves as breathless discoveries.'[1] His thought has not grown old; it is not, like the Palace of Versailles, a monument to an age that is past, for his project was never completed like a building, but grows organically. It is not an accumulation of theorems nor an aggregation of parts.

Then as regards procedure, St Thomas himself compares wisdom and play,[2] and there is much to be said for philosophy being conducted like sport, and largely by amateurs. May they still thrive, 'the race of scholars who read Plato with their feet in the fender,' if only to bear witness to the union of science and letters. A smile is no enemy to truth; so are there sound reasons why a book on philosophy, which touches so many points of human interest and is implied in every adult experience and problem, should not be, to quote Doctor Johnson, 'a gay and vigorous dis-

---

[1] *The Condition of Man.*   [2] Opusc. IX, *de Hebdomadibus*, Prologue.

sertation,' easier reading than the treatises on economics and psychology the week-end student is offered? The subject is neither so tricky as the policies of Queen Elizabeth nor so taxes the memory as learning a new language. The reader will judge for himself, though he is warned that his start is beset by the grey thickets of logic. Having passed through them, he will find himself in more open country, well-watered and fertile, commanding wide views with mountain ranges in the distance. Some equipment of technical terms must be shouldered, nevertheless we are not out on an archaeological expedition. 'The less,' muses *Night Thoughts*, 'we copy the renowned Antients we shall ressemble them the more.'

A pictorial guide cannot miss some of the subtlety of the analysis, though the enlargement of purely logical details will be omitted as far as possible. The dialectic of probabilities verges on rhetoric, and we will risk mixing our metaphors instead. But the temper is direct, the statements of ordinary careful speech are taken as signs of philosophical thought, and the advance is not committed to mathematical transport. The process is neither a programme of formal logic nor an organization of stylized rhetoric. As one who begins with Xenophon may end with Plato, so a student of St Thomas, despite an early impression of burly and agile commonsense, soon discovers more than first meets the eye; many second thoughts to reflection; an ardour and refinement beneath the apparent composure and simplicity; an invitation to the specialist; even a readiness to enter the labyrinth of sophistication; and certainly more echoes than this book will sound. Dick Swiveller asked the Marchioness if she had ever tasted beer, and when she replied that once she had had a sip remarked, 'She has never *tasted* it. It can't be tasted in a sip.'

All the same, first reactions do fairly represent one side of a tradition of thought still alive, and even kicking, among people of no academic standing. St Thomas, however, remains a many-sided author, who cannot be known merely from consulting the indexes. To some scholars he is the last of the Fathers, to others the first of the moderns. He can work in a laboratory and yet renew the open-air discussions of the Greeks. His elaborate abstractions go with a decent respect for the common convictions of mankind. He can be imagined as one intent on far horizons, or, like a farmer, running soil through his fingers. Able to soar, and yet willing to walk, he spoke with pure intelligence and still remained an impenitent materialist.

His philosophy is never meant to remain a professional occupation. The Basques say that the devil devoted seven years trying to learn their language, and then gave it up as a bad job. How many have studied St Thomas for seven years, only for his philosophy at the end to be left in the class-room covered with chalk or treated as a kind of staff-college doctrine.[1] An account of his topics may prove to be not merely of biographical interest to those outside his tradition. For while their chief fascination is for the Christian whose customs are defended and mysteries so daringly yet soberly made reasonable, we would avoid here Charles Lamb's encomium on the man 'who did pretty well, upon the strength of being a tolerable antiquarian, and having a brother a bishop.' Whatever the historical and psychological antecedents, his attempt to take reason to its farthest frontiers, is a free and untrammelled operation, substantially devoid of special pleading. The appeal to authority is relegated to the lowest rank[2]: there is no inclination to adopt a deferential tone in any rationalist company.

This first volume is no more than a free commentary on the traditional logic according to terms, propositions, and arguments,

[1] The standard course of studies in scholastic philosophy begins with *logic*. Neglecting mathematics, the student then embarks on *natural philosophy*, which seeks to discover the general and enduring reasons at work in our physical environment, reasons beyond the power of a particular or passing technique to uncover. The first part of natural philosophy is often called *cosmology* and is concerned with the inanimate world; the second part, which considers animate things and chiefly human nature, is called *psychology*. Both these philosophical sciences differ from the experimental sciences of physics and psychology in that they do not stop at the data of observation and experiment and their correlation in a mathematical scheme, but, while preserving sensible qualities, go on to interpret them by the common principles of thought, which are the special interest of the science of *metaphysics*. The effort here is to elucidate reality as such, in the most general and simplified way, abstracted from the changes and particular problems of the material world. In the first place the student enquires into the validity of knowledge in the science of *epistemology*, goes on to analyse the content, properties, and consequences of reality in the science of *general metaphysics*, and finally investigates the existence and nature of the first and the last cause of being in the science of *natural theology*. He then descends to apply his metaphysical conclusions to what he knows of the nature of man from psychology, and in *moral philosophy* studies human activity as a means to fulfilment.

[2] *Summa Theologica*, 1a: I: 8, ad 2.

which, in stressing the dialectical rôle of analogy, describes the temper of a method, and pauses at some of the positions. Following its hero's advice[1] it will leave aside what is trifling, obscure, or highly technical in the teaching of the schoolmen, and will be directed to where, as Dante sings,[2] there is good nourishment if there be no straying.

[1] *Summa Theologica*, Prologue. Footnote references are to the works of St Thomas unless otherwise stated. Though his logical works are the two great commentaries on Aristotle's *de Interpretatione* (*Perihermenias*) and *Analytica Posteriora*—would that he had commented on the *Topics*—the majority are to the *Summa Theologica*, while probably the most important are to the fifth and sixth questions of his exposition on Boethius, *de Trinitate* (*Opusculum XVI*). The numbering of the *opuscula* follows the order established by Pierre Mandonnet, *Opuscula Omnia S. Thomae Aquinatis*, Paris, 1927.

[2] *Paradiso*, Canto 10.

PART ONE   LIMITATIONS

FIRST catch your hare. Before dialectics can be described, a theory must be secured; what logic is and what not must be defined before its extension into ordinary discourse can be considered. This preamble, or section on proemial logic, will amount in effect to a self-denying ordinance. For contrary to a widespread opinion, logic does not flood the bed of dialectics; it is but one stream, or rather, one channel for the flow. People sometimes have misgivings because unconsciously they exaggerate its force. The scholastics are supposed to have suffered from an overwhelming logomachy; their masterpieces, however, display a method well under control.

It is, in fact, an instrument for a humane and critical spirit indispensable for civilized thought, but insufficient by itself. Reflect on some examples: as a razor is used for shaving and a horse for hunting, so logic is used for the processes of connected and communicable thought. You may, indeed you should, grow so accustomed that the instrument is taken for granted; a keen razor passes without advertence and a fine rider is one with his mount; and so a practised thinker does not trip over an over-conscious logic. A rattlesnake does not listen for his own rattle. Training becomes second nature[1] and operates almost unnoticed. By logic a man thinks swiftly and accurately without wary anxiety about his mental states; his thinking has style; and style is effortless and confident, as you find to admiration in gentlemanly Georgian buildings and the despatches of Nelson, in the well tempered clavierchord and FrankWoolley making a century for Kent.

One must allow for the danger that a primer on etiquette may produce intellectual stammerers, who, according to Hazlitt, are delivered of their good things with pain and effort; and consequently what costs them such evident uneasiness does not impart unmixed delight to the bystanders. This book, however, is rather a defence of the scientific status of alliterative thinking than an

---

[1] *Summa Theologica*, 1a–2ae: XLIX: 3.

exhortation to qualified and grudging speech; though even so, when logic luxuriates into dialectic, some limits should be set.[1]

> Bind me, ye woodbines, in your twines;
> Curl me about, ye gadding vines;
> —But, lest your fetters prove too weak
> Do you, O brambles, chain me too,
> And courteous briars, nail me through.

When written up as a special study, logic may appear to be a nagging discipline, yet its purpose is to ease, not to cramp; to make for grace, not gawkiness. There is a proper way of thinking as there is a proper way of walking; you can shamble and still be able to move from place to place, just as you can have untidy thoughts and still be able to reach conclusions.

Our mental processes, then, need to be trained. Though dialectic will give the suppleness, nothing but logic will give the poise. The discipline can be learnt, for human minds are more apt to think logically than fingers are to play the pianoforte: the result is by practice out of nature. If our thoughts are to be read they must be legible; dialectics will illustrate them, but logic is required to set them in the appropriate severity of type. This is not for scholars alone but for the people: the need is past politeness; survival is at stake, not merely elegance. We dare not give in to majority moods, nor fall for the catchwords and personalities and scoops, but must set ourselves to converse from a lively and humble sense of the facts we are certain of: there will be no rebuilding from the ruins around us unless we begin from the personal integrity of exact thought: humanly speaking there is no other foundation for civilization, nor for religion. Unreason is more cruel than hate, for then law itself becomes the dictate of desire acting according to opportunity, not the measure of encouragement and restraint according to meaning.[2] The universe yields a law and a logic. We do not make them up for ourselves, what we contribute is probably the dialectic and certainly the rhetoric. Now moral effort alone is unable to correct intellectual error; the

---

[1] *Summa Theologica,* 2a–2ae: CLXVII: 1.

[2] Here, according to Hans Frank at the Nuremburg Trials, was Hitler's most serious shortcoming; 'every legal expert to him was a disturbing influence.' For reason in law, cf. *Summa Theologica,* 1a–2ae: XVII: 1. XC: 1.

cure begins in the will to think scientifically. This is not cold comfort, for of its nature the mind is the least lonely of powers,[1] and reasoned meaning, more intimate than affection and more lasting than passion, is the condition of companionship.[2]

---

[1] *Summa Theologica*, 1a–2ae: III: 4.

[2] Logic is part of the courtesy of conversation, attaching to the virtues of friendliness (*Summa Theologica*, 2a–2ae: CXIV: 2) and pleasantness (2a–2ae: CLXVIII: 1, 2), which are bound up with truthfulness (2a–2ae: CIX: 3), for without ease, modesty, and exactness men cannot dwell together.

CHAPTER I

ORGANON

LOGIC is no more a special doctrine than English grammar is a peculiar language; indeed it is to thought what grammar is to language. But while you can learn to write good idiomatic English without applying yourselves to grammar from a careful reading of English letters, as children can learn to feed themselves without a knowledge of dietetics, it is doubtful whether useful argument can be sustained without conscious reference to the rules. You can be understood even if you speak ungrammatically—like the little girl's reply, 'er ain't a-calling we, us don't belong to she,'— but if you are illogical there are no secure communications. Logic amounts to a social duty, though the precept is probably affirmative, which means that the obligation, like that of honouring one's parents and unlike the negative precept of doing no murder, is not continuously binding. We are not always required to speak in a sober and severely rational spirit, and a humane logic of concepts will tolerate the dialectic of fantasy, for we are not in a world of types, but of things half-meaning, half-movement. What may be called logical spoonerisms sometimes strike a light; nonsense verse may be an escape for the univocally-minded scientist who has not yet discovered freedom under the law of analogy; inconsequence may be instructive as well as charming. Yet a temperate logic composes the standards of appreciation. Even madness, as in *King Lear*, must be set against a background of sanity. While admitting that the formal schemes of argument, as displayed in the old classical logic, may have to be stretched to accommodate the freest play of philosophical understanding, and that new modes of statement and inference have since been developed or explicitly recognized, nevertheless we cannot conclude that the ancient models are obsolete.

Aristotle is the father of the science of logic, the systematic reflection on the purely mental patterns of thought; his work on the subject survived to exercise a profound influence on the West before his other treatises were recovered. His texts formed what was

4

known as the Organon, the instrument or method; a means, there-fore, and not an end in itself. It is a servant, and not a master science; logical entities, says St Thomas, are not taken for their own sake but as props for other sciences, and he quotes Boethius with approval, logic is not so much a science as an engine of science.[1]

Perhaps too much was claimed in the later middle ages and afterwards, as too much was feared some centuries before when the Abbot of Cluny could write to Heloïse; 'Well hast thou changed thy pursuits, and like a wise woman hast chosen the Gos-pel instead of Logic,' adding in the same vein, 'the Epistles in-stead of Physics, the Cloister instead of the Academy.' Logic indeed may be taken to comprise a collection of doctrines on all manner of subjects, from metaphysical criticism of knowledge and psychological enquiry into the conditions of consciousness, to purely mental analysis and linguistic discussions about the origin and application of words. In the strict sense it stands for the study of the figures of valid inference and scientific method, and as such need assume no attitude with regard to the nature of existing reality. Though the subject of this book is dialectic, looser, richer and more conversational, including the practice of myth, analogy, and the convergence of probabilities, we must still consider the central logical forms round which all dialectical processes revolve.[2]

Clearness is not enough. Logic itself does not compose the picture, it is not even the lens through which things are seen, but rather the appropriate aperture, focus, and exposure. For this reason one hesitates over classing it among the sciences, for *scientia speculativa*, an achievement of the theoretical reason, is the habit of seeing real and objective truths in their principles, of discovering conclusions about existents.[3] The effort of constructing arguments in correct form is the work of the practical reason, *intellectus prac-ticus* or *operativus*,[4] a function of art rather than of science. There is, of course, a theory of purely mental form, apodictic logic,

---

[1] Opusc. XVI, V *de Trinitate*, 1, *ad* 2.

[2] Commentary, VII *Metaphysics*, *lect*. 17. *Summa Theologica*, 2a–2ae: XLVIII.

[3] *Summa Theologica*, 1a–2ae: LVII: 2.

[4] *Ibid.*, 1a: LXXIX: 11. 1a–2a: LVII: 3. Commentary, I *Posterior Analytics*, *lect*. 1.

logica demonstrativa or *logica secundum quod est docens,* concerned more with the coherence of concepts, and perhaps with their elegance, than with their correspondence to an existing environment; nevertheless our main interest is in its application, *secundum quod est utens,* and this *dialectica tentativa,* as St Thomas notes, withdraws from the restraints of science.[1]

Can we conclude that logic unadorned is a tedious subject for special discussion, all manners and no substance, all plot and no passion, the study of possible shapes without heed to what is shaped, a piece of abstract art—almost a contradiction in terms; or shall we not recognize that it is an essential factor in human expression and satisfaction? The system of thought should be treated as an internal skeleton, not a carapace; minds should be like bodies, bony not filleted, and the supple tissues of dialectic should clothe the pattern of logic. There are shapes in the movement of intelligent intercourse.

Logic is the art and science of thinking correctly, especially on subjects that admit of cogent demonstration,[2] while dialectic is its companionable extension into matters where we must be content with descriptions and probable assents. We shall consider dialectic later; so far as logic is concerned, there are three terms to be seized on, namely art, science, correct.

Arts and sciences are settled mental qualities enabling us to grasp and direct the objects of experience and respond with ease to a given situation.[3] By arithmetic we are ready to deal with figures, or by the art of small boat sailing we swiftly appreciate wind and tide and only less swiftly make the necessary muscular adjustments. But whereas a science is a theoretical cast of mind, a habit of drawing conclusions from premises and assenting to their truth, an art is a practical bent, a rooted aptitude for effecting something useful or enjoyable. Science deduces but art produces. Though art works through technical skill, the scholastics insist on the intellectualism of this ability; it is the *recta ratio factibilium,*[4] the right idea of things to be made, the effective plan of realizing a conception. Logic is the art of arts, liberal and not mechanical, directed to produce aright a quasi-externalized object,

---

[1] Commentary, IV *Metaphysics, lect.* 4.
[2] *Summa Theologica,* 2a–2ae: XLVII: 2, *ad* 3.
[3] *Ibid.,* 1a–2ae: XLIX: 4.
[4] *Ibid.,* 1a–2ae: LVII: 3.

that artefact or *opus aliquod* which is the proper arrangement of reasoning, a job as enduring, though not so solid and visible, as anything in marble or bronze.[1] The emphasis is on the thing to be done, not, as in the moral virtues, on our personal dispositions in doing it. Our expressed thoughts are the material of this art, and logic is no less practical than an escort vessel making order from a tangle and shepherding the merchantmen through the swept channel.[2]

Now the mind is single despite the diversity of its interests[3]; how we act is explained by how we think. A human operation is attempted according to a theoretical plan. The activity of art, unlike happy doodling, is controlled and presupposes forethought and speculation. Consequently there is a scientific side to logic, the study, detached and reflective, of the proper rules of thought and the analysis of their forms.[4] And previous to the expectation of any practical advantage from its adoption, logic can share with mathematics and metaphysics the characteristics of pure understanding, and, like all the sciences, be animated with a disinterested curiosity that does not require that knowledge should be turned to profit.

Men caught a glimpse of the claims of truth beyond their immediate advantage when they left astrology for astronomy. Their impulse was to theorize, to know for the sake of knowing, to find out the answer regardless of safety and comfort. This trait still characterizes the scientist. Yet the early philosophers can scarcely be called unpractical dreamers: Thales, the first of them, was shrewd enough, it is reported, to make a corner in oil, though another legend recounts how he fell into a well; Aristotle, who closes the golden period, was statesman, doctor, dramatic critic, and field-naturalist into the bargain. The British philosophers, from Alcuin and Anselm, through Bacon, Herbert, Hobbes, Locke, to Haldane, Balfour, and Smuts, have played a notable

---

[1] Commentary, I *Posterior Analytics*, *lect*. 1.   *Summa Theologica*, 1a–2ae: LVII: 3. V *de Trinitate*, V: 1, *ad* 3.

[2] Dialectic deals rather with the strategy than with the tactical disposition of thought, or, to continue the comparison, it is the convoying of serviceable thoughts from one place to another.   *Cf.* Aristotle, *Topics*, Bk. I, ch. 1–3.

[3] *Summa Theologica*, 1a: LXXIX: 9, 10, 11.

[4] *Ibid.*, 1a: XIV: 16.

part in public affairs; even Berkeley's idealism went with a bishopric and preaching the panacea of tar-water. The medievals, too, sought restlessly for the elixir of life and the philosopher's stone, and, less ambitious, translated their theories into government and worked out a system of social and economic relationships that may still excite our envy. Albertus Magnus, the master of St Thomas, was a legendary magician, occupied with elaborate technical contrivances well in advance of his time; St Thomas himself, at the time of his death, was composing a treatise on aqueducts and a commentary on the *Song of Songs*. Yet all of them took for granted that truth was its own reward, and theoretical, or as they would say, speculative, was for them a term of praise, not of reproach.[1]

Since then has grown the fashion of dealing with theories, and especially moral theories, as though they were utopian. Hardheaded men of affairs are supposed to be deterred by no ideals from getting what they want. But on reflection it is seen that a successful *Realpolitik* starts from a clearly defined theory; an exponent such as Bismarck had a strong ideal, not necessarily a good one, but so plain and paramount that all else was subservient. It is ideals that are persevering and ruthless, and opportunism that must give way or be content with the shifts of expediency. The peacemakers of Vienna appear to have had at once a clearer plan and a more temperate sense of practicality than those of Versailles, and their work in consequence was more lasting. There is a theory behind the traditional practice of British foreign diplomacy. Or again, think of Richelieu, then pass on to Metternich, Cavour, and Roosevelt, and the same lesson is brought home. While who exceeds Lenin, that *homme très théorique*, as a shaper of contemporary history?

The successful realists are the convinced idealists. Yet we tend to over-emphasize the division between theory and practice, forgetting that strong ideas bubble over into activity, and that unless backed and fed by centres of pure research the institutes of technology would go no further than to refine the current applications of physics. There is a similar need for higher studies in all departments, not least in theology. We think of idealism as noble enough but remote, while realism becomes expedience, a flexible

---

[1] *Summa Theologica*, 1a: XIV: 16. XXIX: 11. 1a–2ae: III: 5. LVII: 1, 2, 3.

accommodation to the turn of affairs. Yet our choices are chaotic unless directed by a principle. We recognize of course that theories are often prompted by practical needs, as in the case of the mathematical treatment of probability, which arose from the problem of how to divide the stakes in an unfinished game of chance. Part of the trouble is that contemplation no longer appears to us, as it did to the Greeks and St Thomas, as the highest form of vitality; knowledge has become cerebral and opposed to strong and vivid action, reason has flown to our head. 'No, Sir'; said Dr. Johnson, 'were Socrates and Charles the Twelfth of Sweden both present in any company, and Socrates to say, "Follow me, and hear a lecture in philosophy"; and Charles, laying his hand on his sword, to say, "Follow me, and dethrone the Czar"; a man would be ashamed to follow Socrates. Sir, the impression is universal; yet it is strange.'

Behind the cunning of constructing cogent arguments, the art of logic, there lies the theoretical science, the elucidation of conclusions demonstrated from their proper principles, in this case, the conditions, canons, and consequences of the correct orchestration of thought. Both must be set in the wider plan of dialectic, and both, the craft and the theory, should go together, though sometimes they are found apart. French peasants may be practical logicians without being versed in the rules; learned men may be well informed about theories and yet jump their proofs. The art comes from practice, the science from examination of the modes of argument, and here correctness is called for, rather than truth.

There is a difference between the two, as between stage property food and real food. You can argue correctly from a false position to a false conclusion, you may start with a mistake and end with one, and yet not be logically awry. As a logical performance the demonstration may be faultless, as when a thorough paced pantheist infers that individual responsibility is an illusion, or an old-fashioned marxist sets out to abolish organized religion.

Nearly every article in the *Summa Theologica* sets off with objections against the position the author is going to establish; and usually the cutting edge of the logic is neither bent nor blunt. Take an objection almost at random against the simplicity of God: the best must be attributed to God, but rich diversity is nobler than simplicity, compounds are higher than their elements, and

therefore we should not say that God is wholly simple.[1] The reply
must turn on the meaning of the term simplicity. Or take another
example of an argument in which all the statements are doubtful,
if not false, and which is yet free from logical flaw: I am told that
people devoid of humour cannot appreciate *Punch*—moreover I
believe that no Scotsman has a sense of humour—then I infer correctly that no Scotsman appreciates *Punch*.[2]

When arguments can be strong and their conclusions inadmissible, the inadequacy of logic alone in the search for truth is revealed. Unlike the other sciences, it provides no food for thought,
though it prepares the food. It works indifferently with true and
false doctrines, with sobriety and whim. People who are mentally ill sometimes argue without deviation to the most bizarre
conclusions, there is a perseveration in their train of thought lacking in the healthy-minded; their sense of fact is at fault, not their
logic. At a less morbid level we are rightly suspicious of doc-
trinaires with little knowledge of history, familiarity with the lives
of ordinary families, or respect for the inarticulate. To be definite, but not informed; to draw the uttermost conclusions from
imperfectly established premisses; to be clever without a sense of
proportion; to impose a simplified scheme without discrimination;
to plan arguments untested by experience and hatch principles to
suit already adopted conclusions; these are instances of logic
running by itself without anything to bite on, with results similar
to those of racing an engine in neutral gear.

The beautifully wrought constructions and the smooth and
excellent finish Saint Saëns applies to sound are not sufficient to
arouse and prolong our interest; and so logic alone will not provide
the sense of reality, nor even the zest for discovery. It has no
special message in comparison with living literature, it is like the
book of the film of the book. There are Christian thinkers who
base their conviction of the existence and providence of God on
mystical rather than on rational grounds, and who hold that
Christianity is valid as a vehicle of experience, not for its manifestation of intellectual evidence; they sometimes refer to the

---

[1] *Summa Theologica*, 1a: III: 7, obj. 2.

[2] Here, as frequently hereafter, we shall make use of what St Thomas calls
exemplary arguments, adduced to illustrate a pattern, not to expound a thesis.
Opusc. XLIII, *On Fallacies*, ch. 1.

classical theology of Catholicism as though it were a system of
Hegelianism aiming to reach the truths of divinity by pure logic,
whereas in point of fact logic is about as important to the *Summa
Theologica* as the cage of masonry is to the architectural, social, and
religious purposes of a contemporary Gothic cathedral.

A prime minister once warned the Commons to beware of
needless innovations, 'especially when guided by logic'; he was
warming to a truth, namely that logic is all very well, but there
comes a stage when a man is not a logician, but just a crank, when
he would construct schemes without reference to real conditions,
and exact shapes from material that will not tolerate them. There
are limits to what logic can do; it is but the mould of rational discourse, empty of itself and needing to be filled from the other
sciences. A man may train himself to logic and find himself in the
fix of the visitor in *Walden* who was earnest to be introduced to a
distinguished deaf sibyl, but when he came to be presented, and
one end of the ear trumpet was put in his hand, then had nothing
to say. To be in possession of the instrument, but of little else,
will impart the unreality, but not always the felicity of Marjorie
Fleming's lines to her pug:

> I could not get a rhyme for Roman,
> So was obliged to call him woman.

The schoolmen of the decadence may have tried to torture the
data of experience into their categories, but if they are accused of
logic-chopping, we shall be more accurate if we mean that they
chopped with, not at, logic. For their logic does not pretend to
reflect on existents, but on mental modes and connections in our
abstract consciousness. As somebody has said, somewhat un-
kindly, it is the ability to rush round and round inside without
getting dizzy. There was always a steady tradition of humanism
among the scholastics, going back to the school of Chartres, and
the awareness of the artificial quality of logic kept many of them
from the chicanery of verbalisms and provoked their criticism of
the *nugiloqui ventilatores,* as John of Salisbury called them, the fans
of futile phrases.

Yet logic will assist in the correct conduct of our approach to
real objects of scientific enquiry; it sets the measure for all
reasoned knowledge, and as such is the first part of scientific

discipline.[1] We shall be warned against mistaking ejaculations for
explanations, particular instances for general rules, intuitions for
demonstrations. Few interests need more to be supplemented by
experience and resource, such as prompted the reply of the Duke
of Wellington to Queen Victoria; incommoded by the nuisance
committed by the sparrows in the glass palace of the Great Exhibition, she asked for a remedy, and had the reply, 'Sparrowhawks, ma'am, sparrowhawks.' It cannot supply good sense and
good feeling, nor, to take the widest view, can it work without the
play of dialectic; nevertheless logic is indispensable if realistic
thought is to be controlled and communicative; what has been
said about its insufficiency applies in a less degree to all the
sciences, which enclose but a part of reality. The business of living
requires that we venture and sometimes jump beyond the demonstrated evidence; the management of everyday affairs cannot be
exercised with scientific reticence; on many issues theoretical certitude cannot be sought and probability is enough for decision.[2]
Risks must sometimes be taken, and as both Horace and St
Thomas have noticed in their different ways there are occasions
when a sufficient motive for virtue is that it's foolish but it's fun.[3]

---

[1] V *de Trinitate*, 1, *ad* 3.
[2] *Summa Theologica*, 2a–2ae: LXX: 2.
[3] *Ibid.*, 2a–2ae: CLXVIII: 4.

If correct logic does not guarantee truth neither does incorrect logic necessarily spell falsehood. There are bad arguments for the truth, even when all the
statements taken by themselves may be true enough. Yet together they compose
an ineffective proof. Frequently arguments are cast in this form: *a* is *b*, and *c* is *b*,
and therefore *c* is *a*. For example: wishful thinking is a comfort, and religion is
a comfort, and so religion is wishful thinking.

CHAPTER II

LIMITED OBJECTIVE

THINKING goes through the successive stages of conceiving a thought, passing a verdict, drawing a conclusion. God—is our refuge—therefore we will not fear. There you see the three parts, the apprehending, the judging, the reasoning, or, in scholastic terminology, the *simplex apprehensio*, the *judicium*, and the *ratiocinium*, which are, as it were, the logical chassis to which our thinking can be stripped, whether the style be ornate, or as economical as Jane Austen's opening: 'About thirty years ago, Miss Maria Ward, of Huntingdon, with only seven thousand pounds, had the good luck to captivate Sir Thomas Bertram, of Mansfield Park, in the county of Northampton, and to be thereby raised to the rank of a baronet's lady, with all the comforts and consequences of a handsome house and a large income.' The treatises on the traditional logic are usually arranged according to this threefold division; they start by considering terms, pass on to the sense of propositions, and end with an examination of arguments.

As we have already noted logic is occupied, not with the alleged correspondence of mental and verbal forms with reality, which is the burden of critical philosophy, nor with ideas and words as responses to environment, which is a subject for psychology, but with their muster and arrangement. Though it will help to give the hang of a situation, the primary function of logic is to tidy whatsoever is presented without discriminating between the true and the false, the useful and the futile, the handsome and the drab. It can do this because like all specialized aptitudes it makes an abstraction[1]; indeed the abstraction in logic is more extreme than in the other sciences.

Abstraction and distraction may suggest the same mood of woolgathering, yet they are quite different, for one is a concentration and steadiness, the other a dissipation and wandering away. Abstract is like extract; you draw off what is wanted, and leave the rest. One aspect is kept in view without reference to other sides

---

[1] *Summa Theologica*, 1a: XL: 3. LXXXV: 1.

and accompaniments; the object is considered as a flat form, and not in the round.[1] Thus at a show a judge first takes the points of a dog one by one before taking him as a whole. Notice that such an abstraction marks only a temporary period. For unless checked by a regard for the many-sidedness of things,[2] and inspired by a desire to hold them complete and entire, the process may produce an attenuated object.[3] Abstraction can go so far as to arrive at what is quite unreal, curvature without a line or chastity without emotion. Abstract can be piled on abstract, and never yield the concrete.[4] To mistake an isolated form for the real thing is a false substitution,[5] so also to treat the abstract form as the substantial form.[6]

Here we touch on the perennial opposition, implicit in scholastic dialectic as in human experience, between types and things, between the contemplation of separate substances and the embrace of the living God, between the rational animal and historical man, and between a formal logic and a living dialogue. And yet by a paradox the greatest achievements seem to demand a certain fanaticism and narrowness of mind. Though he was speaking in another connection Heraclitus may be recalled; the dry soul, he said, is the wisest and best. The human mind is, for the present, incurably formal[7]; there is an accent of abstraction in all our know-

---

[1] We speak throughout of *formal abstraction*, the fixing of one form in a complex subject, as when we consider the hue of a rose without attending to its scent or shape; not of what is called total *abstraction*, the establishment of a simple idea that may include many things, as when we try to consider the essential meaning of humanity without reckoning with individuals; some such abstraction from mere individuality is the condition of all knowledge. *Cf.* V *de Trinitate*, 2, 3. Opusc. X, *de Causis, lect.* 10.

[2] St Thomas recognizes that separation is too strong a term for abstraction, which, while understanding one note without another, implies that in reality they are compounded in the same reality; and so we do not speak of abstracting *animal* from *stone* when we conceive the two apart. Commentary, III *de Anima, lect.* 12. V *de Trinitate*, 3.

[3] What is mingled, says St Thomas, charms more than what is uncompounded, as harmony more than a single bass or treble note. Commentary, III *de Anima, lect.* 2.

[4] *Summa Theologica*, 1a–2ae: LIX: 5.

[5] *Ibid.*, 1a: LXXXV: 1, *ad* 1.

[6] V *de Trinitate*, 3.

[7] Disputations, X *de Veritate*, 5.

ledge, even the freshest and most lyrical; in the rational examination of any subject a selection must be made between foreground
and background, between what is significant, special, and to the
point, and what is supernumerary, general, and taken for granted.
The old scholastic dualism of formal and material is present in all
enquiry. All the activities of knowing would stammer together
in one inarticulate experience but for this discrimination.

One science or art is discerned from another by the distinctness of its own special abstraction.[1] The instructor in geometry
draws triangles and circles on the blackboard heedless whether the
chalk be yellow or white, for his science makes abstraction from
colour. The engineer does not dwell on the beauty of the view
from the top of the bridge he is designing, for his art is oblivious
of the picturesque. The boundaries of the particular sciences must
be accepted as conditions of their effectiveness and independence,
inside which they have their proper field of freedom, and beyond
which they are trespassers. How far they are subordinate to a
general science, if such exists,[2] is another question, and one of the
purposes of dialectic will be to show how they are all penetrated and
may be illustrated by communicating analogies. Yet without an
initial limitation, our reasoned approach to the nature of our environment will be as aimless and wasteful as loosing off ammunition at random. Every discussion becomes muddled unless it
starts with a definition: take, for instance, the subject of nationality; we have to decide whether we are treating it as a juridical
concept, or a historical, or a psychological, or a biological, or what.

All rational science lays this formal emphasis. And one thing

---

1 V *de Trinitate*, I. Commentary, I *Posterior Analytics, lect.* 41.

2 In his original distinction of the sciences St Thomas adopts the three Aristotelean degrees of abstraction. In the first degree the mind makes abstraction
from individuating conditions and considers material things in general as subject
to change, *ens mobile*; this is the level of natural science and natural philosophy.
In the second degree, a further abstraction is made to objects purely as quanti-
fied, *ens quantum*, as when from the physical abstraction 'snub-nosed' you proceed to consider 'curvature.' Beyond this, in the third degree, metaphysics
begins; reality is freed from all material notes and considered simply as being,
speculat ens in quantum ens. The division does not rule out free communication
nor the existence of border sciences, such as mathematical physics, or symbolic
logic, or metaphysical morals. *Cf.* Commentary, I *Physics, lect.* 1. II: *lect.* 3.
VI *Metaphysics, lect.* 1. V *de Trinitate*, I. VI: 2. *Summa Theologica*, 1a: XLIV: 2.

at a time, the habit of sticking to the point, of keeping your eye on the ball, is no whit less necessary in the conduct of affairs as well, and marks the difference between the elder Moltke's campaign that led to Sadowa and the clumsy lungeings of Austrians and Russians in the autumn in 1914. Our world is not in such a flux, says St Thomas,[1] that we can fasten on nothing; the blame for wavering knowledge lies on us, not on reality. We are prone to change the subject or shift the ground, perhaps more so with theoretical discussion than with practical decision. A dentist is not chosen because he is a good companion, but because he stops teeth or takes them out efficiently and painlessly. St Teresa of Avila applied the same rule when she bade her nuns seek the direction of an expert theologian not conspicuous for his sanctity in preference to that of a devout ignoramus. The natural faculties have an inborn drive, the sight goes directly to colour and the hearing to sound; the acquired habits have to be disciplined to a similar concentration, otherwise there is dissipation in miscellaneous activity: lacking a trained appreciation of relevant features, a power of keeping our head and dealing with the immediate object in an orderly manner, we go milling about, like the man St Paul speaks of, threshing the air.

The special target of a science or of any activity is called by the scholastics its formal object, *objectum formale*.[2] This is the business in hand, and everything else must be forgotten for the moment. Warmth and hues disappear in the polar light, and the various sciences are fixed in the nipping air of abstraction[3]: the traditional mathematician freezes everything to numbers, the logician everything to internal coherence and mental relevance; both are studiously remote from the juice and humours of life, yet both recognize, if they be wise and humane, that their self-denying ordinance is a temporary phase of asceticism and that they are insulated from anxiety and disturbing experiences like a man under vows. But lean and spare from economy, and even frugality, the mind practises self-denial and simplifies a complex reality only that a rounded reality may be born again; a dull calm precedes the many-twinkling smile of ocean. Mathematics leads to the discovery

---

[1] Commentary, II *Metaphysics, lect.* 1.
[2] *Summa Theologica*, 1a: 1: 1, *ad* 2. 1a–2ae: LX: 5. 2a–2ae: I: 1. IX: 2, *ad* 3.
[3] *Ibid.*, 1a: LXXVII: 3. 1a–2ae: XVIII: 2.

of real patterns in nature, logic to the dialectic of conversation. All special activities start by making a selection from what seems a welter, they take to pieces and single out, and then, in association with one another, rebuild the very thing from which they seemed to withdraw; once a puzzle, an incident of fragility and perhaps of pathos, whereas now become a meaning and a presage.

Poeta nascitur, non fit, is a tag not seldom abused; aesthetical philosophy and mystical theology alike bear witness that discipline is indispensable to achievement; apart from good fortune or extraordinary favour, there are no spoiled darlings, but only the invitation to drudgery and denial.[1] The life of reason calls for solitude and poverty of spirit as much as does the life of perfection: indeed at their best are they different? Yet the detachment is but a method; the drive is to attachment, no longer furtive and fugitive, but open and enduring. The sciences make an enclosure, but true as they may be their abstract objects are not complete, they are rather means than ends; though mind holds the primacy in happiness,[2] its final joy is not to be found in the thoughts of the speculative sciences.[3] Towards the end of his life, St Thomas said that his theological writings were *sicut palea*, like chaff; logic is even dustier; yet both are necessary if ultimately we are to be caught up into the vision where nothing is wanting.[4] In the meantime logic should go into dialectic as theology goes into liturgy and mathematics into music. The course of studies at a medieval university may be recalled: the *trivium* of grammar, logic, and rhetoric, preparing for the *quadrivium* of arithmetic, geometry, music, and astronomy.

In practice the separation of the sciences is sometimes difficult to maintain; the medical psychologist is exercised to keep off morality and the spiritual director to decant sin from neurosis; while in theory there is a similar difficulty as well; organic chemistry shades off into physiology, physiology into psychology,

---

[1] Commentary, VII *Ethics, lect.* 1. III *Contra Gentes,* 92.
[2] *Summa Theologica,* 1a–2ae: III: 4. Commentary, X *Ethics, lect.* 11.
[3] *Ibid.,* 1a–2ae: III: 6.
[4] *Ibid.,* 1a: XII: 1, 2. 1a–2ae: III: 8.
Nelson knew what he was doing at Copenhagen when he turned his blind eye to the admiral's signal. A special scientist must have a similar *docta ignorantia.*

psychology into ethics, and, in a sense, general philosophy covers them all. Moreover, the non-professional approach and the free play of dialectic offer advantages; guerilla warfare is not subject to the rule against crossing lines of communication which governs the movement of organized armies. Nevertheless the principle remains good that the world cannot be scientifically worked without specialization, and this spells the methodic exclusion of what is not relevant to the formal object.

Such are the demands of practical necessity and academic refinement alike: oblivious of them, naval architects in the beginning of the century built the large and heavy cruisers that were to prove so useless and unfortunate. In the words of Brassey,[1] 'For if a cruiser is to be so powerfully built as to be capable of taking her place in a battleship action, it would surely be more sensible to go the whole hog and build her as a battleship; while if her true function is to act as a scout, there would seem to be no need to place her in rivalry to the capital ship. Confusion of object was beginning to creep in.' Those were the days of John Fisher, but the Germans made a similar mistake in the design of their pocket battleships at the beginning of the war, when also confusion of object reigned over the design of British naval aircraft, which were crammed with apparatus for reconnaissance, fighting, bombing, and delivering torpedo attacks, with the result that they were efficient for none of these purposes. One specialized instrument must be limited to one job. General intelligence, it is true, has the quality of being an all-rounder, but this does not come from overloading, but from a strong and flexible central control, the power of co-ordination and adaptation, of seeing the analogies linking apparently disparate things, of resolving the anagrams of reality, of taking logic into dialectic.

It is probable that we are witnessing a reaction against specialization, understandable when we reflect how dangerously the specialists can drive their processes when they have no regard for others on the road. But the reaction goes too far when it invites physicists to descant on religion, and divines to dogmatize on physical science. A man who is both physicist and theologian is to be envied, so long as he respects the integrity of his two distinct

---

[1] *Naval Annual,* 1939.

sciences, and, while trying to harmonize them, resists the temptation of merging them. He will refuse alike to prove the existence
of God in terms proper to physical science, or to grind empirical
research with religious conviction.

In dealing later with analogy, which is the blood-stream of
dialectic, we shall indicate how the different aspects of things may
be seen together in one serene yet exciting vision,[1] for there is a
society in contrast,[2] a variety to be resolved into unity, a motion
into rest. Yet distinguish in order to unite; the parts must be
taken separately for the whole to be possessed. Specialization,
however, can be taken too far. 'If you know only medicine,' said
an old Spanish physician, 'you don't know that.' There is some
excuse for the pell-mell of the sciences; all are functions of one
and the same human nature, divergent and mixed in its elements,
untidy and ambitious in its energies, more apt to jump and flounder
than pick a dainty way.[3] The organism is single yet compound,
moods colour the motions of the will,[4] sensibility enters understanding, and the mind would play with a great variety of notes.
Normally constituted people find it difficult to pursue one track
of enquiry without gazing at the landscape or exploring other
paths. Some degree of oscillation is a condition of mental health.
Life thrusts us beyond our original premisses. What begins as
mysticism ends as politics, moments of vision and decision develop into accommodations with convention, philosophy runs into
the line of literature, biology into religion, psychology into ethics,
mathematics descends to dealing with coupons.

Religious doctrine does not devour metaphysics, nor metaphysics and mathematics the natural sciences.[5] With stronger
reason must the special sciences be kept within their bounds, and
even more the special techniques be prevented from invading
what is not their field. Scientific gate-crashing can be detected
with fair ease in many cases; but sometimes it may be covered with
the prestige of powerful names. There have been insufferable
attempts to explain the whole of life in terms of one half-educated

[1] *Summa Theologica*, 1a: I: 3, *ad* 2.
[2] *Ibid.*, 1a: XIII: 4.
[3] *Ibid.*, 1a–2ae: LXXII: 1, 3. LXXV: 3.
[4] *Ibid.*, 1a–2ae: X: 3.
[5] V *de Trinitate*, 1, *ad* 6.

way of knowledge. Sects have claimed the name of Catholic, but
laboratory workers as well as church workers have been parochially
minded; and if religious people have been accused of counting only
those persons or things of value that could be set on the path of
salvation painted in revivalist colours, a very narrow path with
steep tumbling slopes to perdition on either side, the schools of
science, notably of psychology, have like-minded votaries, with
similar pretensions to conversion and exclusive righteousness. But
it has been left for modern totalitarianism to produce a cramping
political theory and a ruthless practice of government to which
every human interest must be subservient. Galileo was not the
last scientist to be subjected to an inquisition; the Planned State
threatens to dictate in the name of tame comfort and efficiency all
the public motions of the mind, and to condition its intimate
convictions into the bargain. Nazi biology and Marxist history
have been more of a menace to the expanse and freedom of science
than bibliolatry ever was, though all three are inadmissible. The
declaration of a Russian medical institute—'we stand for the
purity of Marxist-Leninist surgery'—is fallacious as well as intimi-
dating. The notion of Catholic medicine is not free from the
same confusion. Mother-love is just manganese, that is another
example from the days of confident materialism of mixing the
sciences; while earlier there was the substitution of piety for
hygiene when cholera was treated with resignation to the wrath of
God and left at that.

Yet all activities are at work on the same raw material, and all
the sciences take their start, more or less directly, from the world
we experience through the senses. This is the common stuff,
worked up and elaborated in different fashions, called by the
scholastics the material object, *objectum materiale*.[1] Though they
manufacture their own esoteric terms, 'uphill words,' as the canal
boatmen would say, such as isotherms, enzymes, neutrons, mute
of malice, hypostasis, syllogism, and so forth, all sciences have
this same humble origin, which can be disavowed only at the peril
of sterility. There is one common foundation for the whole of
scientific enquiry; sciences so different as meteorology and mystical theology work at the same world; there is continuity from

---

[1] *Summa Theologica*, 1a: I: 3.

London Clay to Longinus on the Sublime. To each science there is a proper formal object, yet each, if possible, should be set in the symmetry of the same general philosophy. There are special subjects, but also, in the analogy of being, the promise at least of a universal science, of a comprehensive education that marks one difference between a university and a polytechnic.

Even abrupt changes of metaphor and example, while they jerk the reader from situation to situation, may serve to show him one common philosophy beneath. St Thomas was a true aristotelean in basing his natural philosophy on the study of sensible objects and in applying an appropriate dialectic to match their movement and variety, a dialectic that is not just the uncoiling, link by link, of formal meaning; nevertheless he commanded a dispassionate, almost a mechanical style, seemingly indifferent to the excitement. He is neither high-flown nor allusive; yet his thoughts are not so case-hardened as his terms, they are susceptible to many influences and move easily and without offence from the highest subject to the lowest. Emotion becomes tranquil through intelligence. With no sense of shock he illustrates the natural law, the image of God, and the divine perfections from the humblest animal operations;[1] a philosophy open to the revelation of God's mystery moves in the mustiest questions.

Like statesmen, scientists and philosophers have the great task of drawing the frontiers of the sciences, and while preserving the proper independence of each, breaking down the barriers and putting them in free and open communication. Scientific autarchy cannot stand; morals and economics and politics and psychology should comfort and borrow from one another; even theology, while it may run for a time as an impressive system of arbitrary law, stiffens into a conventional code unless nourished from humane biology, graced by literature, and tempered by a sense of history.[2] The lover of wisdom, says St Thomas, is a lover of myths; individual substances, he also says, are truer than universals. Deficiency diseases come from an unbalanced diet, mental illness from confinement; and so there is no science so exalted but is not better for being racy of the soil. Formal objects, therefore, must

---

[1] *Summa Theologica*, 1a: I: 9, *ad* 3. XIII: 5. XCIII: 2. 1a–2ae: XCIV: 2. 2a–2ae: LVII: 3.

[2] *Ibid.* 1a: I: 3, *ad* 2.

be grounded in the material object; and we have laboured the
point because, whatever the austerity of logic, the rôle of dialectic
is to work with analogies in the different orders of knowledge.
Whatever else it may be the *Summa Theologica* is certainly not a
complicated system of deductions from purely ideal principles.

Intelligence is the general ability of seeing connections everywhere. Spinoza ground excellent lenses, Borodin was eminent in
medicine, and it is well to go travelling in arts and sciences off
one's professional route. One recommendation of the thomist
philosophy is that nothing is too far-flung to engage its interest;
there is a place for all the sciences; it offers an organization without friction under a law that is polite and not despotic, in a
society rather than a community.[1] As we shall see later, this
generosity springs from the sense of analogy. The formal objects
distinguishing the sciences are distinct abstractions, but all derive,
and are known to derive, from one and the same material object.
Sight perceives russet, taste enjoys the savour, through hearing
and touch one shudders when the teeth skid at the first bite; all
these are different forms, but there is only one thing, one apple.[2]
And so formal logical analysis itself must be set in a more spread-
ing dialectic; between the significant forms arrested and observed the flow of events must not be forgotten; historical science
in particular should not be restricted to the high-lights and cul-
minations of affairs but must study diaries and convey the sense
of how our ancestors lived and felt in the weeks and months
between great events.

With this warning against over-simplification in mind, we
must still say that each science must begin by minding its own
business. It works from a special standpoint and aims at a limited

---

[1] *Summa Theologica*, 1a: LXXXI: 3, *ad* 2.   1a–2ae: LVI: 4, *ad* 3.

Note that some of the sciences start by being more closely related to one
another than by helping in the management and investigation of the common
material object of our environment. Their special interests may lie very close
together. Agriculture is based on geology. The anatomist and physiologist take
the human body, and so also, if they are wise, the psychologist and moralist include the same object; but severally they study the human body under different
aspects, as a structure of muscle, sinew, and bone; as a working, living organism;
as the embodiment of consciousness and desire; as an essential part of a creature
responsibly adapting means to the ultimate goal of human life.

[2] *Ibid.*, 1a: LXXXV: 2, *ad* 2.

objective. It should not extrude the other sciences. Take heed from the economic interpretation of history, the explanation of all human events in terms of the development of the means of material production, which may be carried to such lengths as to abolish political, constitutional, social, even ecclesiastical history. Then history becomes unreal, a marginal illustration of economic laws, uninterested in Cleopatra's nose, except as an effect of diet and climate, and in all the human whims that have shaped the course of events, such as the refusal of the Comte de Chambord to give up the lilies for the tricolour in the very lifetime of Marx.

CHAPTER III

CORRECT AND TRUE

ST THOMAS remarks that two matters cannot easily be coped with at once, there is the danger of falling between two stools, and consequently he deprecates investigating together the content and the method of the sciences; he suggests the logic should first be taken as yielding the common procedure.[1] The separation of logic from the science of reality is, however, but a temporary and methodic phase, adopted, like the enclosed life, for the sake of society. More than the other sciences, and certainly more than dialectic, logic is aloof from the rough and tumble of events, and is therefore all the more likely to be dry and tedious. Thoughts will be tested according to their mental configuration rather than by the laws of evidence; with indifference alike to their sobriety or excitement, to their good sense or silliness. The eye is as frosty as the Iron Duke's reviewing troops, and not betraying whether he was thinking they were scum, or the steadiest fighters in Europe. Cordiality and colour must come from elsewhere, from philosophy and the play of dialectic and the arts.

> Balk logic with acquaintance that you have,
> And practise rhetoric in your common talk;
> Music and poesy use to quicken you.

Even the strange processes of the madman may be logically impeccable. Stanhope relates how Wellington was at a loss to deal with Blücher's fancies: 'When I went to take leave of him he positively told me he was pregnant. And what do you think he was pregnant of?—an elephant! And who do you think he said had produced it?—a French soldier! That is the human mind, added the Duke. He said, striking his side, *Je sens un élèphant là!* And what could you say to him. I could only say, *Je vous assure que vous vous méprenez*, and that he would get better.' It is not the business of logic to decide whether final propositions are true or not, but

---

[1] Commentary, II *Metaphysics*, lect. 5. Opusc. X, *de Causis*, lect. 1. Commentary, VI *Ethics*, lect. 7.

whether they are conclusions. Nor can it decide when fantasy is legitimate or not, though it may detect the purely formal flaws, as in the account of the laughing hyaena Peter Simple saw at Portsdown Fair, 'who cried like a human being in distress, and devours those who come to its assistance, a sad instance of the depravity of human nature, so the keeper observed.' Nor can it appreciate its expressiveness; we are a fast ship in a slow convoy, and a stoker has just gloomily observed that he reckons our fuel must be gaining on us.

Yet despite this concern for the patterning of thoughts, logic should not become an elegant trifling with no sense of intellectual responsibility. Its concepts derive from a living experience, and its purpose is to serve as an instrument for the scientific knowledge of real things. Correctness is the form, but truth is the intention. All scientific systems must observe the connections which are its study. Once in possession of true facts or principles, any conclusion that follows logically from them must be true; if a false conclusion is arrived at, then bad logic is to blame; in other words, the rules of correct thinking guarantee profitable development given well-founded first positions.

That an initial truth can be expanded when treated according to certain mental laws assumes, of course, that the human reason is knit into the fabric of reality, and this can be proved, or rather defended, only by invoking a critical theory of knowledge. On this count logic cannot justify itself, but must borrow the force of its fundamental assumptions from elsewhere, and then proceed in the confidence that we can know real truth, not merely in flashes of intuition, but also by patient exploration and piecing together of the data of humdrum experience. It is engaged more with our reasonings than with out first convictions, it is more important for conclusion than for premisses; it is a frame to build round, rather than a foundation to build on; like British socialism, it is a programme rather than a doctrine.

When an argument proceeds from true principles to a false conclusion then the process itself will invariably be at fault. God is the cause of everything—we are not God—therefore we are the cause of nothing: something has gone wrong somewhere; the first two statements are true enough, moreover they are connected; yet the process of development is wrong, and the conclusion does not follow. Aristotle notes the constructive and destructive rôles of logic.[1] The former is to enlarge our field of knowledge by genuine arguments that are right in their design, whether they be as flat-bottomed and unhandy in appearance as a spritsail barge or as dainty as a naval gig; the latter, often more prominent, is to pull down bad arguments. The general reader may lack expert information about a subject, but he should be able to recognize logical consistency or the lack of it. This is his protection against the expert.

Cardinal Cajetan, perhaps the most famous commentator on St Thomas and a very close thinker in his own right, was dubious about the authorship of the Epistle to the Hebrews because he thought the argument was too loose in places to be worthy of an apostle. But logic can be too exacting, when the occasion calls for tolerance and imagination. People may speak out of character, they sometimes think with their heads and sometimes with other parts, but are not thereby involved in crime against the reason. 'Words,' said Lord Keynes, 'ought to be a little wild, for they are assaults of thought upon the unthinking.' It is here that logic becomes dialectic, lying easily with metaphorical and affective statement, pressing hard only against what purports to be scientific demonstration. Even there it must be prepared to follow the twists and turns of analogy, proper to the processes of philosophical thinking, which are not bound to the lines, fixed points, abrupt edges, and unyielding quantities of a mathematical method. The firmness of machinery is required without the stiffness; *monumentum aere perennius*, yet springier than fine steel coil, suppler than muscle, ready to modulate itself to meaning even when couched in some such phrase as, 'the French General Staff always prepares for the last war, not the next.'

Yet in pure logic the first and final distinction is between what is correct and what is incorrect. A correct argument may be true, or false, or nonsensical; an incorrect argument likewise may be of the same three kinds.[2] Correct arguments of all three kinds are

---

[1] *Topics*, Bk. V, ch. 2.

[2] Every argument conforms to one of these six fundamental types. A sound or correct argument may be well-founded, for example: the spring of bodiless activity cannot dry up—but the human soul is a spring of bodiless activity—and therefore can survive medical death. The first two statements are well-

admitted or rejected as the case may be, not by logic, which is equally complacent with them all, but by other habits of judgement. And so the side that scores the logical points in a debate is not necessarily in the right; facts are sometimes improbable, and not always bound up in what has gone before. Pure logic is not the criterion of evidence; but it does ensure that a conclusion has the force of its premisses; that and no more. While the distinction between correctness and truth must be made clear, too sharp a separation in practice may lead logic into discredit. The elaborate rules of thought have one purpose, and that is to serve singleness of mind and a happy end. To be absorbed in them to the exclusion of real dialectic is to be as set for failure as Philip II matching shadow with shadow in the Escorial.

Although the theory of pure logical form may well make us pause at internal coherence, we should allow ourselves to be carried on by its purpose, which is to shape judgements about reality. Accordingly St Thomas treats it as a method of science rather than a science itself,[1] as an instrument to be directed at existents, and therefore adapted to work not merely with the ideal necessities of ontology, but also with first interpretations of the moving and

---

founded according to the philosophical psychology of St Thomas (Cf. *Summa Theologica*, 1a: LXXV: 6. Disputations, *de Anima*, 2, 14. II *Contra Gentes*, 79). The same logical cogency is possessed by the following argument, which is nevertheless unfounded in both its premisses: a closed system does not need God —but the human community is a closed system—therefore it does not need God (Cf. *Summa Theologica*, 1a: XCIII. 2a–2ae: II: 3). Thirdly, there is the type of argument that concludes, 'for the bong was a boojum you see,' a coherence in absurdity that is the difficult art of the great drolls.

Unsound or incorrect arguments are likewise of three types. They may be composed of propositions true enough in themselves: British armies muddle through—Lord Raglan's army muddled through—and therefore his army was a British army. This fallacy often passes unnoticed when we are in sympathy with the drift of an argument; we are readier to pounce when we disagree or when we approach surrealism in a rationalist temper: Waterloo was won on the playing fields of Eton—and the Southern Railway will carry greyhounds—therefore the captain of the *Mauretania* reads Greek.

In scholastic disputation, one of the deadliest retorts is to accept the premisses of an opponent and show that they have nothing to do with the conclusion they are alleged to prove. Approximately one-third of the *Summa Theologica* comprises objections against the position of the author; they are not always serious attacks, but they are mostly sound arguments, and treated as such.

[1] V *de Trinitate*, 1, ad 2.

sensible facts of experience. It begins already with physics, which cannot be wholly resolved into self-evident propositions. Even a metaphysic that claims to be related to facts cannot dispense with the dialectic of extrinsic and probable factors. Certainly flesh and blood problems cannot be settled by the logical application of naked reasons, as in the argument that parents should be loved before wives because we should love our neighbour more than our body.[1]

We distrust the fanaticism that would press the principle of nationality to its utmost conclusion in the delimitation of frontiers, and may suspect such simple solutions as that the British should clear out of Asiatic territory just because they are Europeans; the extremeness of the abstraction is more pronounced than the regard for the well-being of inarticulate millions. If we care to use logic like this we can spare ourselves much solicitude, not least in moral matters, where a rule accepted in the first place for good reasons, can suppress the workings of a robust and personal conscience. But we shall not be dealing truthfully with the world of individual things. Prudence is necessary as a virtue because pure theory is not a sufficient a guide to action.[2] The abstractions of the mind are related to our immediate environment through the activity of a *ratio particularis*[3]; after somewhat the same fashion, pure logic continues into dialectic.[4]

One may stumble across the truth and this may happen more frequently than a devoted logician likes. In the end the cavalry doctrine of Edwardian Aldershot broke the Hindenburg Line. But we should remember that thoughts may be more logical than their utterance; an appreciation may be true at its source yet betrayed in formulation; perhaps some truths cannot be expressed except through the queerer lines of Christopher Smart. Then also we should allow for the influence of traditional lore; patterns of thought and action are inherited from the wisdom and prudence of our ancestors; there are racial myths behind our civilized history: a momentum from the past may continue to supply with decreasing force what is wanting in our own responsible enquiries; we spend a capital we have not earned, and use conclusions that are

---

[1] *Summa Theologica*, 2a–2ae: XXVI: 11, *sed contra*.
[2] *Ibid.*, 2a–2ae: XLVII: 3.
[3] *Ibid.*, 1a: LXXVIII: 4. LXXIX: 4.
[4] Commentary, IV *Metaphysics*, lect. 4.

not strictly speaking our own. Yet to light on a truth as the result of an unsound argument is an accident, a fortunate chance, but still only a happening which belongs to the scientific way of thinking no more than to take off in a faulty aeroplane is part of the proper method of aviation. Scientific logic is not directly interested in singulars, still less in oddities or incidental conjunctions, but reserves its attention for the proper effects and necessary implications of an argument; it deals, in scholastic speech, with what is *per se,* not *per accidens.*

Hence the qualities as well as the defects of strictly apodictic logic and the need of supplementing it by dialectic, just as justice must be supplemented by equity.[1] I recall the eighteenth century Naval Order of Battle: Byng kept it, and was shot, Matthews broke it, and was censured. Strict science establishes measure and control, orders our thoughts into symmetry and makes a pattern of meanings; but always there is the inherent weakness because insistence on the rationally significant alone must neglect much else of what is presented; the world of fact is a great deal untidier than the world of thought, fugitive, recalcitrant, suddenly surrendering, full of surprises. The sciences work a sort of kaleidoscope, patterns of lucid meanings are displayed and objects thrown into various arrangements; a grid is projected on our environment, which else would appear swirling and blurred. There must be a relatively fixed frame of reference and this is partly supplied by formal logic. But natural science, says St Thomas, must keep the sensibility of motion, and a natural philosophy, or indeed any philosophy that is working with 'historical' reality cannot remain with the explication of essences, but must embark on mixed demonstrations, that is combinations of necessary propositions and observations of fact, and cast about all round any subject it is considering. Here dialectic will operate, to show the arrangement of a scheme of things, a design that, in a sense, is untidier than the internal connections exhibited by pure deduction. The difference between a sense of humour and wit may light up some of the difference; logic is laconic, but dialectic can be extravagant in its humour. Logic will sheer away from passages of sheer absurdity; 'You may well call Stratford Stony Stratford because I was never

---

[1] *Summa Theologica,* 2a-2ae: CXX.

so bitten by fleas in all my life.' Nevertheless nonsense has its standards, and there is a grotesque logic in the best shaggy-dog stories; 'Don't worry about me,' said the head in a bowler-hat bobbing in midstream to the worried man it had followed from Chelsea to the Victoria Embankment, 'don't worry about me, you see I'm riding a bicycle.'

CHAPTER IV

FORMAL AND MATERIAL

FORMAL logic turns on correctness, material logic on the content of thinking. The terms, formal and material, express their difference, which also appears from the two main classes of fallacies, some of which belong to formal logic and consist in not observing the mental conditions of argument, while others come from an imperfect appreciation of its subject and belong to material logic. If I draw affirmative conclusions from negative principles my formal logic is at fault; but if I misapprehend a negative element as a positive and argue accordingly, as when from the evil at work in the world I infer the existence of a supreme principle of evil contesting dominion with the supreme principle of good,[1] then my material logic is at fault. To decide whether the defect be formal or material is sometimes difficult, as in the case of a driver who accelerates when his petrol is running short in order to reach a filling station the more quickly. At other times both may go together, as when a complete determinist abuses his opponent.[2]

Taken in the widest sense material logic includes all the critical sciences of reality. It raises questions that are more absorbing than those of formal logic. They range from the trustworthiness of our senses to the place of general ideas in the real world, they open perplexing issues, the relationship of our mental categories to the non-mental world. From such heights it descends to the play of dialectic and the common or garden sense of fact and proportion,

---

[1] *Summa Theologica*, 1a: XLIX: 3.

[2] The logical works of Aristotle are divided by St Thomas as follows (Commentary, I *Perihermenias*, lect. 1, Commentary, I *Posterior Analytics*, lect. 1):—

I. Formal logic. The *Categories* or *Predicaments* treat of simple apprehension; the *de Interpretatione* or *Perihermenias* (first ten chapters commented on by St Thomas), of judgement; the *Prior Analytics* of reasoning.

II. Material logic. The *Posterior Analytics* (commented on by St Thomas) represent a *logica judicativa* devoted to the processes of demonstration; the *Topics*, a *logica dialectica* of sufficiently grounded arguments, to which are subordinated the *Rhetoric* and the *Poetics*.

such as made the old architect remember that 'a good Parlour in Aegypt would make a good Cellar in England.'

Formal logic on the other hand is concerned with the mode of predicating, not the act of existing.[1] Without deep searchings of mind it proceeds briskly to the examination of terms, propositions, and arguments; conscientious, but not tortured, like Anthony Trollope sitting down to write a novel. It is like someone who is interested solely in the mechanics of music and who therefore accepts the *Messiah* and the *Elijah* in the same spirit. The absence of philosophical fret appeals to certain casts of mind: we read in Trevelyan's *Life of Macaulay*, 'Some of the great metaphysical philosophers, both ancient and modern, were among the authors with whom Macaulay was most familiar; but he read them for the pleasure of admiring the ingenuity of their arguments or the elegance of their literary manner, and not from any sympathy with the subject-matter of their works.' But in fairness we should add that Macaulay also exclaimed: 'How oddly we are made! Some books which I should never dream of opening at dinner, please me at breakfast, and vice versa.'

Even formal logic alone is not without reassurance. There are moods when the mind doubts whether it dwells in a dream world of unreality, or a fine-meshed system of mathematical cages, or the familiar scene of common-sense facts; what was fresh and friendly in the forenoon has become sullen and hostile by the afternoon; and still the mind can be imperturbable about the laws of strict and consecutive thinking. Nor is it without a sense of sociability, for whatever our tenets, there can always be this minimum of agreement on the form and procedure of rational intercourse.[2]

Though formal logic can be discussed in an euclidean temper,[3] its motions differ importantly from those of quantitative mathematics, for they are not confined to transactions conducted in magnitudes and numbers; they reach to identities not merely to equalities. When taken into material logic and a dialectic living in the vicissitudes of philosophical thinking, these identities are implicit in every communication of reason with reason, and in the shimmer

---

[1] Commentary, VIII *Metaphysics*, lect. 17.
[2] Opusc. XI, *de Regno*, I, 1.
[3] Disputations, VI *de Potentia*, 1, *ad* 12.

and glances of analogy. So logic must be seen, not just as the dilucidation of symbolic form, but as the shaping of natural signs and the mental modes of the passions of being, *passiones entis*. Like mathematics, logic is clear, but it has more of a sparkle. Yet logic is like soda-water, made to a formula; but dialectic is like champagne, and cannot be resolved into its elements. It is not restricted to the motionless exactness of figures and diagrammatic patterns, nor to the relational bearing of numbers. On this account it may be doubted whether a mathematical training is altogether a help in the study of philosophy. A steady application to one line of thought is encouraged, but also an exclusive concentration on one type of certitude. Mathematical studies were not held in such importance in the middle ages as in later centuries, they were kept to functions of quantity, but this is not the main reason why the profound sympathies and differences engaged by the philosophy of St Thomas cannot be rendered into crystalline concepts, the *idées claires* of Descartes. For a similar reason his moral theology cannot be exposed by purely legalistic casuistry. Despite the exhibition of logical form, the sympathies of dialectic in the lowest degrees of abstraction are with the motions and sensible qualities of physical nature, and in the highest degrees, with the simultaneous unities and multiplicities of being.

The logical fibre of a branch of science is shaped to every bend of exposition. To the extent that a quasi-geometrical morphology can be exposed a mathematical logic can also be exercised, but a humane discipline of experience also calls for a lively dialectic that will give grace and measure to liberal thought, not harsh and crabbed, but 'musical as is *Apollo's* lute,' curling with the ebb and flow of intelligible being. In something of the same way biology must do more than match chromosome numbers in order to appreciate the propagation of life by the fusion of cells. We shall not, therefore, treat logic as the abstract composition of empty shapes, an elaboration such as a solitary might make for the sake of his own mental clearness, but as a discipline charged from the real sciences and habits of knowledge and governing the stresses of minds conversing with one another about a sensible and moving universe.

While logic may do for soliloquy, dialectic is certainly for

2

dialogue. Therefore we must take for granted that language is expressive of thought, that thinking itself is an admirable and profitable form of activity, that the purpose of thinking is to discover real meaning, that different minds can share in the same meaning, and that this meaning is not just a label we write out, but part of the stuff of reality.

These rules of old discover'd, not deviz'd
Are Nature still, but Nature methodiz'd.

With such a conviction dialectic is committed to statements that are part of general philosophy. For we are not engaged on the one hand with a close analysis of logical form, nor on the other with the demonstration of the principles, but with a description, largely by a convergence of analogies, of how a rational spirit may cast about and accumulate knowledge about a world not wholly reducible to severely logical structures,[1] and that, like Ravel's *Tombeau de Couperin*, by offering a tribute rather than by attempting a close imitation. For one merit of the thomist philosophy is its pervasive rationality, interpreting yet not reducing, ordering yet respecting apparently recalcitrant elements. The cherished positions of common sense are adopted, yet there is a readiness to defend them with uncommon sense; the multitude of things, for instance, is not left as a statement of experience, but taken into the heart of its metaphysics. There are no untouchables in the hierarchy of being. Plain yet recondite, all things to all men, philosophy should be ambitious to explore doubt with the sceptic, penetrate to multiplicity with the monist, establish duty with the hedonist, and exceed a materialist in earthiness. And consequently there is a co-operation between contrary forms, a sympathy with the whole range of reality. Hence formal must warm

---

[1] Commentary, IV *Metaphysics, lect.* 4. I *Posterior Analytics*, I, *lect.* 1. *Compendium Theologiae*, ch. 102. When the logical form of the perennial philosophy is examined we are looking, as it were, at the veneer, not the core; the rational finish, not the substance. Yet though we insist on the thomist *dialectica utens*, the reader will not need to be reminded of the scholastic zeal for the analysis of possible modes of propositions and argument. Purely logical controversies were rarely more dour than after the time of Ockham; the *Logicae Compendium Peripateticae* of Javelli, who closes the period, adumbrates forms that were to be approached three centuries later as though they were hitherto unknown.

to material logic.   It is a control rather than an impulse[1]; a servant
of real philosophy but, like Ariel, lacking the touch of feeling,
needing to be kindled by dialectic at play in the world of sensibility, probability, and motion, and differing from rhetoric,
not because it is cold, but because, instead of an audience, it has a
friendly opponent.

[1] V *de Trinitate*, 1, *ad* 2.   Its action is that of a rudder, *adminiculum quoddam*,
ineffective unless you already have steerage way.

CHAPTER V

FICTITIOUS BEING

THE business of logic is not with historical facts and real things
but with the purely mental relations set up when they are syste-
matically considered; the concepts thus fabricated should make no
pretence to produce external existents, otherwise a realist might
well ask, 'You use the snaffle and the bit all right, but where's the
dangèd horse?' To rate its power, therefore, we must consider the
value and bearing of abstract generalization, and so treat in parenthesis of the scholastic doctrine of universal ideas. *House* is such
an idea, applied to things so diverse as the birthplace of Burns and
Blenheim Palace; *thing* is an idea even wider: and what is *diverse* and
what is *wider*? Some generalizations are closer than others to individual objects, others are more remote and tenuous; some are the
very stuff of the serviceable sciences, others, the purely mental
compositions of reverie; but abstraction is present, at varying
pitches, in every phrase of human conversation.

Now the forms in which logic is versed are not mental processes considered as exhibitions of the thinking subject, for these
belong to the distinct discipline of psychology.[1] Nor are they the
patterns of natural realities, for these belong to dialectic. Logic
takes mental processes neither as responses to one situation and as
presages of another, nor yet as explorations into the working of
things; but primarily as manifesting inner coherence.

I am with a friend on the cliff, watching terns through binoculars; I am more than a casual, if interested, observer; I am a bird-
watcher, let us pretend, a keen naturalist who knows better than
to call them sea-swallows. I recognize certain facts—the word is

---

[1] Psychology includes in its field of study the workings of consciousness, an
object as real, if not so easily measured, as that of any of the other sciences:
states of consciousness are at least as positive as purely impersonal physical conditions, and much more urgent. In a sense, all scientific phenomena are psychological data, else we would not notice them; and in consequence, psychology is as
well-founded as any mechanical or purely objective science, such as ballistics
or biology.

used without prejudice—about terns; the red bill, the dusky distal third, the white shafted outer primary, and other notes of the scientific catalogue: I am more interested in the general marks of the species than in any one particular bird, yet while I do not completely identify myself with the living fluttering object, for I am not enjoying a poetic experience, nevertheless let us admit that my mind is occupied with certain real characteristics.

Then laying down my glasses I cease thinking about birds and turn to myself; from watching terns I begin to reflect on myself watching terns. Why this interest of mine? Is it, I wonder, just an escape to the Orkneys from the noise of the town? I find myself analysing my motives, and then presently considering the springs of human activity in general. I have left ornithology and am now engaged in the science of psychology. Its data are not entirely internal and subjective, for while I was watching the terns and then thinking about myself, my companion has been watching me, reading my thoughts and feelings, studying me as an outside fact in the same fashion that I was studying the terns: psychology can be pursued from without as well as from within.

So far the scientific musings of both of us have been keeping fairly close to the facts. I was intent on the special characteristics of terns, through the use of scientific apparatus, in this case my binoculars ; I may have missed the grace and vibrating poise of that slender body in the air above the isles, and when I turned to self-analysis my introspection may have deprived me of the most direct awareness of myself at that moment: such is the penalty of the scientific approach. But let us shift our knowledge away another remove from our primary perceptions. Suppose I cry, 'Look, there's a skua! A great skua!' and we both see that drifting flight and the sudden stoop. We go on to discuss the nature and habits of skuas, unpleasing piratical characters we agree, 'quite a different kind of bird from a tern,' I observe. There we pause, and ask ourselves, what do we mean by saying *a different kind of thing*? We are constantly classifying in that fashion, perhaps not always scientifically, but still with sufficient justification and approximate accuracy. We group different things under the same heading, and put this tern and that tern in the same kind or species; we also group different things under different headings, and put this tern and that skua in different species.

There can be no systematic treatment of knowledge without
the concept of formal object, of *kind* of thing; so much so, that in
recent years, a new discipline, called Systematics, has been introduced to aid the science of general biology, by separating and defining species, and to ensure that the same name shall always have
the same meaning, as nearly as possible, when applied to one
organism or group of organisms.

Yet is a species as such a real entity? Is it a physical nature or
is it a mental category contrived for our own convenience? Is it a
thing or a thought? Out there is a thing we call a tern, now walking awkwardly on the shore; also a thing we call a skua, poised
against the clouds; also two things called men, I lying on the
heather, my companion seated on a tussock. I strive to make the
situation circumstantial and particular, yet watch how generalizations throng—shore, clouds, heather, tussock, and so forth. But
let us keep our attention on the tern, the skua, myself, and my
companion. We agree that there are four diverse things here; we
also agree that two of them, myself and my companion, are of the
same kind, and that the other two are each of different kinds. Yet
both are birds and therefore closer to one another than to the seals;
and both belong to the same family of *laridae*, and therefore are
closer than to the ducks and geese.[1]

But are species real? The natural scientist may well evade the
question, and concentrate on deciding what are the special characteristics of select examples; he may continue his search for the
classification of species without bothering overmuch about their
final status in a general theory of reality. But if the question be
faced, then the realm of material logic and critical metaphysics
must be entered.

We have raised the major problem for the early scholastics,
the problem of universals, over which we must skate lightly. The
condition of logic is involved, also the exercise of dialectic. A universal idea represents a nature communicable to many individuals;

---

[1] In terms of the old natural philosophy, they are of different species, but
of the same proximate genus. The traditional classification of objects, as will
be seen in a later chapter, proceeds according to the distinction of genera and
species; the nomenclature has been changed, so that now the naturalist speaks
of orders, and families, and sub-species; but the ruling conceptions remain
the same.

thus tern, skua, man. The problems are whether and how such a
nature exists in reality, or whether no more than a mental concept
or verbal label is affixed. One of the most vexed questions in
philosophy is released, appearing at different times under different
terms, and flashing in the debates of Abelard. In between the
two extremes of ultra-realism and nominalism there are many
shades of doctrine; fairly in the middle lies the position of
Aristotle and St Thomas, the mean of temperate realism,
realismus mitigatus.[1]

At one extreme are the ultra-realists, inspired by the elevated
strains of platonic philosophy, more devoted to exemplars than to
examples. Ideal types, they say, are of everything the most real
and lasting. Purified by the asceticism of philosophy, the mind
can contemplate with peace and security the pure forms of beauty
and of justice, undistracted by the passing gleams of loveliness and
by the shady and shifty claims to particular rights. Who can
doubt the nature of triangle, what more certain and serene; but
who can be sure that the figure he draws is truly a triangle and not
an approximate sketch? What is more unconvincing and troubled
than the intellectual attempt to demonstrate particular and
material facts? Lift up your eyes to the calm and eternal hills from
the turmoil of temporals down in the valley: universal ideas endure, but individual things no sooner are born than they begin to
pass away: here below there is only opinion, if not downright de-
lusion; there above in the heavenly places you will find certain
truth; to seek it here is but 'to carve in snow, on waves to write.'
We are invited to escape from the flux of history to the changeless
world of ideas; no wonder that marxists have discovered Plato as
their great enemy—yet is not their temper similar when they
would have us substitute devotion to humanity, or near-humanity,
for a tenderness towards individual human beings? Yet by a mysterious compensation no philosophical tradition has sung this
world more graciously and lyrically than platonism. Where are
the poets from an aristoteleanism which intellectually holds it
more dear?

At the other extreme are the nominalists, who would keep close
to the physical world and refuse this flight to the ideas. An ounce

[1] Commentary, VII *Metaphysics, lect.* 13. *Summa Theologica,* 1a: LXXIX: 3.
1a: LXXXV: 2, *ad* 2. Opusc. VIII, *de Ente et Essentia,* ch. 4.

of fact is worth a ton of theory; our business is to deal with the things we experience here and now; we must get them into order without taking refuge in dreams. At least two currents converge on nominalism, one setting from empirical science, the other from poetic sensibility. Empirical science rightly resents any attempt to short-circuit its own patient examination and elaboration of facts by a swift reference to a supposedly ideal type; it cites the pseudo-scientific conclusions that have followed from the sedulous application of metaphysical concepts to the physical world unchecked by physical verification; and sets its face against the contemplations of metaphysical entities as a substitute for the effort of grouping and re-grouping in useful constellations the results of exact and prolonged observation and experiment. Indeed there are good grounds for suspecting any mysticism or philosophism that would deprive natural science of its dignity, or deny that the material world can furnish objects of real and certain knowledge.[1] Scientists are joined by poets in resisting the overbearing reality claimed for general ideas, particularly by those with an immediate and sensuous appreciation of the spurts of individual life, an acute response to the moment that will never return, a sense of the frail and fugitive, expressed in the lament for mortality, which, to read between the lines and relate to his loving respect for creatureliness, St Thomas appropriates to the highest gift of science.[2] Abstractions appear but shrouds wherein to wrap dead thoughts. Behind the scientific and the poetic protest alike lurks the conviction that things are utterly individual and distinct; they must be grouped in classes, of course, for the sake of mental tidiness, but the general natures thereby formulated are little more than verbal or mental tags, names, *nomina*, covering a collection of individuals. Better if we can see things just as things, and not as examples. A scientific theory, says a scientist, is not a dogma but a policy. Hang up philosophy, says a poet, unless philosophy can make a Juliet!

The material world is real and consists of particular and individual things, and these, though elusive to the purely rational sciences, are beings in the full metaphysical strength of the

---

[1] V *de Trinitate*, 2.

[2] *Summa Theologica*, 2a–2ae: IX: 2. On the sadness of science, and the promise in the second beatitude: *Blessed are they that mourn, for they shall be comforted.*

word, a set of stubborn facts that cannot be suppressed. A high-flying philosophy takes off from nowhere unless it starts from them. A logical theory is sterile unless it is joined to such existents; the universal reason must work from the *ratio particularis*, which means that logic must be united with a dialectic. Yet these particular things are embodiments of different natures; they exist in different types, few or many as the case may be. Such natures, expressed in our minds by universal ideas, are real, though they do not exist as universals outside the mind, but only as realized in physical individuals. Humanity as such is not real, but human beings are real; there is more there than an orator's gesture. According to a scholastic adage, a universal idea exists formally in the mind, fundamentally in things, *formaliter in mente, fundamentaliter in re*; it is not an ultimate object of contemplation, but a means to particular knowledge.[1] And therefore, as Gilbert should be sung to Sullivan, so logical theory should be taken to dialectic.

From this issues the aristotelean view of the world; a pattern of real kinds composed on a common ground and repeated and multiplied in many individuals; neither a series of disconnected incidents, nor yet a set of shadows cast from another world. There is here a true synthesis, for the facts of experience, cherished by the nominalist, are safeguarded; indeed they are lifted from the plane of appearances and become objects of metaphysical solicitude; while the universal forms remain constant and certain, and are yet brought close to the world of physical science.

Most of us take for granted, often without reflection, that the world contains real types, besides much that is highly individual. I am watching *birds*, and recognize a *tern* and *two* skuas, then with my companion I *consider* the *different* foods of animals and what *causes* them to grow, etc., etc.; our thoughts abound with such general ideas, and there is not a word that could not be italicized; unreal or not they are certainly among the earliest data of our rational consciousness. Tell me, said Tertullian, how can you indict names? and logic, said Boethius, *non de rebus sed de vocibus est*: it is neutral in the issue whether deductive philosophy is an inference from language to non-linguistic facts.

The human mind works continually with general ideas, and we

---

[1] V *de Trinitate*, 2, *ad* 4.

2*

shall assume that in the main they represent real kinds. The scholastics call them first intentions, *primae intentiones*, for to them the
reasoning reason first tends; they are its first readings of the sensible
world.[1] As we have seen, there is disagreement about their real
status, but that begins to close when we push the abstraction to
another remove from the individual objects of experience, and
enquire: what do we imply mentally and what conditions are demanded by the very laws of thought without overt reference to an
outside reality when we group objects into the same species or
divide them into different species? What is the meaning of such
classification itself and what are the rules?[2] What is meant by
genus as such, not bird-genus nor mammal-genus; what is the
result of a specific difference imposed on such general mental
patterns; what do we signify by *species as such*, not *tern species*
nor *human species*; what is the principle of discrimination between
a proper characteristic and an incidental quality; what are the tests
for such abstract notions as sequence, and connection, and sharing
in common?

Now whatever the verdict about the first intentions of the
mind, there can be little doubt that in the outside world there
are no such things as genericity, specificness, differentiation,
peculiarity, idiosyncrasy, all precisely as such. As the Dormouse
said to Alice: 'You say things are much of a muchness—did you
ever see such a thing as a drawing of a muchness?' They are conceptions formulated by the mind and cannot exist outside the
mind; their stuff is mental, and not real.[3] They are described by
the scholastics as second intentions, *secundae intentiones*, secondary
thoughts and marginal readings. They enter into all thinking;
there are few phrases, even of poetry, where words cannot be italicized which represent such fictitious entities, though they are not
usually the subject of separate study. To treat them apart from
their subject is like trying to draw without colour, yet pure logic
must make the attempt, and address itself to thoughts about

---

[1] There may be an experience of a concrete thing, some cognition on and
just over the threshold of consciousness, before such a term of the first intention
is articulated.

[2] Disputations, I *de Potentia*, 1, *ad* 10.

[3] *Summa Theologica*, 1a: XXVIII: 1.

thoughts, a procedure no closer to reality than is a course of instructional technique to the actual business of teaching.[1]

A logical entity, or notional being, is termed an *ens rationis*. The term is not rarely misunderstood and taken to mean a fictional or imaginary being—such as one from the litany in *King Goshawk and the Birds*, 'Mr. Pickwick and Don Juan, Rosalind and Lady Cicely Waynefleet, with the Chimaera and the Hippogriff, the Squirryphant and the Mock Turtle, Puss in Boots and the Whangerdoodle, and the Dong with the Luminous Nose.' But none of these is a purely logical entity, for they could exist outside the mind; improbable they may be, yet they belong to the metaphysical order of possible being. They differ in degree and historical completeness from Goliath the Philistine and Diogenes the Cynic, Julian the Apostate and the Man in the Iron Mask, the Merry Monarch and the Boy who stood on the Burning Deck. Anything that can exist, even if only on the most extravagant supposition, is not a creature of logic. But an *ens rationis* is a condition of meaning that can exist only in the human reason and nowhere else, a generality lacking the perfection of the real.[2] It is mental through and through, though a remote foundation in reality must be allowed it, for the notes of nature are the ground bass on which logic is scored. Authentic examples are such notions as genus, species, sequence, syllogism, undistributed middle, and a host of others that will occur throughout these pages.[3] They are but the ciphers of music, the other sciences must sound the notes, and dialectic must carry the undertones and overtones, the echoes of analogy.

There is divergence, then, between a science of things and a science of notions,[4] and yet they are related. Here another parenthesis, on the main divisions of being according to the thomist philosophy, will be found helpful. Being is a grand and metaphysical word to be sure, putting us in contact with all existing things, referring to everything that is not nothing or nonentity,[5] from the eternal supra-substance of God to the lemony tints in

---

[1] Commentary, IV *Metaphysics, lect.* 4.
[2] I *Contra Gentes,* 75.
[3] VI *de Trinitate,* I, first question. *Summa Theologica,* Ia: XIV: 9.
[4] IV *Contra Gentes,* II.
[5] *Summa Theologica,* Ia: XIV: 9.

Cotswold stone, from necessary forms to vagrant incidents, from real events to rational modes. Some are more real than others, for being can be differenced from within by its own intensity or relaxation.[1]

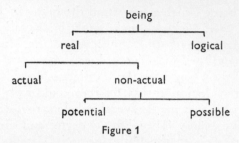

Figure 1

A man walking and alive is a real and actual being. Is a corpse there? No, not actually, but potentially; it can, and will be there, unless high explosive does its work. Is a radiant winged creature there? No, not actually, not even potentially, for within a man are no real dispositions to such a transformation. But the prospect is not inconceivable, at any rate it is just possible, and to that extent it does not speak nonentity.[2] Reality stretches from the most solidly established substance down to the least likely possibility; wee has a sense in metaphysics; everything is included, from the one before the first comer to the one who never arrives. Once upon a time, a Christian believes, this world and everything in it was merely possible.[3] Was it real then? Yes, in a manner of speaking, for possibility is a mode of reality, and is eternally in the divine mind and power.[4]

The difference between potential being and possible being lies in the existence of a real subject[5]: a potential being is already related to existence in a present and actual being, as was recognized by the old countryman to whom caterpillars were always butterflies-as-is-to-be; but a possible being is powerless to be born, there are no real grounds or material for its existence. There are shades of possibility, from the nearly-might-have-been to the not-an-earthly,

[1] *Summa Theologica*, 2a–2ae: LII: 1, 2. *Cf.* Figure 1.
[2] Disputations, I *de Potentia*, 3. III: 17, *ad* 10.
[3] *Summa Theologica*, 1a: XLVI: 2.
[4] *Ibid.*, 1a: XLVI: 1, *ad* 1. 1a: XXV: 3.
[5] Opusc. IV, *de Aeternitate Mundi*. *Summa Theologica*, 1a: IX: 2.

from what Christopher Marlowe might have written had he lived longer to a theologian with the body of a sea-lion; just as there are shades of impossibility, from the metaphysical impossibility of an uncaused composite substance, through the moral impossibility of a white lie and the mathematical impossibility of a square circle to the physical impossibility of powdered water. The world of possibles opens out endlessly, for they are infinite in number, kind, and degree; we cannot imagine the creator using up all his reserves, though there seems reason to believe that the world of actual and potential beings is limited.[1]

Now logical being does not even touch the fringe of reality proper to possible being, for omnipotence itself cannot make an *ens rationis* emerge outside the human mind. Yet it deserves the title of being, as having a mental existence as a notion and conditioning our reasoning about real things. Though an abstraction from an abstraction, it is the special object of logical discipline, without which knowledge does not begin to be systematic and classical. Here is no twilight or shadow world; the thoughts of logic are bright and clear. Hence the danger that a logician may be like a medical psychologist who remains interested in the diagnosis and understanding of mental illness, though sceptical as to the value of treatment, or like a medieval jurist who forgets the law for the gloss. Yet given the humour for analogy, logic is the instrument for the liveliest and highest philosophy; given the realist and scientific impulse, it will help restore the nobility and good sense of the ancients, and recover what J. W. Mackail described as ' the Greek genius for asking the right question, and the Roman genius for finding the practical answer.'

---

[1] *Summa Theologica*, 1a: VII: 4. 1a: XXV: 3. 1a: XLVI: 1, 2. Potentiality is sometimes called *potentia subjectiva*, that is a potential in a real subject; while possibility is *potentia objectiva*, that is as an object of consideration it is not a contradiction in terms. Commentary, IX *Metaphysics*, *lect*. 1.

DEFINITION, enunciation, and argumentation,[1] these are the three
periods of our discourse. First, objects or notions; then their relations by judgement; finally their generations by reasoning: subject,
predicate, and conclusion: man, woman, and family. One mental
process is no sooner completed than another begins anew; the
teeming population of thoughts is always breeding. The first
specimens, which we shall call notions for that denotes their
mental form,[2] though discernible in the complex data of consciousness, are caught with difficulty. Psychologists rightly
hesitate before treating them as if they were like elements in
chemistry from which compounds are built up; many postulate
instead a single response to a situation more ample than can be represented by one meaning. We move all of a piece, and not in a
series of connected jerks like a goods train starting with the coup-
lings clanking as they take the strain. Logic, on the contrary,
begins from units; it is like the shunter, and its concern is with the
pieces, not the flow of life.

A notion is formed in an initial perception, *simplex apprehensio*,
before any crisis of acceptance or rejection; the reaction is merely
the registration of an object, the *intelligentia indivisibilium*, the
glimpse of what has not yet been composed,[3] the state of having
a thought rather than of thinking. A notion is expressed as a
term.[4] One term may consist of a number of words, for instance,
lust-considered-precisely-as-a-morally-neutral-motion-of-the-
sensitive-appetite, or lust-considered-in-the-augustinian-sense-as-
the-manifestation-of-depravity.[5] Before examining such forms let
us revert to the supposedly stilted figure cut by logic, as though it
were a marionette, twitched this way and that by mechanical con-
trivance, but not really alive.

1 *Summa Theologica*, Ia: XXXII: 2. Ia–2ae: XC: 1, *ad 2*.
2 *Ibid.*, Ia–2ae: XC: 1, *ad 2*. Commentary, I *Perihermenias lect.* 1.
3 Commentary, III *de Anima*, *lect.* 11.
4 *Summa Theologica*, Ia: XIII: 1, 4.
5 *Ibid.*, Ia–2ae: XXIV: 2. Ia–2ae: XXX: 3. Ia–2ae: LXXXII: 3.

From the psychological point of view the mind can scarcely be pinned down at the point of an initial simple perception, a perception, moreover, which is expected to contain one defined meaning; its attitude may be still perhaps for a moment, then it hurries to build up a response. When for example I exclaim, 'ah! the sea,' then at once I begin, if I do not anticipate, a judgement to the effect that the sea is in some way real, and already the notion and term are entering into complex relationships with other objects of my experience and setting off a series of meanings. Only in logic can the mind be arrested at the stage of the simple apprehension, and only there can we stop to consider terms as though they did not beckon further, but resembled the façade of an Italian church, unrelated to the interior or the building behind. Not merely an abstraction is produced, but also a fixation.[1]

Here, then, is the phase of set terms rather than of transitions and meanings in motion. Movement can be marked, or at least allowed for, indeed St Thomas requires an appreciation of *ens mobile* as a condition of the difference between physical and mathematical science, and dialectic must plunge into the flow, but so far as a severe logic is concerned the terms employed will be constants, like insoluble particles in a fluid. In accounting for change there is a sideways gesture towards the motion in between, then the gaze is steadied on the fixed points, the *terminus a quo* and the *terminus ad quem*;[2] the becoming is almost forgotten for the being that starts and the being that arrives. The manner of such logic is that of a stiffly formal dance, a succession of set attitudes not the billow and eddy; Lady Hamilton in her tableaux, not Emma in private. It gives the impression of working on a series of pauses, or states of being. This is inevitable but need not be regretted; no error results so long as dialectic makes the correction. Settled

---

[1] Take the term *cheese*: in pure logic accepted as the point of departure for a process of straight or crooked thinking, not as the manifestation of a reality. By making an abstraction disregarding the probable nature of the external world suggested by the thought of cheese, and uninterested in the tastes and inclinations of those who conceive it, we can concentrate on the fitting shape of the notion for the purpose of argument. When we go on to reflect that 'Yorkshiremen like plumcake with cheese,' logic is content to rest on the purely notional shape of the thinking; for all it cares, we might as well have said, 'Bosnians like peaches with pork.'

[2] *Summa Theologica,* Ia: IX: 1, 2. Commentary, III *Physics, lect.* 1. V, *lect.* 1, 3.

periods must be established even in a never-ending movement, as in Peter Simple's observations on the Royal Bengal Tiger, 'only three years old, what growed ten inches every year, and never arrived at its full growth.'[1]

Scholastic science is alleged to deal with the position of objects rather than with their speed. Despite some flexibility and modulation, the elements of its processes are nouns, not adverbs,[2] while *to be* and *to have* are the verbs.[3] The effect is that of a man who has a firm command of Basic English. There is great clearness and firmness of outline about the argument, especially when conducted in the Latin language; the work may be fine and delicate, yet the result is like an etching without half-tones and tints. The thomist philosophy in general has been supposed to suffer from this stationary quality: various causes have been suggested; it is a statuesque achievement, say some; it has been adopted as an official doctrine, say others. Not seldom there is a failure to appreciate its intellectual humility and self-criticism, its vitalism, and the depth and range of the analogies in its reasoned dialectic.

---

[1] The likelihood of an indefinite evolution must be left to natural philosophy, where the scholastics favour definite and achieved types, and a time when growth must stop. *Summa Theologica,* 1a: XLVI: 1, 2.

[2] Namely, categorematic terms, or terms standing by themselves, such as man, dog, cause, and congenial to the lapidary style of *laborare est orare* and *dulce et decorum est pro patria mori*; not syncategorematic terms, or modifications of another term, for example humorously, faithful, effective, etc.

[3] Usually cast in the present tense, when they are not made into nouns by the use of the infinitive.

CHAPTER VI

SIGN AND SYMBOL

IT is commonly taken for granted that a simple conception in the mind somehow exists in the outside world as well; that *cheese* enclosed in our consciousness when we think of it can also be enclosed in a rind on the larder slab. Let us suppose that this indeed is the case; it is not a finding of logic alone, but requires a close analysis of sensation and a critical philosophy prepared to take the examination of knowledge to its ultimate grounds.[1] Do our thoughts correspond to things or not? Are there things, or are there merely thoughts? Or as some would say, are there not only things merely? Is being the same as being perceived? To such questions, in so far as he attends to them, St Thomas replies in no subjectivist strain, for he holds that the mind is a part of reality, that concepts are sympathies, *passiones animae*,[2] that knower and known become one.[3] He compares their union to the action and passion of male and female,[4] and speaks gently of the early Ionians—divining the truth, but from afar off[5]—who described the situation as a physical assimilation. Let us admit for the present, that conceptions involve a double existence, *duplex esse*.[6] First, there is cheese really and physically existing, cheese in its natural being, in *esse naturali*, and secondly, there is cheese perceptually and mentally repeated in my consciousness, cheese in its significant being, in *esse*

---

[1] Whether ideas be purely subjective or not is of little consequence to logic. For the sake of explaining the scholastic terminology we shall adopt what is called the position of commonsense. Incidentally this is not a term of praise in learned circles and some look down their noses at naïve realism.

[2] Commentary, I *de Anima, lect.* 2. I *Peribermenias, lect.* 2.

[3] Disputations, VIII *de Veritate*, 6, Exposition, and *ad* 3.

[4] Opusc. XIII, *Compendium Theologiae,* ch. 38.

[5] Commentary, I *de Anima, lect.* 12.

[6] Note that in scholastic usage the term physical is not restricted to the merely bodily, but includes everything that is natural and real in the material universe. Thus the human soul, the substantial form of body, is a physical being and the object of that part of natural science and philosophy called psychology.

intentionali.[1] The word comes from *intendere,* to stretch out, to direct towards, which indicates that the mental form or concept of cheese must be treated not as a thing and a final term of direct knowledge, but as an open relation and a medium.[2] Through its passion or affection the mind conceives a similitude or likeness. The form is not opaque, but transparent; the mind does not stay there, but looks through it to the thing that is signified.

Let us shift from the senses to the presence of cheese in the mind as an intelligible nature, or in scholastic terminology as a *species intelligibilis,* a significant likeness of its nature, a form rendering cheese understandable.[3] Such mental forms, though the stock-in-trade of logic, are no more than currency for other sciences, useful only for what they bring in. In themselves they are entirely secondary to and derivative from real things.[4] Thinkers inevitably flounder in subjectivism when they treat these representations as terminal, not penultimate or mediate. They are like economists who make an idol of gold. But as money is important for food, clothing, shelter and the amenities, so these mental forms are important to the sciences, including psychology but excluding pure logic, only because they signify something beyond themselves and beyond a mental state.[5] An idea consists in beckoning or pointing; in other words it is a sign; not a facsimile but a means to knowing another.[6]

Now there are two kinds of sign, natural and artificial. The force of the former does not depend on convention, arbitrary agreement, or previous instruction; instinctively and directly the attention is transferred from the sign to the thing signified. Thus

---

[1] *Summa Theologica,* 1a: LXXXIV: 2. 1a: LXXVIII: 3. Disputations, XXII *de Veritate,* 12. The distinction is between the *immutatio naturalis,* the process of birth and decay, and the *immutatio spiritualis,* where, even in the lowest knowledge, there is a becoming another without ceasing to be oneself.

[2] *Summa Theologica,* 1a: LXXXV: 2. IV *Contra Gentes,* 11.

[3] Various terms are employed, enumerated here but not sorted: concept, idea, intelligible form, *eidos,* species, meaning, *intentio,* representation, *ratio,* mental word, *logos,* notion, likeness, abstract nature, concept. We use the word notion, for that, more than others, suggests a logical form. *Summa Theologica,* 1a: XV: 1, 2, 3. I *Contra Gentes,* 53. IV: 11. Disputations, III *de Veritate,* 1, IX: 4, *ad* 3.

[4] Disputations, XI *de Veritate,* 1, *ad* 2.

[5] *Summa Theologica,* 1a: LXXXV: 2.

[6] Disputations, IX *de Veritate,* 4, *ad* 4.

a skull-and-crossbones notice-board by the roadside warns the driver to take care; the footprint told Robinson Crusoe that he was not alone on the island; some tones of laughter manifest gaiety of heart, some cries suffering, some glances affection. If I point with my finger you will look along the required direction; though even here there are variations and degrees; we point with the first finger, but Red Indians with the second; we beckon with an upward curve, but they with a downward; dogs will look to where you are pointing, but cats merely glance at your finger tip.

With artificial signs, however, the pointed meaning is settled by agreement and custom; there is no intrinsic likeness between the symbol and the thing symbolized, and the relationship between them is conventional, *ex institutione*. Thus, says St Thomas, a trumpet is a herald of war. *Achtung!* on a mountain road means little to the driver ignorant of German, though he may pause at the exclamation mark; in the nature of things there is no more reason why a red-white-and-blue pole should signify a barber and not a confectioner. The words of spoken and written language are the commonest examples of artificial signs; they refer to reality only through the concepts they are invented to represent[1] and, unless accompanied by appropriate natural signs, such as gestures and noises, or invested with a magical charm, they do not inevitably resemble what they describe. There are words, such as cuckoo, ping-pong, twang, and children's words especially, such as puff-puff, moo-cow, bow-wow, that shade into natural signs; onomatopoeia enhances the power of words and many lines of poetry surpass artificial significance; 'the curves of the purple hills of Tusculum.' Dialectic will seek to rouse this sympathy in rational philosophy; the evocation goes beyond the signification. By association words become charged with emotion: how much adolescent sentimentalism is psychologically conditioned by their look and sound, how much political thinking? Yet in general all symbolism requires an initiation into the meaning; for the true significance of an artificial sign may be at variance with the natural impact of the situation, as when a glamorous secret agent winks across the restaurant in morse code.

The question arises whether our ideas are in the category of

---

[1] *Disputations*, II: 1. XXII: 7, *ad* 5. *Summa Theologica*, Ia: XIII: 1, 4, *ad* 1. Commentary, I *Perihermenias*, *lect.* 2.

real or artificial signs. Some hold that the mind throws its own light like a headlamp on the surrounding fog. They cannot admit that our ideas are natural likenesses of the world outside. Ideas may perhaps have a symbolic value and practical utility; but the existence of an objective natural world is doubted, or if granted, then any guarantee that we can know it is despaired of. Nevertheless, they say, let us make do with what we have and arbitrarily agree to attach the same useful meaning to the same idea so that we can engage in harmonious transaction together. Ideas are like words, and we must use the same dictionary.[1] A realist and vital philosophy, however, if it is a rationalism as well must claim more, it cannot be content with a let's pretend or with knowledge that has no roots in the physical world. Such a doctrine, doubtful of its contact with what is real, dries thoughts into artificial specimens and makes the communication of ideas just the exchange of convenient counters. By affirming that ideas are natural signs we break out of ourselves and find company.

---

[1] Reference is here suggested to the psychological doctrine of Behaviorism, that ideas in fact are initial speech movements and the words themselves mechanical reflexes. Language is then not the vehicle of meaning, but rather, as it were, the noise of machinery.

Chapter VII

IMAGE AND MEANING

Objects may be summoned up without being disclosed, for instance in the valediction to romantic philosophy in the music of Mahler. Many evocations are possible in a heightened sensibility; English nonsense-verse even has meanings where explanations cannot be attempted—

> Far and few, far and few
> Are the lands where the Jumblies live.

Here's richness indeed, and opportunity for a generous dialectic, but off the track of didactic logic, and so for the present we must neglect hint and keep to open avowal. At once a capital distinction, between image and meaning confronts us.[1]

A natural sign of a sensible situation, called by St Thomas a *vox*, though more than an animal spasm, may not exceed an interjection; but human speech, *locutio, sermo,* or *verbum*, renders an intelligible situation,[2] and that not merely by its arbitrary linguistic figure. That is to say a natural sign may point either to an occurrence or to a meaning or to both; we may catch the early morning summer mists, the glintle of rain on leaves, the note dying on the wind, or we may possess the laws of vaporization, of the refraction of fluids, or the theory of acoustics. In this contrast between fugitive perceptions and enduring generalizations, the former perhaps may be counted better worth the having, indeed there is some justice, the reverence we owe living substances, in our defiance of abstractions that stale as they last. Fortunately there are more humane durations.

> Past ruin'd Ilion Helen lives,
> Alcestis rises from the shades;
> Verse calls them forth; 'tis verse that gives
> Immortal youth to mortal maids.

---

[1] Commentary, III *de Anima, lect.* 4, 5, 6. *Cf.* Figure 2.
[2] *Summa Theologica,* 1a: XXXIV: 1. Commentary, I *Perihermenias,* I: *lect.* 2, 3, 4. I *Politics, lect.* 1.

For verse substitute wisdom, or rather let it mean the know-ledge most closely sharing in the creative and sustaining mind of God, the knowledge which is the aspiration of philosophy and of which logic even at its severest is the preparation.

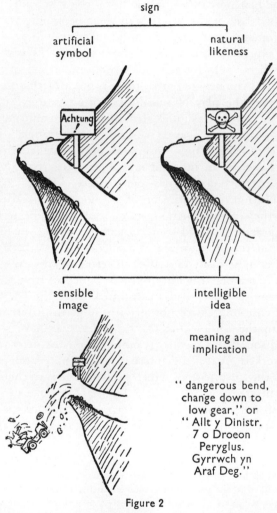

Figure 2

Corresponding to the contrast between an event in space and time and its lasting and universal meaning, there is a difference between a natural sign that is sensible and one that is intelligible.

This is the difference between image and idea, the dual symbolism running throughout all human consciousness.[1] To stop at the momentary responses of sense is difficult; the fleeting flash of king-fisher blue along the Regent's Park Canal, the first taste of Double Gloster, the first note of a hunting horn, the first sniff of estuary mud, the first feel of the fire. From their beginning they signify something outside, but until the mind takes over there is nothing lasting to express to ourselves or communicate, however imper-fectly, to others. 'Oh for a life of sensation and not of thought,' said Keats, and you may urge that there is no call either to heighten or to interpret the play of sensibility into a rational statement. That may be, but the point is that there is no enduring signific-ance until it is born again: sensations are strangled by space and time, they happen only once, and unless charged with reason they reflect merely an incident no sooner born than dying, and though we may avoid smugness our posture is less than human.

The reflection, or impression of phenomena, is called by the scholastics the sensible likeness, *species sensibilis*. The term *species*, sight or appearance, would seem to denote a predominantly visual character, but this is mainly a convenience of speech, since most knowledge is most easily described in terms of the sense of sight, the nearest to reason.[2] Lucidity must be banished from knowledge if this means distance, and made murkier if this means more warmth. Sense-images are not all visual but in different degrees according to the complexion of the individual have shape and texture and sound and savour. Coming from the external senses, they are worked up by the internal senses and received in the mind from the imagination, which presents them in the form of a composite image.[3]

It is also unfortunate that the term *image* suggests something rigid and statuesque, though every image as such is altogether

---

[1] Illustrated by the narrative pictures of the English painters from Hogarth to the pre-Raphaelites. In addition to the representation of a scene there is a lesson or moral, as in the picture of Napoleon sailing to exile in *Bellerophon* the grain of the planking is scrupulously drawn, every line of the rigging, the crease in the waistcoat, but the figure holding the centre conjures up the idea of genius in defeat.

[2] *Summa Theologica*, 1a: LXXVIII: 3.

[3] *Ibid.*, 1a: LXXVIII: 4. *Exemplar* is preferred to *image*. 3a:XXV: 3.

derivative and relative[1] as such. *Effigies*, a term also used, has a similar disadvantage. The scholastic term phantasm, *phantasma*, is perhaps happier, so long as the sense of the weird and fanciful does not enter. We shall follow the usage and speak of images, always remembering they are, as the case may be, luminous, murky, blaring, whispery, fluent, jagged, gentle, sharp, bitter, sweet, scented, stinking, earthy, airy, and with other appropriate qualities of sensuousness.

Human consciousness is not entirely enmeshed in the flesh; prolonged and solitary sensations do not always relapse into daydreaming. What starts in the senses is quickly infused with meaning, delicate or coarse, tenuous or harsh; musings are framed and related. Seeing a flash of blue we conceive—kingfisher! and immediately have a sign that does not uniquely point to the halcyon flight, but can send us to a bird-book to ponder over the same object in an entirely different context and in terms more general and lasting than the particular occasion by the Regent's Park Canal. So, too, from tasting the Double Gloster we may expatiate on the catalogue of cheeses and narrate encounters unlike the elevenses we had that morning at a Cotswold inn; the horn wakens echoes from history; the smells lead us to the science of soil; the fire kindles reflections on the future sources of industrial energy, and so on. We penetrate beyond sense images whenever we perceive a rational meaning and pass a judgement. The adult mind does not merely register a series of jottings, but is constantly deciphering and in its waking consciousness arranging experiences according to a system of intelligible relationships; organizing them in some sort of plan, though this may be incomplete, limited, expectant, or hopeless; for all logic can tell, merely perhaps the solution of a grammatical puzzle. A man of principle is he who upholds a meaning however distracting and various the circumstances: a liberal journalist, who believes in freedom and human dignity, will attack tyranny from the Left as from the Right and see the menace both of the boss and the bureaucrat, the magnate and the manager. The drama of human character lies in the conflict between the here and now on one side and the general plan on the other.

'Look! a kingfisher.'—'Where?'—'There!' Consider that

---

[1] *Summa Theologica*, Ia: XXXV: I, *ad* I.

simple dialogue, which is not just exclamatory, but explanatory as
well; and while pointing then and there to a particular fact, implies
and uses knowledge previous to and not bound up with the immediate event; it presupposes that the speakers have a common and
general idea of kingfisher, of location, and of relative direction
from where they are standing. Such notions may be similarly
operative in entirely different sense situations; for we may look up
the term *kingfisher* in an ornithological dictionary: and what could
be more unlike the green canyon than a column of print? Or the
dialogue might run: 'Hark! a lark.'—'Where?'—'There!' Or
again: 'Ouch! hurts.'—'Where?'—'There!' In all these situations,
and many others, so different sensuously and emotionally, there is
a common meaning. We shall speak later of the grasp of analogy
under various and complex circumstances which is the essential
strength of intelligence: if we are inclined to dismiss this abstract
and formal significance as pretty thin stuff, we must remind ourselves that on its web is stretched out the entire texture of human
consciousness.

The pure logician is not perturbed by the supposed lack of
richness and satisfaction. He is not out to be full-blooded but
correct; his aim is not to work a confidence trick or to be persua-
sive, but to be exact in his handling of the shapes of interlocking
meaning; he is as indifferent to rhyme and enchantment as to ridi-
cule, sarcasm, invective and the forms of satire. It is for a higher
philosophy and dialectic to show that abstract truths are not like
evaporated milk or denicotinized tobacco or non-alcoholic beer, a
substitute and an occasion for wry reminiscence. We are not
moved or drawn to universals: it is not humanity that is healed, as
Aristotle says at the beginning of the *Metaphysics*, but this man or
that man; St Thomas however notes in this connection that the
universal is the *ratio* of things that move and must therefore be
tracked down.[1] Eventually, philosophy should sing, but our present demand is that it should sing in tune, and for that we must
have a common pitch and key.

Take the sensations and emotions evoked by the term *sea*: how
different they are, and how changing in one and the same individual. For the landsman it separates places, to the seaman it joins

---

[1] V *de Trinitate*, 2, ad 5.

them; a menace to the conscript, an opportunity to the navigator, a holiday to the yachtsman, a field to the fisherman: yet all can take part in a common discussion of what is at stake in the command of the sea. A meaning is fixed and enlarged amid the numerous images and emotions that are set loose by the sight or sound of the word. The idea of the thing must also be separated from the idea of the word, for words are bad travellers in geography and history: liberal is not the same in England and Quebec and Belgium; *Falange* is different in Chile and Spain; enthusiasm was deprecated in the eighteenth century, but admired in the nineteenth; political whiggery has gone into abeyance, though fortunately the spirit is not dead yet; charity has become patronage; and who likes now to be called respectable or amiable?

Now logic is exclusively concerned with signs that point to a rational meaning, *species intelligibiles,* the forms that express the enduring and general characteristics of the universe, not its passing and particular attractions. Furthermore these are subjected to a more refined abstraction, so that only their mental bearing remains. 'Ah! spider!'—you shudder, but I like spiders, and have cherished them as pets, steering bluebottles into their webs. Our images are different, our emotions are conflicting, yet the idea means to you what it means to me. And what is more, when we forget about the nature of spiders, and merely consider the notional quality of the concept, we can be more unanimous, as when you ask: 'What do you mean, a spider, or some spiders, or all spiders?' For all the world as if I had said, 'Ah! celery,' or 'Ah! topaz,' or 'Ah! kangaroo.'

And there, like a dowager winning the hundred yards in a burst of speed, was old *Ramillies* coming up, pushing a white bolster beneath her bows, with a high plume of smoke from her funnel and her guns cocked up at maximum elevation—but the real reassurance was that she was heavily armoured and could deliver a broadside of about eight tons, and that the Italians now had no stomach to interfere with the convoy. The adoption of the distinction between image and idea is indispensable for scientific thinking. For the imagination is always present, and however lively, fresh, and clean, its images are thick and solidified compared with the subtle and fluent reality of meaning.[1] Until we can separate

---

[1] *Summa Theologica,* 1a: LXXXIV: 6.

intelligible forms and partial but essential characteristics from the mixture we can scarcely be said to be engaged in rational reflection and discussion.

It is for philosophical psychology to elaborate on the difference between sensation and intelligence: how the former is individual and only approximately communicable; how the latter is universal and, when pains are taken, exactly communicable. I say *cat*; one sees tabby, another feels claws, another hears meowings, another remembers Lord Roberts, and so forth; but all can consider the same meaning, and the stronger our grasp on this the less we are at the mercy of stray sensations. Here is the clue to the old-fashioned catch, 'Yesterday I saw a cherry-coloured cat'; while we remain with sense-associations we smile at the absurdity, and not until we abstractedly think of *black* do we see the connection, why, black cherries, black cats. The distinction between imagination and meaning is at work even in trivialities.

That's the wise thrush; he sings each song twice over. Ideas and meanings can be communicated; they can be tested and related and examined and discussed and agreed over; they are social and civilized of their nature. But images and experiences are personal and cannot properly enter into psychological commerce; they can be suggested but not explained; in a sense, they always remain solitary. It is true that masses of people can be moved by rhetoric, and that skilful declamation and repetition of an image can mesmerize a multitude into a course of action. Rabbles do not respond to ideas; we have witnessed this in our own time, and not only with the nazis. The look and sound of a word or phrase is often used as a substitute for its meaning—worker's revolution, schoolgirl complexion, social security, people's justice, equality of opportunity, civilization, barbarism, daring; then, to go back, mysticism, science, evolution, General Gordon, property, free Briton, the Bible and the Bible alone, divine right of kings, hellfire: there are many instances where the strength of terms spoils their original sense. To pretend that we can live by reason alone or that logic requires no aid from rhetoric would be priggish; but it is well to insist that of all our faculties we are least lonely by the reason, even the loving will may only seek but never lay hold,[1] and sensations and emotions are, as we have said, private and particular.

------

[1] *Summa Theologica,* 1a–2ae: III: 4.

High happiness can be grasped by no other act than that of knowledge: in the meantime there is no substitute for the reason if we
would enter into pleasant intercourse with our fellows and deal
sociably with them.

Words have to be looked at quietly and discussion has to begin
with a definition. In theory at any rate one would expect ideas to
be most surely communicated when they are purest and least
mixed with sensation and passion. It is difficult to render them
when charged with feeling. A. E. Housman said that this single
line from Milton always moved him to tears:

> Nymphs and shepherds dance no more.

I consult the first dictionary to hand, and translate: legendary
lesser and mortal divinities imagined as beautiful young maidens,
or rather, since the dictionary adds *poetical*, young and attractive
women together with men employed in tending, feeding, and
guarding sheep are no longer engaged in leaping and stepping with
motions of the body adjusted to the measure of a tune. All that
can be said is that something of the meaning remains. In imaginative utterance you can scarcely alter a vowel sound without
breaking the sense; so much so that, according to Cardinal Newman, the multiplication table is one of the few things that can be
translated from one language to another without detriment to the
original. There is here a pure rational meaning: nevertheless exact
communication need not be limited to mathematics nor demand
the pedantic awkwardness of our exegesis of Milton. There is a
deft separation of sensible and intelligible signs in all the sciences,
and it is peculiarly the doing of logic. Afterwards they may be
re-united, and that largely is the doing of dialectical philosophy.

For the security of communication creeds are best set in dead
languages and recited in monotones. Consider the Catholic
Church merely as a contemporary organization without ranging
to periods that have passed and regions that have been lost: despite
the great variety of religious experience, wealth of diverse cultures,
gradation of moods and contrasts of individual types, even differences of theological accents, there is a unity in a common dogmatic and disciplinary idea. Sensation and emotions pass away,
but thoughts and meaning endure with logic as their bone.

> Bones, never vivid as blood, longer resist the sucking
> Of mould and worms.

It is difficult to strip ideas from their sensible manifestations, however meagre these may be: distracting emotions may be set up by
initial letters, such as l.b.w., l.s.d., LST, or LMS. Yet a logical
habit will seek to pierce beyond the appearance of words and
images, and will unconsciously use what an American critic has
named a fog-index to journalism.

Ideas cannot be assimilated until they have been made palat-
able, and this is the work of rhetoric, which treats of the possible
ways of persuading people on any given subject. The method of
logic is proof, not persuasion; and here it differs from the art of
swaying the imagination and the passions, and which may be employed even to recommend logic by a display of allegory and alli-
teration. But just as rhetoric may have the effect of exciting a
strong emotion, often of reprobation, instead of an idea, of using
words as nicknames, which, says Hazlitt, 'are the talismans and
spells that collect and set in motion all the combustible part of
men's passions and prejudices,' so logic may have the effect of
chilling warmth with a platitude. Both effects however are
abuses, particularly indefensible in the case of logic, for it is the
servant of the human reason; every idea should be a biological act
in the widest sense of the term and stir the appetite.

We speak of cold logic, and there is an austerity about the
purely logical treatment of a subject; though the old physicians
sought to cure excess by excess, the *Summa Theologica* is no cure for
spiritual dryness. In a way, logic is a puritan among the sciences,
killing colour, suspicious of the senses, even of the magic of such
terms as Coromandel Coast, Aphrodite, debonair, threnody, the
Downs and Christmas Eve. It would protect us from the racket
of catch phrases and bogy words; it is disdainful of what are called
loaded terms, and of verbal effects where the emotional fringe does
duty for the meaning, such as retribution, communist, appeasement, Jew, prelate, feudalism, fascist horde, sex, officer class,
freedom, dogma, democracy, Poona, progress, high finance, Vati-
can, and others that crop up in the high-brow periodicals, itself
a term of the same sort. Yet though we are now going to consider
the purely mental shapes and figures of ideas, we must not forget
that our real interest is with the extension of logic into an exciting
and untidy environment.

Chapter VIII
SHAPE OF NOTIONS

'Look! a kingfisher'; before the phrase is finished, the speaker has surpassed sensation and touched an abstract nature. When he makes such a pronouncement as 'kingfishers swallow fish tail foremost,' and asks himself, 'does that mean *all* or *some?*' then interest is temporarily transferred from the real idea to its mental form and figure. The enquiry now is whether the idea is general or particular, and the purely logical interest is the same as if the observation had been to the effect that whales or razorbills or sea-lions or Andaman Islanders swallow fish tail foremost. In other words no attention is paid to the real significance nor to the psychological notes and echoes of our concepts; they are admitted solely as notions to be subjected to the tests for correct thinking. In consequence logic can appear intricate and contrived, not simple and direct; the bird is left for the notion; the electric blue, the swift low flight, the messy nest, all forgotten for a mental pattern.

Yet even those mainly interested in the bird may profit from this logical excursion; for say they are told that kingfishers frequent ponds, and this on the strength of two or three observations; then should they be on their guard against changes in the logical form of the idea which may start up together with illogical inference from the habits of few to the habits of all, as in the flat statement, kingfishers are pond birds. Few periodicals will not provide examples of this jumping from few instances to a universal rule; from some religions to religion itself, from one swallow to the summer. One particular object is used to prove another; the features of Salazar are delineated from Hitler's. There are other logical fallacies to be treated later, of which one of the most frequent is to argue from association to identity—'the philosophy of Aquinas is subsidiary to his theology, and therefore his proofs for the immortality of the soul are special pleading.' Often the reader is not in a position to check the conclusions from his own first-hand knowledge; but even when he is off his own beat, say on some such subject as the psychology of the Russians, the politics of the Spanish clergy, or the beliefs of primitive races, he may yet detect a logical fallacy and treat the argument with appropriate reserve.[1]

Ideas and notions are qualities that can vary according to area and intensity, conditions of quantity applied by analogy to quality.[2] Area is measured by the number of units comprised, thus we speak of acres more or less wide, of fleets more or less large, of ideas more or less embracing. Intensity is measured by the penetration effected, by the degree of possession or domination over the material, thus we speak of colours more or less bright, of sounds more or less loud, of ideas more or less exhaustive. Both measurements may be used when qualities are compared; we can say that there is more white in the cliffs of Dover than in this page, meaning that there is a greater extent of whiteness, but that this page is whiter, meaning that there is a greater intensity of whiteness: similarly as regards love, for benevolence may be judged both by its range and by its localization and force. So also knowledge may be rated according to span and to depth, by sweep and fullness, extent and penetration, or, to use scholastic terminology, by *extensio* and *comprehensio*—in this context the latter term contracts a narrowing sense.

The area or extent of an idea is judged by the number of objects contained. *Man* covers millions of individuals, but *animal* is wider still, for to the multitude of human beings are added the innumerable members of other species, mosquitoes, golden plovers, limpets, giraffes, minnows and all. The three following progressions represent ever widening notions: *Renown*, battle-cruiser, man-of-war, ship; Thomas More, Londoner, Englishman, European; Sukie, cocker-spaniel, mammal, animal.

---

[1] In some cases, of course, special knowledge is required; the following argument can be met only by a practical acquaintanceship with the business of publishing: if the expenses of an edition of a thousand copies will cost one hundred pounds, then I suppose an additional five hundred copies will cost fifty pounds more. Yet the field of purely logical criticisms remains large. We have been warned against identifying meanings because they conjure up much the same picture; a political Christian may be a man of the Right in some countries, a man of the Left in others. We should be warned against confusing ideas of different shapes because their core of meaning is the same; one is not some, and some are not all; nor does a contingent connection establish an essential predicate.

[2] *Summa Theologica*, 1a–2ae: LII. 1a–2a: III: 1, *ad* 1.

The intensity or penetration of an idea depends on its completeness as the representation of an object, on its ability to express the special characteristics as well as the general features. The idea of *Renown*, if narrower, is deeper and contains more notes than does the plain idea of ship; so also in this sense the idea of Thomas More is richer than the general idea of man, and the idea of Sukie more vivid than that of mammal. The sense of the special and peculiar is for the literary artist to cultivate, rather than for the philosopher; it must be confessed that scholasticism displays a preference for ideas that are wide and general. This is partly because its congenial method of deduction works from the covering general idea to the particular case, partly because its bent is to systematize from broad principles, partly because a universal nature is more tractable than a many-sided individual to brief and convenient definition. The abstract is easier to deal with than the concrete, the act of existence more mysterious than any essence.

Unless an epigram succeeds in hitting them off—

> Death the Skeleton,
> And Time the Shadow—

the description of features becomes prolix; logic is shy of such contrasting wealth as in the old blazon of *Mortalities Atchievement*:—

'He beareth for his coate Armour in a sable field, or land of Terroure and darknesse, dead bones in the midle layd crucifix, between a Skull and a crowne Imperiall, turned Topsy Turvy confusion-like proper, ensigned with Mortalitie on the Prince of Terrours head, environed with a wreath of snakes or poisonous wormes, crawling through the eye holes and out of the mouth; where there is fixed an houre glasse between a Turffe spade and shouell supported by Two Skallitons, or Images of death, one holding a dart the end reuersed, the other a syth, with top over his heade, Mantled with Oblivion Lined with Obscurity; standing Vpon the Brink of eternity, whereon is engraven this everlasting Motto by the hand of Truth, *Triumpho: Omnia Mihi Nihil.*'

Without prejudice to higher conditions of knowledge, at once more universal and more profound, it will be noticed that the extent and fullness of rational ideas vary in inverse proportion. The wider-spread they are the thinner they are, like butter on toast. The more intense they are, the less they cover, all the butter is at

3

one corner. The more diffused means the less intimate—tallying with the reproach, something about everything but everything about nothing. On the other hand, the more penetrating and total an idea with respect to one, the less applicable it is to others. Johnson said of Cowley that he pursued his thoughts to the last ramification, 'by which he loses the grandeur of generality.'

Merely to know *ship* conveys nothing of the lean strength and speed of *Renown*; while merely to know *Renown* tells you next to nothing about tunny boats or trows or stern-wheelers or luxury liners or junks.[1] *Man* defines part of the Duke of Marlborough, but will not explain his charm and military genius; he provides few clues to the understanding of Beaudelaire, Isaac Watts, Kant, Fra Angelico, or Aristophanes. Or again, religion is a more extensive idea than Christianity, but not so intensive; and Christianity is wider than Catholicism, but not so deep; and so on down through Latin Catholicism to Dominicanism, and to Savonarola, Catharine of Siena, Lacordaire, and Lagrange. The more latitudinarian, the less comprehensive; it will be noticed that the usage of the word is different in logic and in broad-minded religion.

In life and learning there is a tension between the wide and the deep, the general and the particular, the common and the private. Logic notes the difference, but not the suffering. Philosophy is at odds with poetry. Everything goes flat when seen from above, the higher you are the less apparent the valleys and eminences. But this is to speak of the reasoning reason not of knowledge itself, for the divine Logos embraces all things at once and enters the recesses of each particular.[2] There not shallow the wide nor narrow the deep. But the double and contrasted measures of human ideas according to extension and comprehensiveness determine a notional figuration which is the particular concern of logic and which must now be examined.

'Caroline,' said Mr. Helstone smiting the mahogany, 'understand this: it is vulgar and puerile to confound generals with particulars; in every case there is the rule and there are the exceptions.' The extension of a notion is here in question, its power to encompass many objects; ship and animal have been given as examples of

---

[1] *Summa Theologica,* 1a: XIV: 1, *ad* 2. 7. 11, *ad* 1. 1a: LVIII: 2, 3, 4. Opusc. X, *de Causis, lect.* 10.

[2] *Summa Theologica,* 1a: XXXIV: 3.

very extensive notions, but *Renown* and the Great Duke of Marlborough, though comprehensive, are highly exclusive, they do not
communicate with other things but keep to themselves.

A singular notion indicates an individual, one alone and no
other[1]; it indicates, neither exposing nor explaining; for rational
knowledge can make no more than a gesture towards such a one.
The individual is but the occasion for formal abstraction which
stays with types. Science, says Aristotle, does not treat of singulars; a remark often quoted by St Thomas, from the opening of
the *Summa Theologica*,[2] where it is used as an objection against the
scientific status of a theology engaged on working with historical
fact, namely the Christian revelation, and often repeated, especially
in the treatises on morality, where the impossibility of guiding
conduct merely from scientific habits of mind is often affirmed.
The reason is first concerned with general forms, and a set of them
grouped as a pointer reading to a unique substance and associated
with a particular image of that substance does not amount to a
direct knowledge of its heart. Logic, less perhaps than other
sciences, is occupied with individual events, save as they relate to
the proper patterning of our thinking. Examples of singular
notions are the man who broke the bank at Monte Carlo, Herne's
Oak, Harriette Wilson, W. G. Grace, the Star of India diamond,
Bucephalus, Immanuel Kant, the *Summa Theologica*, Tintern
Abbey, Crete, the opinion of Aristotle on a given point, and so
forth. The sciences do not fasten on such singulars, except by way
of example or citation of an authority; their movement is with
general natures, with the proprieties rather than with the actual
observance. To pin oneself to what Aristotle affirms and to follow faithfully what Boethius says in such or such a place is to be
a commentator, a biographer rather than a philosopher.

Singular instances may serve as the beginning of an argument,
but even then they are more an occasion than a cause. Logic
watches lest they become illegitimately particular or general, and
the discourse widen out into statements about women in general,
cricketers, precious stones, gamblers, trees and so on. We cannot
with safety argue from the behaviour of one individual to that of
another, from Harriette Wilson to Harriet Martineau.[3]

---

[1] *Summa Theologica*, 1a: I: 2, obj. 2.   [2] *Ibid.*, 1a: XIII: 9.

[3] *Ibid.*, 1a: LXXXVI: 1.

The position of singulars is uneasy in a philosophical assembly, though they don the uniform of general ideas—and wear them in a peculiar fashion. All the same, when ideas strive to express the singular they approach more nearly than do sweeping generalizations to that intuition of whole existing substance without which knowledge is imperfect. Though the most problematic object of experience the singular is also the most intimate.[1] Here in philosophy is found the story of Cinderella, with the same moral and ending.

In contrast to a singular notion stands a universal notion expressing a meaning that can be repeated; a form that is, or can be, possessed by more than one thing, for example, woman, diamond, horse, gambler. Common signifies what can belong to many, thus common room, common land; but universal adds the sense of being multiplied and identified with its members.[2] Such a universal notion is called a particular or disjunctive notion when restricted, and a general notion when unrestricted.

A particular notion is a universal limited to less than all; for example, one woman, two diamonds, three horses, most gamblers. It differs from a singular notion in that a communicable nature is expressed, whereas a singular notion is private and cannot be transferred from one object to another. There is but one Harriette Wilson, but the notion of a woman expresses a general nature not limited to one person, though a qualification is added which attaches it to one individual conceived in general terms, or to what the scholastics call the unattached individual, *individuum vagum*.[3] That most and many, as well as one, two, or some, are restrictions should be noticed.

For particular notions must be treated guardedly if they are not to set off a train of illogical thinking. What is true of some horses is not true of most; what applies to most gamblers does not apply to all. We shall return later to the use and abuse of particular notions when we come to deal with the conduct of argument; there we shall see that the inductive sciences work with the idea of the usual and the most, not with the idea of the necessary and the all, and that their generalizations are approximate and

1 *Summa Theologica,* 1a: XIV: 11.
2 *Ibid.,* 1a: XIII: 9.
3 *Ibid.,* 1a: XXX: 4.

neither truly universal nor lit by insight into natures. There is no harm in this, but only benefit, so long as the restriction is recognized.

In a general notion there is a universal meaning applying without restriction to all members of a class; to all women without restriction, all trees, every cause, all copper, all water, all truthfulness as such, every top, every column—the pages of any book, even Bradshaw, will provide examples of notions used without limitation. As may be imagined, the finding of truly general ideas is the ambition of science, the search for the law without exception. This is most certainly the case with philosophical science and with logic. A good syllogism, the straightforward expression of the logic of the schools, is based on the principle that whatever can be predicated of a general nature can be predicated also of each and every subject possessing that nature.

CHAPTER IX

COMMUNITY AND SOCIETY

THE disposition of general notions under collective and distributive headings, primarily the affair of logic, enters deeply into social philosophy. Contemporary totalitarianism, which ominously substitutes human masses for the individuals composing them, was prefigured by the giant effigy on the title page of the *Leviathan*, and preceded by a liberalism according to which the human group was just an aggregation of independent units or a collection of numbers enclosed in a bracket; an individualism, curiously reverent of the voice of the majority. The purely notional categories of collective and distributive wholes will be of assistance in framing such topics.

Nouns of multitude indicate collective notions; a flotilla of destroyers, a covey of partridges, a stack of hay. All the members of a group taken together in the lump are signified, but not each one of them taken singly. There is always something about the whole that does not belong to the parts; in the composition another entity is produced, over and above the components, of a character different, and sometimes less admirable: the voice of the mob, the yell of the crowd, and even public policy, these are less than human. When real and individual personality is merged into a pack, then take care. The group is sometimes termed with unconscious irony a *moral person*, but moral is an ambiguous term and as a rule the actions of a group, even when composed of people individually estimable, tend to be irresponsible and defective by the standards private persons would set for themselves; this is borne out by the history of corporations and religious institutions. It has been said that the speed of a fleet is that of the slowest vessel; in fact it is slower.

But there is another type of generality set in sharp contrast, namely a distributive whole expressed by a distributive notion. Here all the members of a class are signified, and also each one of them taken singly. Man, cause, animal, quality, plant, these meanings are applied wholly and without diminution to each and every example. Every particular is a microcosm of the general whole. Human nature—a distributive notion—is entire in one man: the human race—a collective notion—is not. Distributive universals are most useful in logical argument, for an easy passage can be made backwards and forwards between the general and the particular. Collective notions are trickier though they are at a lower level of thought; you cannot identify a man with the bank to which he belongs, and it is difficult to pin down who is responsible for the acts of a nation. Of course distributive notions as well must be used with diffidence; it must not be thought that a generalization completely finishes off the particulars it includes; in the case of generalization according to genus and species there is much

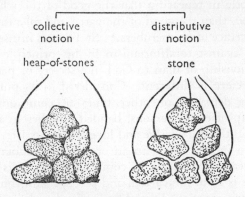

Figure 3

left out of account, for no particular is merely a type; in the case of a generalization by analogy, the interior iridescence of the notion is recognized. 'Is not the name of Englishman a general term,' enquired Hazlitt, 'as well as that of man? How many variations does it not combine within it?'

The difference between collective and distributive is of capital importance: the former is gross and applies to all the parts, or most of them, when taken together in the lump, it may be large, but is not truly universal; whereas the latter can be multiplied and shared without loss, and be wholly applied to each and all its parts. A good huntsman not only knows his pack, but each and every hound by character and proper name. The difference is more than a matter of logic, its applications in the contrasts between community and society powerfully affect human relationships. A human community is composed of individuals, all of whom have some share, usually unequal, in the common property; this common whole is greater than the parts and we conceive it existing as a kind of supervening entity[1]; the parts are entirely subordinate and, as it were, cede their own private inclinations in return for the benefit of belonging to the group. This kind of common good, *bonum commune*, is compared to a living organism, the well-being of which may sometimes require the amputation of a part.[2] There is something godlike about the claims of the community; we have read about, and suffered from the extravagant exaltation of the nation-state, but long before Hegel, the scholastics were but following Aristotle in repeating that the good of the whole is more divine, *divinius*, than the good of the part,[3] and tolerates, and even exacts, the sacrifice of its members.[4] St Thomas himself sterilizes this doctrine against totalitarianism by his principle of the immediate relationship of man to God in a society of persons.[5]

Now a society is different. Considered in its pure state and free from the demands of other types of communion, it is a companionship of equal persons, banded together in a friendship in which, as in the knowledge and love that is its life, there is no surrender,[6] no incorporation in an organism or subordination of parts to a greater whole, as in community. Life is here at its highest; there is communication, and perhaps gain, but no expansion at another's expense. Friend finds friend without loss of himself; the society exists only in and through them, there is no overriding *tertium quid*, their association has created no superior power to which they are subject. Such an analysis of friendship

---

[1] Commentary, I *Ethics*, lect. 1. *Cf.* Figure 3.

[2] *Summa Theologica*, 2a–2ae: LXIV: 2. 2a–2ae: LXV: 1.

[3] Commentary, I *Ethics*, lect. 2. *Summa Theologica*, 1a: LVIII: 7, *ad* 2. 1a: XXII: 4. 1a–2ae: XC: 2. 2a–2ae: LVIII: 5. Correct 2a–2ae: XXXI: 3, *ad* 2 by 1a–2a: II: 8, *ad* 2.

[4] *Summa Theologica*, 1a: XLIX: 2.

[5] The tempering distinction is found in his defence of consecrated virginity against the biological urge of the group to breed. *Summa Theologica*, 2a–2ae: CLII: 4, *ad* 3: a characteristic example of how his thought is tucked away in unexpected places.

[6] Disputations, II *de Veritate*, 2. *Summa Theologica*, 1a: LXXIX: 2. 1a–2ae: XXVIII: 2, 5. I *Contra Gentes*, 100.

in the strict sense[1] engages the profound sexlessness of love—all are one, and there is neither Jew nor Greek, neither bond nor free, neither male nor female—and supports the saying that charity knows no law, for positive law is essentially a community affair.[2] The contrast between collective and distributive notions applies to many problems of social morality, and touches off the controversy between communism and anarchism. A ruler, for example, is bound by decencies which do not derive from community needs, and may be condemned as a criminal by private law when he outrages them. No alleged national interest can defend the surrender of personal honour or the direct destruction of innocent life.

The examination of the scholastic concept of the common good would take us too far afield, but this at least must be said, and not merely to make a logical point, that to discern when the context refers to a human group taken as a collectivity composed of member-units and when it refers to a society of persons is of great consequence. There is a difference between the good of the community and the community of the good, though a state of pure society is perhaps but rarely and temporarily found in human conjunctions. At periods the relationship may be achieved, then it succumbs to a community base, the level of habit and common ground, of team-work and the claims of our animal nature, only to spring up again: the lapse is inevitable and merits no stricture; there is work to be done, the race and nation to be served, domestic economy established and property administered; perhaps only at moments are lovers actual, though their condition may be, and should be, habitual. Quiet friendship between men is possibly the most level and least taxing; but in present fact all association demands compromise and tends to produce the interim value of community. The companionship of husband and wife should be a state of society; the onset of family responsibilities brings a state of community; through to some extent, as the purpose of juridical authority is to produce a communication within good beyond legislation, so the purpose of this community is to destroy itself and be transformed into a state of society again, by the education

---

[1] *Summa Theologica*, 2a–2ae: XXIII: 1. 1a–2ae: XXVI: 4.
[2] *Ibid.*, 1a–2ae: XCVI: 1.

of the baby into friendship with its parents. Happy the family whose members are bound not by ties of blood and property alone.

The doctrine that things may be entirely united without constraint or fusion or any loss of identity has many ramifications in philosophy and theology, in the problem of how the One can create the Many and how the creature can live in the Creator and yet remain himself, as well as in the study of the implications of the Trinity; yet we must return to the logical treatment of collective and distributive ideas. At least the digression should aid us to appreciate the relevance of philosophy and its accompanying logic to the highest vital processes. There is a freedom about ideas that are whole and entire in each and in many, private yet communicable, distinct in substance yet identical in nature, *non idem numero sed idem specie*, real yet not the victims of physical change, generated without corruption. A thought dear to St Thomas lies behind his use of the term *communication*; there is a confident generosity about such ideas like that of truth itself; they are shared without diminution, given away but not spent, poured out without waste. They are neither statistical averages nor sums of amounts nor results of coalescence; lifted above the additions and subtractions of quantities, they are essential to philosophical thinking.

Distributive ideas are so congenial to the human mind that there is a temptation to set them up in place of collective ideas, as when symbolic figures are used to personify collective groups, the Boche, Marianne, Uncle Sam, and then each individual member treated as an embodiment of the whole. A reverse substitution was perpetrated by the Edwardian bishop who brought himself to bless the movement for women's higher education; addressing Oxford women students he pointed out that they were 'all destined to become the wives of some good man.' He meant each. Special fallacies attend such thinking, namely the fallacies of composition and division.[1]

---

[1] An example has been given in the matter of a publisher's costs. An illegitimate division may be made when an edition, a collective notion, is sorted into equal components; the publisher's costs of the first few books run off the press are far more than a few shillings, while of the last few they are far less. As an example of an illegitimate composition may be taken the argument that because a cinematograph film consists of many 'stills' the perception of a moving picture on the screen is therefore an illusion: or that a society of penitents constitutes a penitentiary.

COMMUNITY AND SOCIETY 75

For this reason any human group, whether it be called the Class, or the Nation, or the Race, or the Social Collectivity, or the Dynasty, should very guardedly be allowed the attributes of human personality: and, in the reverse direction, rulers and subjects cannot shield themselves from blame behind the impersonal irresponsibility of their group. *Moi, je suis l'état*, was a juridical concept of French political theory and practice at the end of the seventeenth century, but Louis XIV was probably too well versed in logic, too little a neurotic, and too well monitored by Madame de Maintenon and his Jesuit confessor to carry the attribution to extravagance.

Mysticism, whether sacred or profane, may be allowed to transcend logic, but not to swamp it. By scrutinizing the nature and limits of a collective whole and contrasting it with a distributive whole, some of the excesses surrounding the social philosophy of totalitarianism may be exposed. In their public lives, still less in their private lives, men are not wholly members of a collective group, religious or civil[1]; nor is any man the head or servant of the whole so as to be empowered to sink his conscience in its irresponsibility: the Duke of Wellington spoke for an old tradition when he warned the Cabinet that if they wanted Napoleon put to death they must find someone else for the job. Justice, as Socrates said, should be written larger and be more discernible in the State than in the individual. Notwithstanding its discipline, medieval civilization recognized that some of the virtues were not to be tested by their direct community value nor recluses to be treated as oddities; the temper of following ages has been perhaps more civic; the ideal of a state-servant stresses the less original qualities of human character.

No human person can avoid responsibility because the community to which he belongs is credited with irresponsibility; the laws of logic and of morals alike should forbid him. The argument:—the Party was composed of these individuals—the Party did not act with criminal deliberation, since it was running out of control—therefore, this individual member of the Party did not act with criminal deliberation, falls into the same fallacy as the following:—this book is composed of these pages—this book is not

---

[1] *Summa Theologica*, 2a–2ae: II: 3.

about politics—therefore this page is not about politics. Great care is called for in any argument from a part to a collective group, from one page to a book, from one human person to his community: and still greater care when the argument is in a reverse direction, above all in questions of social philosophy, lest the claims of corporations be used to suppress the obligations and privileges of human persons.

The situation with regard to distributive wholes is less subject to restriction; there is free and easy movement between them and the particular objects they include. More will be said about this distributive glide when we come to consider the logic of reasoning. Syllogisms themselves are less pieces of clockwork than a cyclic chorus, and their periods are not so mechanically punctual but they can tolerate the free play of meaning. In the meantime we may look at the division of distributive universals into two classes, univocal ideas that express a fixed nature and analogical ideas that express a more flexible and perhaps deeper reality.

CHAPTER X

ANALOGY

A BRISK rationalist method may single out notes of reality without listening to their echoes and consonances. The particular sciences may play with a mute, but wisdom wants richer sounds. Unity in multitude is the signature of beauty; and how shall the simplicity in diversity, the *communiones contrariorum* and the *incommixtiones unitorum*,[1] be declared except by abundance? The measure of philosophy becomes musical, the logic of forms a dialectic of difference and likeness. There is no excellence that is not strange, no thing precious that is not also friendly. Even the Pickwickian sense has a place, for philosophy does not work only with standard fixtures. Neither extreme can be avoided,

> Nor a tall *Metaphor* in the Bombast way,
> Nor the dry chips of short lung'd *Seneca*,

yet the movement does not oscillate between them, as though sometimes it were severely scientific and literal and at other times rhetorical and figurative, but combines them in the method of analogy. There is a literal sense even in metaphors.[2] Anatomical diagrams cannot fairly display this circulatory system of the thomist philosophy; it functions in a living whole.

The account must start from what has been said about distributive ideas. They represent communicable forms. And here we note a major difference. Some may be applied in exactly the same and unvarying sense to the particulars they comprise, in which case they are called univocal or identical notions; whereas others may be applied according to some resemblance or association, more or less profound, in which case they are called analogical or analogous notions. The degree of the likeness will mark the difference between true and forced analogy.

---

[1] Opusc. XIV: IV *de Divinis Nominibus, lect.* 6.
[2] *Summa Theologica*, 1a–2ae: CII: 2, *ad* 3. *Cf.* Figure 4.

A univocal notion, the same word and the same meaning, is attributed to many objects according to the same specific meaning. I am a man in the same sense that you are a man, we may differ by temperament, sex, physique, constitution, background, training, character, social status, yet essential humanity is the same in both of us. In this respect, the notion of man is univocal, so also the notions copper sulphate, crimson rambler, golden Labrador, animal, and probably Old Etonian.[1]

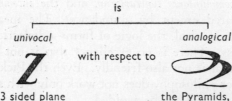

distributive idea

e.g. triangle

is

univocal   analogical

with respect to

3 sided plane   the Pyramids,
figures   the Family, the Trinity,
                        the Archduke Trio, past-present-future,
                    perception-judgment-reasoning, triangle
                        drama, trinitro compounds, etc., etc.

and these may be the cues for such terms as :
threesquare, foundations of society,
eternity, compactness, achievement,
constant flow, fertility, first number
actually odd, common chord, explosive,
tricorne, *San Ho Hui*, magical triad, etc., etc.

Figure 4

A generic or specific nature is here indicated, which would be transformed into another kind were any intrinsic alteration suffered; the idea is so definite that it either is or is not, and there's an end on't; shades of meaning do not enter. There is but one way of essentially being a man, and that is by being a body informed with a rational soul; there is but one way of being copper sulphate, crimson rambler, and so forth. But there are many ways of being

---

[1] *Summa Theologica*, 1a: XXIX: 4, ad 4.

true or good or beautiful, ideas that cannot be enclosed in univocal notions. Taken as a univocal idea, *man* applies equally to all men; no individual has more of the abstract substance of human nature than any other human individual, though as regards the accidents, which are much more prominent in social intercourse and morality, there is great variation.[1]

Egalitarianism therefore is justified in the logical realms of genus and species; by a similar abstraction the legal concept of the equality of all men before the law is established. But at once higher and lower than this exact scale is the inequality of being, to be engaged only by the use of analogy. There is a favouritism in creation—shall he that contendeth with the Almighty instruct him?—and God does not make all men equal except in the essential and abstract requirements of their nature; otherwise there would be one level of happiness, all would be equally virtuous or wicked,[2] and, more bothering, we should be called upon to love all equally.[3]

Univocal forms are invariable in themselves, though they can be extinguished by mutations in their subjects[4]; that is to say, they are present in no intermediate or ambiguous sense. In this they promise well for research; they have a fixity of meaning which ensures neat exchange and a ready calculation; the security and convenience of a money standard, and also the limitations; the fool-proof framing of a questionnaire on a government form, and also the stringency of detail.

Specific natures, observes Aristotle and St Thomas often repeats the comparison, are like numbers[5]; their differences are of kind, and not of degree. Nine, ten, and eleven are, as it were, specifically different, but arithmetically you cannot have one ten *tennier* than another: ten just men are no more ten than ten green bottles; the notion falls on both sets with exactly the same stress; which goes to show how limited is this mode of thought, but also how safe and secure. Rose is the same for all roses, dog for all dogs, man for all members of the human race; there are differences between *Gloire de Dijon* and Dorothy Perkins, between a Pomeranian and a bull-mastiff, between a Bantu and an Eskimo, but

---

[1] Opusc. XI, III *de Regno*, 9.
[2] *Summa Theologica*, 1a: XX: 3, 4.
[3] *Ibid.*, 2a–2ae: XXVI: 6, 7.
[4] *Ibid.*, 1a–2ae: LII: 1.
[5] Commentary, VIII *Metaphysics*, *lect*. 3.

the differences are extrinsic to the central univocal idea; there is an identical core of meaning. From the point of view of scientific classification, no man is more human than another[1] and though, according to morals, a good man is a better man than a bad one, the difference lies not in their radical nature, but in their habits and final end.

The clearness of univocal notions will be appreciated; they are definite and edged; they chart a fixed and rational clearing in a confusion of hints, but do not explore the recesses of reality.[2] They suit those sciences that build up their effects in layers. High philosophy transcends them, nevertheless they remain the goal of the natural scientist and philosopher who sets out to classify and establish the formula which shall express with exclusive and unvarying meaning the nature of the wild convolvulus and the mountain goat and vitamin D; and then to relate the finding in a general system of knowledge. How far he can seize the heart of things is another matter, but at least he can affix a label sufficient for recognition. Perhaps, as in experimental biology, the concept of a species is scarcely more than a test applied to a group of individuals that breed true within their own limits. The detection of species and the claims that are made by that token must be left to the naturalist who, with perseverance and modesty, may train himself to perceive essential identities and differences or their methodic equivalents, and may reach the quickness of an observer who can spot eight different varieties of bats on the wing. The logician as such is solely concerned with the mental rules of classification and of predicating a general nature of a particular object: whether the concept represents a real specific nature or whether it is but a symbolic approximation does not worry him; what he insists on is that the term should bear the same sense whenever invoked and should be invariably treated as carrying a univocal notion.

Now we must broach the subject of employing meanings hard to catch and conquer. As the personal character of St Thomas was made up of contrasts for comparison not for contradiction—

---

[1] In philosophy, by the way, women count as men, though the scholastics, influenced by the aristotelean physics and the ethics of the stoics, are not wholehearted in the admission.

[2] I *Contra Gentes*, 32.

gentle yet drastic, self-effacing yet majestic in the vigour of his
Norman and Hohenstaufen blood—so his philosophy cannot be
appreciated without the dialectic of likeness in difference. For
him analogy is not just a method of arguing by examples, but is
a response to the interrelatedness of heterogeneous things and
an exposition of their affinities; it has a metaphysical weight
and ring. It may be mentioned in anticipation that the noblest
ideas are analogical, beauty and justice, truth and love, comedy
and tragedy, life itself,[1] indeed all the perfections engaged by the
fourth proof for the existence of God.[2] 'To understand a proverb,
and the interpretation, the words of the wise, and their dark sayings,' to describe a spirit, elusive and free and yet revealing, not
confined to the track of univocal predication, a mixture of metaphors must be risked. Philosophy and literature alike employ
ambiguity, for the objects they engage cannot be answered with
simple mental clicks but require variously echoing reactions. To
strike the mathematical proportions is not enough, sensibility and
motion have to be preserved, and yet taken beyond the stage of
rhetoric; it is as though one were required to find a philosophy
intervening between the Pythagorean mathematics and the
Pythagorean mysteries.

Analogical ideas are not so crystalline as univocal ideas; there
is more of a shimmer and a mist about them. They respond to
beings which have an internal variety and degrees within themselves; they express perfections that can be differently pitched.
They are like shot silk compared with plain dull cloth. They start
at the level of ordinary idiom, as when we say as right as rain and
as fit as a fiddle, or speak of icebergs calving; they state a likeness in
such pleasant lines as

> Happy convents, bosomed deep in vines,
> Where slumber abbots, purple as their wines;

they lie at the heart of poetry, and what is more to the point, are
engaged by the philosopher as soon as he gets past the quasi-
mathematical categories of the natural sciences and touches the
everlasting myths. They are deep and far-ranging, lively and

---

[1] *Summa Theologica*, 1a: V: 6, ad 3. I *Contra Gentes*, 97.
[2] *Summa Theologica*, 1a: II: 3.

venerable, promising and variable, beckoning to heaven and re-
calling to earth. The dance is a *gigue triste*; the play a tragi-comedy.
The thought of St Thomas is alive with these settled novelties and
sudden antiquities, its movement is from an interaction of analogies and, despite the appearances, cannot be plotted on a figured
screen. A philosopher, he says, must marvel and be a lover of
myths and poetry.[1] They are beyond calculation by tables, as in
moral philosophy they are beyond the reach of legalism, for justice
itelf is above the written code and finds fullness in the play of
equity.[2] Lacking them the scientific atmosphere grows intolerant
and inhuman.

Analogical ideas are truly distributive, that is they apply to
each of many objects, but, unlike univocal ideas, they do not bear
a wholly identical sense throughout. They attempt to express the
sliding rhythms beneath set terms. They are based on different
strengths of being.[3] Thus healthy, to take St Thomas' example
of predilection, may be attributed to diet, or physical constitution,
or complexion, or game, or habit of mind, or regular motions.[4]
And again, there is beauty in a North Atlantic gale and in the Vale
of Pershore during May, in the Fens and in the Dolomites, in tor-
toises and in hares, in perpendicular gothic and the broken curves
of the baroque, in measured colonnades and Chinese pavilions, in
Lully and in Berlioz; in each case different and in each case
strangely kin. The analogy to an elephant's trunk is found in our
hands and not our noses; feet to us are fins to fish, lungs to us are
leaves to a tree.

One quality of the philosophy of St Thomas is to continue to
be surprised while retaining a sense of order; not to poetry alone is
this all-at-once freshness and familiarity dear, the novelty and the
déjà vu, the remote and the near, the discovery and the memory, the
simultaneous sense of first welcome and that we have been here
before:

> *curru nitido diem qui*
> *promis et celas aliusque et idem*
> *nasceris.*

---

[1] Commentary, I *Metaphysics, lect.* 3.
[2] *Summa Theologica*, 2a–2ae: CXX: 2.
[3] *Ibid.*, 1a: XIII: 5.
[4] *Ibid.*, 1a: XIII: 5.

A great novel does not stand alone in combining a universal theme and an intensely felt local setting. Creation compounded with eternity, the exciting manifold with quiet changelessness, 'full of tumultuous life and great repose,' that is the philosophical mystery of God, the problem of the Many and the One. The simultaneous continuity and discontinuity of all things in the universe including the creator, who yet dwells beyond our categories,[1] that is the guiding principle of natural theology.[2] Variety is more than the spice of life, it is the condition of intercourse within the union of minds and hearts[3]—two distincts, division none. One could continue in this vein; how metaphysics is at once both airy and ponderous, nimble and stately by the adoption, critical yet not grudging, of analogy; but our present interest is the method or dialectic of philosophy and not the after-effects.

If logic is to serve and be present in every play of spirit, guiding every adventure, keeping neither to the rails of univocation nor losing itself in the labyrinth of words, then must it possess a theory and a practice of analogy. This would be an impossible demand were logic but a branch of mathematical science albeit clad in verbiage, for mathematics is strictly univocal. That St Thomas adopts analogy in those very parts of his system exacting the hardest thought should dispose of the prejudice that science can work profitably only with ideas that are plain and fixed, for there it is required to follow every angularity and curve in its examination of the waywardness at the heart of being.[4] Being is not an undifferentiated genus, but enters into every particularity; consequently a humane metaphysics responds to different intensities within its object.[5] It will admit that one and the same idea can exist at different strengths; that some things possess more *being* than others, Suffolk Punches more than mangel wurzels, and Suffolk

---

[1] *Summa Theologica,* 1a: III: 5.

[2] *Ibid.,* 1a: IV: 3. I *Contra Gentes,* 29.

[3] *Summa Theologica,* 1a–2ae: XXVIII: 1, 2, 5.

[4] As will be seen later, any differences that confront the attempt to classify things univocally by genus and species can always be treated as coming from outside the common stock, vertebrate is additional to animal, and mammal is additional to vertebrate, and rational is additional to animal; but there is nothing additional to or outside being, no difference from without.

[5] Commentary, I *Metaphysics, lect.* 9.

farmers and their wives more than their horses; yet all belong
to reality and all are related[1] It will recognize that truth also
is various; mathematics is truer than experimental psychology
and philosophy truer than either; and so with all the variegated
ways of knowing, for they do not deal with lonely truths that
never meet. The purpose of analogy is to emphasize the likeness
while pointing the difference; the shock of surprise lingers after
the inevitability has been established: this runs from top to bottom,
from the statement that all loving reaches out, confidently or
otherwise, for God, to the figure of speech, the rats were that
hungry they even ate the anchors.

The first quality to be noticed about analogical notions is that
they rejoice in interior contrasts. These differences of degree are in-
accurately pictured as differences of size.[2] By resorting to them
the philosopher learns to be cautious with his either-ors in argument, for while you can be downright with univocal ideas, as with
pounds-shillings-and-pence, analogical ideas are not so readily
fixed, and since they express what is deepest and best in reality, he
does well, certainly in the domain of highest philosophy, who dis-
trusts the easy opposition, the slapdash alternative, the heaven or
hell of contrasted attitudes. And here it may be remarked that
moral theory is partly a metaphysical science.

One idea is enriched and strengthened when correlated with
others. In a world where all things are kin, it is the genius of
analogy to throw light on the unknown and still mysterious from
what is known and evident, to find familiarity even in what is
strange. The pathetic fallacy of reading our own affections into the
world must be avoided; but that is not an example of analogy, but
rather of working according to univocal ideas: through the French
windows we survey the garden scene, the moss on the dial, the
thrushes on the lawn, and call it kindly; yet is it also cruel, though
in no moral sense of the term. Sensibility apart, the whole of
creation is all of a piece, shot through with likenesses in difference;
and a world-dialectic must wield the delicate and powerful

---

[1] *Summa Theologica*, 1a: XVI: 7. I *Contra Gentes*, 54.

[2] As in the case of mortal and venial sin: the difference is not between big
and little, though it must be rendered so in the junior stages of the catechism,
but between denying an end and misusing the means. *Summa Theologica*, 1a–2ae:
LXXXVIII: 1. 2.

weapon of analogy. As will be recognized, this means more than
drawing inferences by taking samples. It is the *analogia entis*,
running from high to low, that gives range and penetration to
philosophy, or to speak of more personal qualities, aspiration and
modesty. To sink to bathos may be a crime in poetry, but not so
in philosophy: St Thomas cites the power of rhubarb to illustrate
causality,[1] does not hesitate to draw on the impolitest ideas in
meditating on the nature of God,[2] and in his lines the drop of the
conjuration in the couplet may not seldom be recaptured:

> By princely Bourbon's late recovered Crown
> And by Miss Fanny's safe return from town.

or the mock solemnity of

> There thou, great Anna, whom three realms obey,
> Dost sometimes counsel take, and sometimes tea.

But there is a rise as well as a fall: if he appears profane on sacred
subjects, he will also set the humblest function in theology. Few
thinkers are so continuist in joining everything to everything else;
and the feat is all the more impressive because nothing is excluded
from his range of interest; moreover the harmony does not stop at
purely rational thought but reaches also to the revealed mysteries
of the Christian religion.[3]

Though it may frequent the laboratories, metaphysical science
should be careful not to stay there. A humane tradition associ-
ates philosophy and letters, and it is worth remembering that the
artistae sive philosophi of the University of Paris mourned St
Thomas when he died more than did the students of divinity,
medicine, and law. Complication and obscurity must be risked
if the intention is not to write an elementary text-book; better to
suffer from a confusion of images than to limit a meaning to one

---

[1] Opusc. I, *de Operationibus Occultis Naturae,* written for a soldier.

[2] *Summa Theologica,* 1a: I: 9, *ad* 3.

[3] For this reason St Thomas requires to be read right through. His doctrine
cannot really be selected from under the appropriate section headings. The psychologist must consult the treatise on the Trinity (*Summa Theologica,* 1a: XXVII–
XLIII), the metaphysician must add to that the treatise on the Angels (1a:
L–LXIV), the social philosopher must go to the treatise on the Mosaic Law
(1a–2ae: XCVIII–CIV).

clear sense-experience; philosophers and mystics meet the same problem from very reverence for their subject. The existential value and force of analogy is a matter for a treatise of metaphysics; though prescribing some rules, logic remains on the fringes, for its interest in analogy is almost, but not quite, confined to the validity of reasoning by example or paradigm. Its office is to safeguard the correct and communicable forms of thought; if more critical, its action is also more negative and, in a sense, more unsympathetic than that of dialectic. Yet it will respect the idioms of ordinary speech, neither seeking to impose an unadorned style nor to be apathetic before flights of fancy; after all, the literal sense of a figurative statement is its plain and proper meaning[1]: sitteth at the right hand of God signifies honour, not bodily location: moreover it will entertain analogies when in company with thoughts that are glancing and lissom and agile,[2] too quicksilvery to be exchanged as fixed counters: content to welcome what it cannot disprove and to keep the controls that will prevent analogy landing the mind in ambiguity and equivocation. Greatness, says Longinus, needs the spur often, it also needs the bit. Nevertheless rationalism will be advised to entertain distributive ideas that exhibit such simultaneous identity and diversity of meaning within themselves, and in respecting their general attributions never to treat them with the inflexibility appropriate to univocal forms.

The *Summa Theologica* is one prolonged argument by analogy. Take one bald case. The good is what all desire—but, God is the Good—therefore, God is what all desire.[3] Forget the apparent thinness of the syllogism—in fact it is rich beyond the dreams of commentary—and concentrate on the idea of the good. What differences are included, lying a-bed with the morning's *Times*, bathing while the mist still lies on the water, the taste of marzipan and of horseradish sauce, Saturday night and Sunday morning, to name but humble events: but of all these, and of many more, nobler and more enduring, we say that they are good. The word does not convey all that we mean, for that cannot be said, yet it is not just a conventional tag; despite all the differences between the events enumerated, a profound likeness is also claimed, closer than that, say, between Marlowe and Gounod because both have

---

[1] *Summa Theologica*, Ia: 1, 10.   [2] *Ibid.*, 2a–2ae: CLXXX: 6.
[3] *Ibid.*, Ia–2ae: II: 6, 7, 8. Ia: VI: 4.

written on the subject of Faust. The likeness is not purely verbal, as would be the case in equivocation, but answers to a real relationship.

In the broadest sense, all use of one term to stand for different things is equivocation, but a distinction must be drawn between benign equivocation which is justified because of some real likeness between them and pure equivocation where the resemblance stops at the sound or spelling of the word. Vice may signify depravity or the instrument on the woodworker's bench, and there are many examples—adder, bank, cock, date and so on—of other words having more than one utterly different meaning; they are what the scholastics call the equivocal by chance, *aequivocum a casu*, where to argue from one meaning to another would be an obvious fallacy. But there are ambiguities more lurking; commonsense may mean the practical agreement of most men or the internal power which is the clearing house within the organism for the other senses[1]; democracy may mean anything from the enlightened extension of popular control to the seizure of power by a gang of thugs; political clericalism may cover a programme of advanced social reform as well as the last ditch stand of the black aristocracy. Because the word happens to be the same, it is supposed that the ideas for which they stand are identical, and the result is a sustained begging of the question and other fallacious forms of argument which will be examined later. The ethical treatment of politics, the release of moral indignation, is especially prone to make this mistake, be its cause the defence of or attack on the traditional order of society; there is a kind of uplift writing on international affairs more irresponsibly dangerous than Macchiavelli. The impression of the word is substituted for the idea of the thing, and by repetition becomes a sort of incantation. Words of course play a great part in conditioning our thought, especially in an environment where much of our experiences comes through the printed page, more of our information depends on hearsay, and thought moves in a murmur of ideological chit-chat. Here comes the overworked term of anti-fascist: whom did it not signify in reality?—liberals, freemasons, competitive capitalists, members of the ancient nobility, communists, clerics, socialists, quakers,

---

[1] *Summa Theologica*, 1a: LXXVIII: 4.

anarchists. When such a galley of types can be covered, a word ceases to be useful in argument.

Purely verbal equivocation serves no purpose. As St Thomas notes, the choice of words is largely a matter of agreement, and there is nothing to prevent others terming *stone* what we term *God*.[1] Ideas or things cannot be equivocal, for though an idea may refer to two different things, this is only on condition that they have something in common. If there be a real resemblance, either strict or metaphorical, then it will be found that the same word has been deliberately selected to stand for both, an instance of what the scholastics sometimes refer to as designed ambiguity, *aequivocum a consilio*, and, more frequently and less misleadingly, as the analogical.[2]

Symbolism and metaphor come lowest in the scale of analogy to the metaphysician, certainly during his strictly scientific periods, yet teaching and exposition will draw on them; the philosopher, says St Thomas, should cherish poetic fables.[3] Scholastic theology should be nourished from the Bible and Babylon, and scholastic philosophy, because of its logical polish and complacence, needs to draw on living experience lest it become a pharasaism of forms. Plato recognised the value of myth. The *Bonny Grey Ey'd Morn* supplements the knowledge to be had through meteorology. No gleam, however fitful, should pass unnoticed, nor any spark of contact, nor the strange shadows of primitive myths; but analogies are most philosophically tractable when they express the inner proportions of things. Acquainted with the psychology of art we can begin to know an attribute intrinsic to God when we strike the proportion that as an artist is to his work so God is to his creation.[4] Metaphor is usually not so strict[5] yet together with simile,

---

[1] Opusc. XIII, *Compendium Theologiae*, ch. 15.

[2] *Summa Theologica*, 1a: XIII: 5. I *Contra Gentes*, 33, 34. It is important to note these two senses of the term equivocal, the distinction between *aequivocum a casu* and *aequivocum a consilio*. For instance, a cause of a higher nature than its effect is called an equivocal cause, which may appear misleading since every full-blown cause is of this class. The context will decide the sense: the chance equivocal is either just an identity of terms or the occasion of fallacy: the designed equivocal refers to a real likeness.

[3] Commentary, I *Metaphysics*, lect. 3.

[4] *Summa Theologica*, 1a: XIV: 8.

[5] *Ibid.*, 1a: 1: 9. 1a–2ae: LXXXVIII: 1.

allegory, and parable,[1] it is grouped under the heading *locutio meta-phorica*, and belongs to analogy. Although philosophical dialectic will not eschew the picturesque or neglect anything that will provide a glimpse of reality, and theology will speak of sensuality as the tinder of sin[2] and penance as a plank after shipwreck,[3] yet the analogical ideas most proper to formal and rational enquiry are those that signify the firmest and most abstract proportions and meanings. The thomist system is closer to Dante than to Milton.

The whole body of the organic thought of St Thomas is built round the principle of the analogy of being. Behind the variety we experience, there is not one exclusive, complete, and monotonous reality, but a richness of perfection to which the mind can respond with many and different notes. Nor is there a diversity of fundamentally different and independent units, for the universe is a planned order, composed of multiple systems all closely intermeshed, and none of them closed. Tapeworms illustrate the doctrine of the image of God[4] and even illusory desire is warmed by divine happiness.[5] There is unity as well as difference; things are not completely irreducible, a multitude of windowless monads; nor are they aspects of one unique thing. Pantheism is to be avoided on one hand, polytheism on the other. There is a God whose infinity does not abolish finiteness, whose glory does not extinguish lesser glows.[6] This is not the place to examine the foundation of such pluralism, the distinction within being of

---

1 Various definitions have been attempted of these figures of speech; but for the sake of understanding the scholastic principles of literary criticism, and notably as regards scriptural interpretation, where a strict aristotelean logic meets a rich oriental imagination, it is well to note that an allegory lends itself to more detailed analysis than does a parable. For in an allegory all the parts of the story have their counterparts in the lesson that is intended, an allegory is, as it were, an extended simile: the state is like a ship, the prime minister is like the helmsman, the chancellor of the exchequer like the purser, the rocks to port are communism and to starboard are vested capitalism, or what you will. But a parable tells a story that must be taken all in one piece, without scrutinizing the parts to see if they correspond to parts of the moral: God is like an unjust judge who grants the request of an importunate woman; the point is the need of perseverance in prayer, the supineness of the Lord is not implied: a parable is, as it were, an extended metaphor.

2 *Summa Theologica*, 3a: XV: 2.
3 *Ibid.*, 3a: LXXXIV: 6.
5 *Ibid.*, 1a: XXVI: 4.
4 *Ibid.*, 1a: XCIII: 2.
6 *Ibid.*, 1a: VI: 4. 1a: VII: 2.

essence and existence.[1] Nevertheless at this height, the mind, and logic with it, must find a way; a foothold here, the weight taken there; it is all as delicately poised and severe in its discipline as mountaineering.

Nor is this the place to pursue the metaphysical idea of analogy, and its division into two classes, namely the analogy of attribution, or immediate proportion or relation, *analogia attributionis*, which attributes to a principle or cause whatsoever is found in its consequences or effects, and the analogy of proper proportionality, the

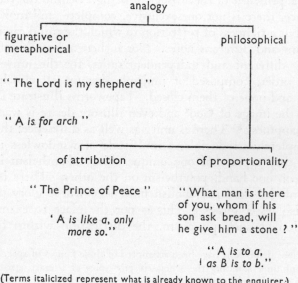

(Terms italicized represent what is already known to the enquirer.)

Figure 5

proportion of proportions or relation of relations, *analogia proportionalitatis*, which is more subtle and profound and from a familiar relationship projects another to a term hitherto unknown.[2] The reader need not strain to grasp the difference, still a matter of controversy among professional scholastics, but he will not go far wrong if he takes it along the lines of the following example. Let us imagine someone who is familiar with the works of Mozart, but

---

[1] *Summa Theologica,* 1a: III: 4.

[2] Disputations, II *de Veritate,* 11. Disputations, VII *de Potentia,* 7. *Summa Theologica,* 1a: XIII: 5. I *Contra Gentes,* 34. I *de Trinitate* 2, *ad* 3. *Cf.* Figure 5.

has never heard Haydn: he asks for information; and you reply that Haydn was Mozart's master and that the younger man was an authentic but adventurous disciple; you are then using the analogy of attribution, and the questioner is left with some knowledge of Haydn. But if you reply that Haydn is to Mozart what bread-and-cheese is to biscuits-and-cheese, then you are drawing a parallel, or using the likeness of proportions, which despite the possible cheapness of the example, taken here not for its justice but as the illustration of a method, is calculated to take the questioner rather further into the musical character of Haydn. An example of the two types of analogy and their comparison may be taken from Canning's squibs. He described Addington as 'happy Britain's guardian gander,' an analogy of attribution; but a deeper and wider historical appreciation is obtained through the analogy of proportion contained in his famous couplet; 'Pitt is to Addington, as London is to Paddington.'

Such attributions and proportions underlie the phrases of everyday speech; the metaphysician simply lifts them to a more abstract plane, while the logician registers their mental form and keeps their development within the limits of meaning. Faces smile, but the term is transferred to landscapes, seas, orchards, and prospects. Wines are called generous, or wise, or discreet. Blood is thicker than water. Beauty shall glide along. We speak of a yellow streak, a bouncing manner, a fruity voice, a wag, a bear with a sore head, a cat on hot bricks. Examples can range from the bizarre to the sober, from the racy to the academic, from the poetical to the scientific. They are drawn upon and worked throughout the *Summa Theologica*; one, already given, is the comparison of the creator to an artist[1]; another, the parallel between mind and will, as mind is to conclusions so will is to objects of choice[2]; a third, the likeness between a criminal and a diseased member of the body.[3]

If logic is to be a fit companion for a lively philosophy then it must welcome, if sometimes hard put to, the habit of ranging abroad and finding familiarity among things at first sight so different. An analysis according to mathematical symbols will not meet the case. There is here a profound steadiness and simplicity

---

[1] *Summa Theologica*, 1a: XIV: 8.   [2] *Ibid.*, 1a: LXXXII: 2.
[3] *Ibid.*, 2a–2ae: LXIV: 2.

when the mind does not run wild with complexity nor allow itself to be bemused with the embarrassment of its riches.[1] 'If Alcibiades was proud,' says Aristotle, 'or Achilles and Ajax were proud, we should find on enquiring what they all had in common, that it was intolerance of insult,' but he also notes that 'it was this which drove Alcibiades to war, Achilles to wrath, and Ajax to suicide.'[2] In fact, according to psychologists, this power of co-ordination is the very mark of intelligence, found alike in the sympathetic discernment of the kinship between people so dissimilar as St Teresa of Avila and St Thérèse of Lisieux, in the ability to translate one language into another and to sort out anagrams and read 'Barchester' from 'there's crab,' in the understanding of the praise from a negro, 'his skin may be white, but his heart is black,' and in the recognition that God is most just because he is merciful.[3] Perhaps this is part of the reason why people with quick and voluble perceptions are apt to mix their metaphors. At any rate, to see a fundamental likeness of meaning is to rise above the level of sensation.

'We become oblivious of the difference between a horse, a steam-engine, and a waterfall,' says Bain,[4] 'when our minds are engrossed with the one circumstance of moving power. The diversity of these had no doubt, for a long time, the effect of keeping back their first identification; and to obtuse intellects, this identification might have been for ever impossible.' It is by the grasp of analogies that our actions are different from those of animals. Their instinct, for instance, will drive them to catch fish in one determinate way, by diving or wading as the case may be; but we can employ all manner of different motions with the same meaning and purpose, we can trawl, cast, spear, depth-charge, or tickle. From this sense of analogy follows the power of adaptation which works from the speculations of high philosophy to such crafts as jungle fighting, where, as military experts have noted, civilized peoples, though they start at a disadvantage, can be trained to be more efficient than primitive peoples because of their aptitude for mastering a subject.

---

[1] Opusc. X, de Causis, lect. 9, 10.
[2] Posterior Analytics, II, 13, 97b. Transl. G. R. G. Mure.
[3] Summa Theologica, 1a: XXI: 3, 4.
[4] The Senses and the Intellect.

In this conception of all-round ability, or general intelligence as it is sometimes called, the word *general* is beginning to recover some of the strength that was apparently denied it with reference to the thinness and flatness of extensive notions; for to be universal reveals a powerful central energy, available for use in diverse departments, an integrating wisdom working throughout profusion. To recur to a point raised in regretting the rupture between theory and practice, eminence in one field of human interest may not leave much time for the cultivation of another, yet the capability is there. Verdi was a proficient farmer and St Thomas himself was an acceptable preacher in the Neapolitan vernacular,[1] an acute observer of human character,[2] and was frequently consulted on administrative problems.[3] Yet his latent allusions make him a difficult author for those who would extract his doctrine by consulting the appropriate headings in the index; he is not really a manualist for he supposes a general background and is often most informative in his asides, his best sayings on a topic not seldom are to be found in unlikely places. A single theme runs throughout the versatility, the passage from one aspect to another is not abrupt, there are no splits in his personality.

We may conclude with an outline of the workings of univocal, equivocal, and analogical terms in a cardinal treatise of the *Summa Theologica*, the problem of the nature of God. The preliminary positions of theism having been granted, the schools of theology fall into three main groups, though there are many shades of detail; there are two extreme positions corresponding to the opposite boundaries of univocal and equivocal terms, and a midway position, *modus medius* says St Thomas, corresponding to the mean

---

[1] Opuscula XXXIII–XXXVI. Most of these sermons are published in English, *The Three Great Prayers*, Burns Oates, 1937.

[2] The detailed analysis of the emotions. *Summa Theologica*, 1a–2ae: XXII–XLVIII; and of good and bad human habits, 2a–2ae: XLVII–CLXX.

[3] Cf. Opusculum XI, *de Regno*, On Sovereignty, to the King of Cyprus; Opusculum XII, *de Regimine Judaeorum*, On the Jewish Problem, to the Duchess of Brabant; Opusculum XX, On the Deferred Meeting of Commercial Bills. What was expected from him may be seen from the heterogeneous questions addressed to him; two bundles, one of forty-two questions (Opusculum XXII) and the other of one hundred and eight questions (Opusculum XXIII) were sent in by the Master General of his Order.

of an analogical term,[1] a mean in the sense, not of a compromise, but as when virtue is said to lie in the mean.[2] Courage is not a mixture of rashness and cowardice though the initial stages of these emotions may be supposed,[3] and in the same way temperance cannot live without passion[4]; so too, an analogical term does not represent a univocal term that has been watered down to meet the circumstances, a half-hearted univocal on the point of surrendering to an equivocal, but stands in its own right, nobler than the one and more generous of evidence than the other.

First there is the primitive method of taking the strongest or best qualities found in the world and attributing them without reserve to God, describing his character in terms of human kindness, vengeance, anger and the rest, perhaps treating his benevolence as though it were good nature, or resenting his vengeance as though it sprang from spleen. Here words are taken univocally; the general picture is that of anthropomorphism, such as results from a crude misunderstanding of the scriptures in English, and especially the Old Testament.[5]

Secondly at the other extreme, are those who hold that nothing can be known about the divine nature, though we must talk about it: if there is a divine justice it must be quite different from human justice and to speak of God being good can only mean, on analysis, either that he is not evil or that he is in some sense the cause of goodness as we know it.[6] Since there is no reliable likeness between the ideas, the terms must be reckoned equivocal; the general theory that results is called agnosticism, which includes not only those who dismiss the subject with a shrug, but also the mingled reverence, reluctance, and ardour of the school of the *theologia negativa*, from which St Thomas came, and the distinguished name of Moses Maimonides, the doctor for those who doubt.[7]

In between lies the *via media*, if one can so speak of the adventurous but calculated synthesis of St Thomas, probably his most

---

[1] *Summa Theologica*, 1a: XIII: 2, 4, 5.

[2] *Ibid.*, 1a–2ae: LXIV: 1.

[3] *Ibid.*, 1a–2ae: LIX: 2. 2a–2ae: CXXIII: 3.

[4] *Ibid.*, 1a–2ae: LIX: 5. 2a–2ae: CXLI: 3.

[5] *Ibid.*, 1a: I: 9, 10.   [6] *Ibid.*, 1a: XIII: 2.

[7] Disputations, VII *de Potentia*, 5. Opusc. X, *de Causis, lect.* 6.

important and certainly his most characteristic contribution to the science of rational theology. For though he opens by saying that we know what God is not, *quomodo non sit*,[1] in the event he surpasses the conditions of his analysis, at least to the extent of attributing positive and absolute perfections in their most proper sense. His instrument is that of analogy,[2] a critical application of the form with a qualification of the mode according to the method of elimination and supercharging, the *via remotionis et excellentiae*. A perfection or idea, such as knowledge, goodness, life, or power, is first carefully examined and purified of elements that may always accompany it in our experience without essentially belonging to its nature, then heightened and related to other ideas, and so attributed to God as principally, properly, and intrinsically his.[3] The method is strictly scientific, but even poetry halts before suggesting the effects.

---

[1] *Summa Theologica*, Ia: II, Introduction, Ia: I: 9, *ad* 3.
[2] *Ibid.*, Ia: XIII: 2, 3, 6. I *Contra Gentes*, 30. VI *de Trinitate*, 2.
[3] *Summa Theologica*, Ia: XXXIII: 3.

CHAPTER XI

COMPLEX AND CONCRETE

AFTER the deployment, the depth of ideas must next be considered. When one nature or kind of thing is isolated, however rich, composite, or many-sided that nature may be, then a simple idea, *conceptus incomplexus*, is formed. Thus octopus, porcupine, man, spirit, fig, efficient cause. A simple notion is the logical form of an idea unqualified by antecedents, accompaniments, or consequences. If however a group of diverse natures or properties is collected in the idea, then you have a compound or complex notion, *conceptus complexus*: a complex designates an accidental whole. There is a *polupatheia* in 'married to a mermaid at the bottom of the deep blue sea,' or 'an amphibious operation,' or 'a disagreeable duty' or 'lymphatic system,' or 'reichsluftschutz-bund.' A military operation is not amphibious as such, nor is duty as such disagreeable; in these cases two simple concepts are united to form a complex.[1]

Simple notions are the elements of logical thought, and by returning to them we turn our back on the occasions of fallacy. Yet terseness of expression does not necessarily betoken compression of thought; there is a kind of simplicity that does not match our environment, uttered in nothing better than philosophical baby-talk. Compound notions are indispensable, but they need to be watched, and for several reasons. They may easily merge into smudged ideas; a compound idea of justice may be adulterated

---

[1] Such an idea may be expressed by a single word, when the genius of the language allows the formation of a richly expressive word, as in Greek and German according to their different manners, or when, as in familiar speech, the additional qualifications are taken for granted, as when sailors talk of the Bay, the Channel, the Straits, or the Service. Usually a compound idea requires a set of words, thus, 'ginger cat up an apple tree in blossom watching a bullfinch on the greenhouse roof.' But whether the terms be few or many, the test for a compound notion is the number of diverse ideas contained.

into the idea of vindictive revenge, so opening the way to equivocation, as when the hunger for justice is used as a plea for the
satisfaction of an angry lust. Again, compound notions can offer
distractions; you may lose sight of the meaning because of the
colour of the context. The trappings of an idea may be arresting
and interesting, but if you take your eye off the ball, the argument
will lose its proper trim as the cargo shifts and so list and founder,
a clear case of talking to the driver at the wheel—and as metaphors
can be mixed, so can arguments, and with no compensating diver-
sion. In other words compound notions may introduce the fallacy
of the irrelevant. Moreover, they verge into judgement and even
into argument, for while a simple notion is clearly no more than
the simple registration of an object without committing itself to a
statement, a compound notion is tantamount to taking up a definite position by associating certain ideas together; a simple idea
calls neither for acceptance nor for rejection, but a compound idea
may give you pause, as you weigh the fitness or otherwise of the
epithet, the probability or otherwise of the scene.

In examining the process of scholastic debate it will be observed
how a simple notion appears to grow more complex as it gathers
more and more qualifications in the course of the argument, but
the accumulation is rather of outward show than of substance, for,
at anyrate in the more responsible disputations, while the terms
appear to grow more complicated, the central idea becomes more
simple.

Yet the difference between simple and complex notions is not
unlike that between the humour of the *New Yorker* and of the Vic-
torian *Punch*, one aims at the most economical statement and will
get a joke across almost without a word, while the latter abounds
in irrelevant detail; brevity may be the soul of wit, but the old
humorists demanded plenty of time and elbow room for their
display of the picturesque and comical. Or another analogy; a
simple notion is like a musical term, which may be a single note
or a chord, but a complex idea is like a musical phrase; the former
is harmonic, the latter melodic.

There is a scholastic terminology governing the use of simple
and complex notions in argument, notions being spoken of as precise, or coupled, or specific. If a notion is so refined that the
nature or note is represented away from an essential part of its

4

reality, then it is said to be precise, and the idea must be taken precisely, *praecisive*: a mental excision has been performed for the sake of clearness, though the separation is impossible in the world of reality. So long as this be recognized there is no falsity; otherwise the argument becomes unreal and profitless. Research sometimes requires the intense purity of these abstract and precise notions, of which extreme examples are curve apart from line, or youth apart from animal, or differentiation apart from differences. We have seen that logical entities belong to this class, which may be called thinned or skimmed ideas.

In extreme contrast stand ideas that represent one nature in conjunction with another, or with many other natures. The notion is, as it were, hyphenated, and must always be taken as coupled, or twined, *reduplicative*. Thus, nodding plumes, Dover soles, a bullet-headed man, a whimsical admiral, speaking as a man old enough to be your father, vitaminized margarine, positive law. Most of our working notions are so mixed; even simple ideas have their echoes and harmonics. Some notions, otherwise single and free, become coupled or tied terms by force of custom or cliché; for instance, bloated capitalist, brutal dictator, flaming youth, impassive oriental, sinful worldliness; or by the artificiality of civilization, which forces us to speak of shell eggs, liquid milk, and Franco Spain. As we have remarked, such complex ideas verge on a judgement, as in the inn-sign, *The Labour in Vain*, and they need also to be watched lest in the course of an argument they suffer an internal change, as when approval for praying-while-you-smoke becomes permission for smoking-while-you-pray.

Keener and more to the point than these conjunctions, and yet without the extreme attenuation of precise notions, are ideas that exhibit distinct and different natures without any trimmings. They represent a specific form, or specific factor; the idea is said to be specific, and must be taken specifically, *specificative*. Discovering such forms is the effort of science, and may be attempted through considerate two-sided discussions, but not through the wrangle of many voices. Yet essential kinds are less than their total implications; to be set on them exclusively may be like taking the postillion without the coach and horses. As we have seen, abstract notes are separately considered only that eventually they may be brought together again in a co-ordinated system of knowledge, as when the anatomy, psychology, social morality, and theology of sex are united in agreement.

In scholastic argument how ideas should be taken will usually be fairly evident from the context: there is a precise notion for every *ens rationis*, a specific notion for every real general nature, a coupled notion for every composition of diverse ideas—matter individuated by quantity, democratic government, lax conscience—and for every fact of history—the battle of Actium, the South Sea Bubble, the Tractarian Movement—and for every note of poetry —sea-shouldering whales, soft Lydian airs, forests of the night. In discussion it is most important to observe when ideas are to be taken as precise, or doubled, or specific, lest we slip from the extreme abstraction of the first to the complete *mise-en-scène* of the second; or from the rich mixture of the second to the formal distinctness of the third.

Recall the fallacy that once upon a time appeared more frequently than nowadays, not through any logical superiority on our part, but because scientists have grown more critical and exact in marking the limits of their terms. In the exploration of the physiological changes accompanying our psychological states it was discovered that when sensation x and emotion y were posited the physiological changes X and Y took place, and vice versa. That was the premiss. Presently the following conclusion crept in, therefore x and y are X and Y. Virtue and vice are by-products like sugar and vitriol: psychology is just refined physiology. In some cases the proof of this materialist conclusion was attempted, more often it was just slipped in. Conjuring of this sort is not difficult for the mind, which, unlike the hand, has to unlearn such tricks of substituting the specific idea of *psychological* for the coupled idea of *psycho-physiological*. Sometimes the premiss itself was modified to meet the needs of the conclusion, and instead of accurately stating that physiological changes accompany psychological changes it was asserted that they are identical, so blurring the distinction between a concomitant and a constituent.[1] A similar fallacy consists in ascribing particular value to a drug because, for instance, it can produce the transport of *Kubla Khan*; but, as Mr. de la Mare observes, the prescription is not opium *per*

---

[1] *Summa Theologica*, 1a–2ae: IV: 1.

se, but opium *plus* Coleridge. Contemporary writing on the philosophy of religion has not been free from this mode of thinking. Starting from the place a parent is thought to hold in the infant's mind, the argument reaches to the idea of God, which idea is then assumed to be a fantasy preserved from childhood. Here again the case may be impressively argued from the concepts of infant and primitive psychology, but not rarely the conclusion is intruded because the descriptive notion in the premisses becomes a definitory notion in the conclusion.

From the point of view of logic the division between concrete and abstract notions bears on the rules of predication; from the point of view of humane philosophy, it rouses the problem of the relationship between general ideas and singular substances.

A concrete idea represents a nature or meaning existing, not as a simple form nor as a pure type, but in a subject, or subjects. A man is a concrete notion, signifying human nature existing in a thing; this thing is a man. Such concrete terms as redshank, policeman, God, cause, are used with the same turn to substance considered as having real existence.[1] The notion may be concrete though the term be plural, thus men, policemen; note, however, a tendency for plural terms to become abstract. A concrete term always indicates a nature as a subject of existence, and since created things are not pure and simple but composite, in that a distinction lies at their heart between existing as a thing and as a specific kind of thing,[2] concrete notions will to that extent prove to be complex notions: concretion, says St Thomas, is a mode of composition. Despite their admixture with fact, always an embarassment to a purely ideal philosopher, they have the merit of pointing to complete and singular substances, and as signifying a real existent they are applied to God,[3] though here there is no question of composition, either of matter and form, or essence and existence, or of being and manner of being.[4] There is more force in concrete notions than in abstract notions; the idea of God is

---

[1] A concrete term expresses a *conceptus absolutus* when referring to a substance, he is *a man*, or a *conceptus consignificativus* when referring to an accident, he is *pasty-faced*.

[2] *Summa Theologica*, 1a: XIII: 1, ad 2.

[3] I *Contra Gentes*, 30.

[4] *Summa Theologica*, 1a: III: 2, 3, 4.

more urgent and claiming than the idea of divinity; it is hard to imagine a fanatical deist.

But with the contrasted class of abstract notions what is lost in vigour is gained in lucidity. A meaning is taken outside any particular subject, or subjects, thus humanity, politeness, causality, and is expressed in a pure and uncompounded state, apart from any determinate embodiment. This purity and refinement makes abstract ideas highly useful in analysing the nature of God.[1] As their name suggests, they are the effect of an abstraction, and a formal abstraction at that. Medieval Latin has a knack of coining abstract terms, but indeed they abound at any period of energetic speculation; they simplify a situation and lend themselves to impersonal treatment. Nevertheless the clearness is obtained at the cost of completeness. An abstract idea is a partial idea of a thing, for either only a form is signified, which is but part of a material substance, though the intelligible and specific principle,[2] or if matter be included, it is but nodded at, *ponitur in obliquo*, treated as a kind of ersatz form,[3] and the unique and profoundly informal singular thing still remains out of the calculation. The scholastics were content to treat form as *quo*, that by or as which, not as *quod*, the thing which; as manifesting type, not intimate individuality. The difference between abstract and concrete ideas has been compared to that between the classical French and English drama, but, replied Dr. Johnson, 'Corneille is to Shakespeare as a clipped hedge is to a forest.'

The logician will be cautious about identifying abstract and concrete notions. The practice is sometimes allowable in ordinary usage and to enhance the force of a sentiment. He was civility itself means that he was exceedingly civil: but the expression is not permissible in strict logical form, for were a man in truth civility itself, it would follow that nobody else could be civil, since civility would be already wholly taken up and possessed.[4] Civility is signified as a form existing apart from any particular manifestations, and in general the rule should be observed of not attributing an

---

[1] *Summa Theologica*, ia: XIII: 1, *ad* 2.
[2] *Ibid.*, ia: III: 3.
[3] Commentary, V *Metaphysics, lect.* 2. VII: *lect.* 3.
[4] Opus VIII, *de Ente et Essentia,* to his brother companions. I *Contra Gentes,* 21.

abstract predicate to a concrete subject nor a concrete predicate to an abstract subject.[1]

---

[1] 'Je suis l'Immaculée Conception,' these words may seem to break the rule, but it must be remembered that they were spoken in patois, and in case the phrase is rightly taken to mean that Mary is alone in the prerogative of sinlessness. So also must be taken, 'I am the resurrection and the life.' In Christian theology, particularly in connection with the doctrines of the Trinity (*Summa Theologica*, 1a: XXXIX: 4, 5, 6) and the Incarnation (*ibid.*, 3a: XVII) strict rulings guard the use of concrete and abstract terms. It is proper to say that man is God, but not, man is the divinity, or God is humanity.

CHAPTER XII
NEGATIVE AND POSITIVE

THE lookout at sea catches sight of a dark gleam on the starboard bow; watching intently, 'No, not a submarine,' he says, 'but it's moving, must be alive; swims like a fish, no, it's a whale, a sperm-whale, I reckon.' He has run through the division now to be outlined of notions by yea and nay. Not a submarine—a negative notion; but it's moving—a positive notion; must be alive—a common notion; swims like a fish—a descriptive notion; it's a whale—a definitory notion, but incomplete; a sperm-whale—a sufficiently complete definitory notion. The process of clarification matches the movement of scholastic exposition.

First, to attend to a negative, also called an infinite or indefinite concept, *conceptus infinitus.*

> Great Negative, how vainly would the wise
> Enquire, define, distinguish, teach, devise,
> Didst thou not stand to point their dull philosophies.

Indeed negative knowledge is not to be despised; points and lines are negatively defined in geometry, and negative ideas put

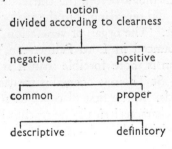

(A simplified version of a more sub-divided scholastic scheme.)
Figure 6

edge to argument; more than that, they imply positive knowledge, for negation supposes an affirmation of some standard. A system of universal denial is impossible.[1] It might be thought that

---

[1] *Summa Theologica,* 1a-2ae: LXXII: 7, *ad* 3. 2a-2ae: LXXIX: 3, *ad* 2. Figure 6.

negative notions can teach no more than Peter Simple learnt about the hiptostamass at Portsdown Fair, 'which the keeper said was an amphibious animal as couldn't live on land, and dies in water.' But in fact negation can be very informative; there are speaking silences in conversation and in music, and gothic architecture is shaped by the preponderance of voids over plane surfaces. There is a new vista when a familiar tree is cut down, an eloquence in the empty seat at table, scholarship in knowing what to skip. You cannot have the idea of a hole without something round it.

The method of elimination, the *via remotionis* already alluded to, is perhaps the most direct route to clearness open to the human mind in its present circumstances, especially in approaching high and spiritual matters.[1] If not the shortest cut, it attracts those who would be at once definite and cautious. There is a sustained application of negative notions in the parlour game of sending somebody out of the room and on his return demanding that he should light on what the company has thought of: the topic, however recondite, may always be discovered by the method of applying negative notions, which is also successful in serious and far-reaching enquiries. Human philosophy starts in a fog, and must pick its way carefully, often starting back, and saying, no, not that. Negative notions played a predominant rôle in the development of rational theology before the thirteenth century, and the results are as quiet and revealing as in the analogous English genius for understatement. 'The organ of veneration,' said Bulwer, 'was not broadly pronounced in Lord Palmerston,' and the effect of the characterization is more forcible than if it had been couched in positive terms. St Thomas opens his treatise on the nature of God with the words, 'in the first place let us consider that God is not,'[2] and though characteristically he reaches beyond to the stage of formulating positive ideas about God,[3] he draws considerably on the *theologia negativa*.

A condition of methodic rejection is that the concepts employed should bear on the question; to start miles away and on the wrong scene is of little profit. The method is closer to the subject than is the clearing away of irrelevancies. Nor should the pre-

---

[1] *Summa Theologica*, 1a: XXXIII: 4, *ad* 1.
[2] *Ibid.*, 1a: III. Introduction. I *Contra Gentes*, 14.
[3] *Summa Theologica*, 1a: XIII: 12.

misses be entirely negative. There was a celebrated flag captain called Pompo Heneage, who was asked, when giving evidence at a court martial on a collision, what he would have done; he replied, 'If my ship had been where she was not, and the *Vanguard* had been where she was not, then I would not have done what I did not.' As will be seen later, no conclusion can follow from two negative premisses; no construction is possible on sheer destruction; even as regards criticism, the most damaging attacks are based on positive convictions. Nothing can be inferred from mere absence: I am reminded of Mr Charles Graves's story about the serpents of Killaloo that St Patrick drove out of the country; they could wrap their necks about a musket and squint along the barrel and both load and fire it with their tails; but the Saint prayed at them and told them to quit, and off they went howling; the proof, said Johnny Maguire, that I'm not codding you is that not a single specimen of the breed is now to be found on the shores of Ireland.

In dealing with the use of negatives, we must consider a distinction that operates throughout the scholastic dialectic, namely that between simple negation, *negatio*, and deprivation, *privatio*[1]; these technical terms recur again and again. Simple negation, or the employment of a purely negative notion, merely excludes a form or note; men are not angels, art is not moral, matter is not created, human law is not comprehensive and all-embracing. But deprivation, or the employment of a privative notion, implies that the quality should be present; men are not virtuous, art is not reasonable, matter is not helpful, this law has not been promulgated. To say of a pig that it is not-winged is to apply a negative notion and not to be very much the wiser; but to say that the pig is not-snouted is to apply a privative notion and to find the subject wanting. Criticism should have a sense of context; as Alice said of a different case, 'If it had grown up it would have made a dreadfully ugly child; but it makes rather a handsome pig, I think.' A similar example can be taken from morals. Simple ignorance, or nescience, which is a pure negation of knowledge, is no crime; why should I know how many stones there are in the Great Wall of China, or the names of all the rivers in order going clockwise

---

[1] *Summa Theologica*, 1a: XLVIII: 3, 2a–2ae: X: 1.

round the coast of the United Kingdom? But if my ignorance is of something that I should know, for instance, of the traditions and laws of my country, then it is privative and culpable.[1]

The teaching of St Thomas on the problem of evil depends on appreciating the position and influence of privations.[2] For evil is not a thing, nor is it just an absence of good; it is the lack of a form that should be present, a *privatio* produced and purposed by a good out of place, and present in a good subject, for there can be nothing sheerly and entirely bad.[3] Evil is rather like poison, a matter of dose. Not from any spirit of kindliness, but by the hard exigencies of his metaphysics, St Thomas cannot allow the existence of a pure spirit of evil nor of a principle of evil at all comparable to the supreme spirit of good; there is no dramatic polarization between the two, for evil is subordinate and secondary to the good, as negation is derivative from affirmation.[4]

An oscillation between negative and privative notions attends the philosophical thinking which treats sin (a privation) as the inevitable consequence of creaturely freedom and limitation (a purely negative notion). Fissures run through reality and there are corresponding veins in our thoughts. Negativeness, the being not that, is the occasion for growth of knowledge, and the student must learn the dialectic of negation, as the seeker after perfection must practise the virtues of abnegation.[5] The principle of contra-

---

[1] *Summa Theologica,* 1a–2ae: LXXVI: 2.

[2] Disputations, I *de Malo,* 1, 2, 3.

[3] *Summa Theologica,* 1a: XLIX: 3.

[4] An example of confusion between negative and privative notions occurs in the following quotation from a cross-examination in a court of enquiry into the loss of a submarine; the switch from *disabled* (a private notion) to *not able* (a negative notion) will be noticed.

The presence of a tug is to afford a greater safety on a trial dive?—Yes.

Its two objects are to take off unnecessary men before the dive and to warn the submarine of approaching vessels which might endanger her?—Yes.

Before you went out you effectively disabled yourself from performing either? —No.

You did not take the men off before the dive?—No, but we were not disabled.

You could not take any men off after she dived?—Of course not.

Therefore, by the time she dived you were not able to take men off?— Exactly.

[5] IV *de Trinitate,* 1.

diction lies at the beginning of rational thought; *to be* is incompatible with *not to be* under the same respect; *is* cannot be simultaneous with *is not*; in a world made up of many things and many thoughts about them, by affirming *is* in one respect you imply *is not* in another; that is a tulip, it is not the Begum of Bhopal. The dialectic of thesis, antithesis and synthesis is not so pronounced as in the hegelian system, yet St Thomas's working processes include the principles that contradictories cannot simultaneously be true and that oppositions can be contrasted to produce a higher affirmation.

But let us return to our look-out. He knows something when he says, no, not a submarine: but he knows more when he says, but it's moving though, reckon it must be alive. He then has a positive notion, *conceptus finitus*. From the point of view of logic, all knowledge must start from such a definite concept. It may represent a minimum to start with, and then the purpose of discussion will be to provide greater clarity and detail. For there are degrees of positive knowledge. To begin with the first division, a positive notion may be common or it may be proper.[1]

A common notion, *conceptus obscurus*, represents no more than the generic character of an object, shared in common with objects of other kinds, or it may not reach so far as that but stop at a general indication of its positive content, as when God is called a being, or a cause is termed a principle or, to quote President Coolidge, the sermon I guess were about sin, and the preacher I guess were agin it. A proper notion, *conceptus clarus*, on the other hand, applies only to one kind of thing. It is not vague but unmistakably distinct and specific, and goes with clear words and ideas. The test of a stylist, Flaubert decided, was to describe one tree in a forest so that it could not be mistaken for any other tree.

A proper idea may not hit off the essential character of an object—everybody knows Kent, cob-nuts, cherries, hops, and women—but may be a description rather than a designation[2] and is called *conceptus non quidditativus*, and also, unhappily, *conceptus confusus*. A lion is a desert coloured animal that looks like Garibaldi, rhubarb is celery gone bloodshot; in both cases the description is peculiar and exclusive, yet does not reach to the heart of

---

[1] *Summa Theologica*, 1a: LXXXV: 3.   [2] Commentary, I *de Anima*, *lect.* 1.

the matter. Many of the pointer readings of the sciences have this quality; they do not, or should not, claim to touch the essential nature of things, nevertheless they fix certain constant and characteristic notes, expressed in the appropriate scientific medium, sufficient for recognition and to serve as guide-marks for deeper exploration. Women are reputed to excel at descriptive notions; they see details that pass unnoticed by other eyes, and the trait that appears irrelevant sometimes turns out to be the one that most matters.

More masculine ideas fasten on the salient features and attempt to isolate an essential meaning. In the event of success, a definitory notion, *conceptus quidditativus*, is formulated, which must be judged adequate, *conceptus adaequatus*, according to the degree of articulation of the essential notes of an object. Our knowledge of any subject, however trite, is rarely exhaustive,[1] but often it can be complete enough to serve exact and scientific enquiry. This, with reservations, can sometimes be allowed to be in touch with the nature of things. We shall refer later to the scholastic doctrine, not seldom misunderstood, that the proper object of the human mind is the essence of material things; for the present, without plunging into the depths of physics and organic chemistry and the philosophy of the sciences, we may assume that a trained zoologist who has specialized in the cats can manage to frame a sufficiently complete definition of a lion. Science, however, like politics, does well to recognize the need of working within limits and of proposing to itself a limited objective.

The advance from negative to positive notions, from common to proper notions, and then, developing proper notions, from description to definition, is the methodic movement of all the sciences,[2] and is clearly displayed in the systematic argument of the *Summa Theologica*. Ideas are there rejected and accepted, then winnowed and refined, until a stage of knowledge about God is reached that amounts almost to definition[3]; definition, that is to say, in the scientific sense, for there is no question of intuition or vision. Comprehension of God remains an unattainable goal.[4]

---

[1] Or *comprehensive* according to scholastic usage. 1a: XII: 7. 1a: XIV: 3. Opusc. XIII, *Compendium Theologiae*, Ch. 106.

[2] I *Contra Gentes*, 14.

[3] *Summa Theologica*, 1a: III: 5.   [4] *Ibid.*, 1a: XII: 7.

But at the beginning there is no such clearness; the religious sense, such as it is, needs the discipline of hard and calculated thinking. The knowledge we have of God, says St Thomas, is contained in some common inborn ideas, inasmuch as he is our happiness, which we naturally desire; for what we naturally desire that also in some sense we naturally know: but this is not to know God properly speaking, any more than to be aware that someone is approaching is to know Peter, though in fact it is Peter.[1]

---

[1] *Summa Theologica,* 1a: II: 1, *ad* 1.

CHAPTER XIII

MUTUAL BEARING

NOTIONS may carry different relationships to one another. They may be identical or diverse; they may be opposites; or they may be complementary.

Terms may differ in spelling, also in psychological impact, yet for logic such notions as the following are identical, equal-sided triangle and equal-angled triangle, scheduled castes and untouchables, actuality and entelechy, person and rational suppositum, end and final cause. Technical terminology both adds to the number of identical notions and fixes degrees of difference. The sameness of notions, as we have seen, when applied to many objects may be univocal or analogical. The diversity of notions is legion, and the conjunction of strange ideas may on occasion be vivid and arresting; yet the severely rational enquirer tends to suspect the violent and strained and to prefer sociable ideas. The temper of logic is nearer to Longfellow than to Edward Lear, until matched with dialectic. For long periods there is a sobriety amounting almost to dullness in the style of St Thomas; but then his purpose is elementary exposition as we are warned in the prologue of the *Summa Theologica* which quotes St Paul, I have fed you with milk and not with meat. Nevertheless strangeness and wonder keep breaking in; logic remains, but kindled with the fire of Ezekiel; the words are quieter than the ideas.

In the second place notions may be opposites. *Contrariorum eadem est scientia*, an object is known from a sufficient account of its contrary, and more will be said later on the value of contrasts as a method of developing knowledge. Here again dialectic completes logic, it is a conversation rather than a soliloquy. Opposition is a condition of advance both in the manufacture of armaments, for new weapons of attack are countered by new weapons of defence, and in the arts of peaceful government through parliamentary institutions, for the party in opposition must have an alternative programme and be set on becoming the party in office. So also in the *sic et non* of thomism, besides the fundamental opposition of the older philosophies which are there resolved, motion and rest, the one and the many, the ideal universal and the material particular, pleasure and duty, great store is set on the employment of antithetical ideas. Difference as well as likeness serves to bring out the character of a subject, as when three representative monuments are taken to compare two periods of history, and the great cathedrals, the old universities, and the Common Law set against the Bank of England, the Stock Exchange, and the National Debt. To restore the balance between medieval and augustan England, one might also contrast the killing of cattle for the winter with the rotation of crops, the restrictions on physics with the Royal Society, a chronicle with the *Decline and Fall of the Roman Empire*.

The principal issue concerns the difference between contrary and contradictory opposition.[1] Contrary notions, such as black and white, have common ground; and contrariety is the opposition of forms in the same matter.[2] So Whig opposed Tory within the common assumptions of eighteenth century England, so Dominican disputes with Jesuit, wife with husband, counsel for the defence with the prosecution, so East is not West. But as there is a Near East and a Middle East between, and as between black and white there are intermediate shades of grey on their common colourable surface, and as between Jesuits and Dominicans there was Pope Paul V, so contraries admit of compromise, a midway house, a *tertium quid*. For this reason they must not be taken too bluntly[3]: the denial of one of two contraries does not entail the affirmation of the other. Because you deem that an object is not black you must not be taken to affirm that it is white—a frequent trick in debate; because you are not Left Wing in politics it does not follow that you are fascist-minded, or even a reactionary[4]; because his monkey liked to tease his weasel, we need not agree with St Thomas More's interpretation that it was because he

---

[1] Commentary, I *Perihermenias, lect.* 11.

[2] *Summa Theologica*, 1a: XVII: 4. 1a–2ae: LXXI: 6. 1a–2ae: LXXIII: 2.

[3] *Cf.* the opposition of right and wrong. Opusc. XIII, *Compendium Theologiae*, Ch. 116. Also the specific character of sins. *Summa Theologica*, 1a–2ae: LXXII: 1. I *Contra Gentes*, 71.

[4] *Summa Theologica*, 1a–2ae: XXIII: 2, 3, 4.

liked to please his rabbit. In a similar fashion a witness may be
pushed beyond the needs of the defence—

When he suffocated that woman, etc., did he know it was
wrong?—No.

At the time he thought it was right?—Yes.

But the case is different with the opposition of contradictory
notions. A contradictory is a blank denial, the contradictory of
black is not-black. Contradictories do not even suppose a common ground, they are like the entrance into the political scene of a
party that abruptly dissociates itself from the traditional customs
and convictions of the country; between them there is no compromise, no intervening stage, no half-and-half.[1] *To be* or *not to be*
presents a complete and final crisis, even when applied to trivial
matters, but in general the issue does little to advance the cause
of criticism. Macaulay said there were two ways of sleeping, with
and without a night-cap; there is no escaping the fact. There can
be a certain recklessness in the enunciation of contradictories;
hence their attraction for decisive and perhaps impatient minds, and
for those who dislike sitting on the fence. Hence also the temptation to make all opposition an affair of contradiction, forgetting
that fences are sometimes there to be sat on.

Generally speaking the opposition of notions in practice should
be approached warily, first to determine whether there be any opposition at all, for frequently parties to a dispute might discover
that they are not really at variance if only they would seek to define the point at issue; and secondly to determine what type of
opposition may be engaged. An apparent opposition is not necessarily a complete exclusion of either, not a complete division of
the possibilities; as in the case of the celebrated academic agony;
the King of France has hair; on the contrary the King of France is
bald; solution, the King of France wears a wig. But to reflect on
more serious matters; it is better to eat your loaf and keep it; to
make the best of both worlds. Or are there two worlds? Such
ideas as body and soul, matter and spirit, nature and grace,
freedom and law, are not really at such loggerheads as they have
been made to appear. As if you could kill time, someone has said,
without injuring eternity.

---

[1] *Summa Theologica*, 1a: XVII: 4. 1a: XIX: 9, *ad* 3.

In the third place, different notions may be neighbourly or complementary to one another, like the two parties of the British parliamentary system. The tension between them must be resolved to a kind of contrary opposition. Relatives imply one another and cannot be understood apart; father and son, Pope and Church, means and end, useful and enjoyable, practice and theory, left hand and right hand, rule and miracle, duty and pleasure. The use of complementary notions is a pronounced feature of argument in the *Summa Theologica*. It supposes a world where many things are kin and rejoices in the oppositions of analogy. In a sense pure logic is solitary in its abstraction, but dialectic has the confidence that there is a friendly opponent to co-operate in the dialogue, unlike rhetoric which requires only an audience.

PART THREE   JUDGEMENTS

THE mind slips almost imperceptibly from notions into judgements—
> Ah happy hills, ah pleasing shade,
> Ah fields beloved in vain.

—and so arrives at the second stage of logical activity, the taking
up of a position. A typical judgement is made up of two notions,
which may be simple or complex, expressed in terms called the
subject and predicate of the sentence and set down either in agreement or in disagreement. Judgement is an affirmation or a denial,
a joining or a splitting, a union or a separation, operating, in the
scholastic phrase, *componendo et dividendo*,[1] by synthesis or diaeresis.[2]
The verbal expression of a judgement is a proposition or sentence,
oratio.[3] The logical relation of subject and predicate is expressed
basically by the verb *to be*, called the logical copula. The Nordic
hero *is*, or *is not*, superior to Mediterranean man: *doctor romanus est
asinus germanus*. All verbal links between subject and predicate are
supposed to be reducible to this form, though it is often latent or
disguised by the complexity of the notions and the richness and
interest of another verb. In the use of an elementary verb lies the
real fertility of judgement, the affirmation of existence which
brings the mind into reality and truth. The logical meaning of
est and *esse* can fairly easily be managed, but the metaphysical

---

[1] *Summa Theologica*, 1a: LVIII: 4. 1a: LXXXV: 5.

[2] Examples of affirmative judgements are, God is omniscient, Waller was
smooth, a stitch in time saves nine, machinery relieves the strain on human
muscles, playfulness can be a supernatural virtue: of negative judgements, animals
are not machines, Cromwell was not king, rhododendrons will not grow on
chalky soil, Marshal Ney did not grasp the strategic plan of the campaign leading
to Waterloo, charity is not bound by prudence.

[3] The scholastics speak of a pronouncement, *enuntiato*, when the form is a flat
statement; a question, or *interrogatio*, when proposed as subject to doubt; a *propositio*, when taken in order to prove something; a *conclusio*, when proved. *Summa
Theologica*, 1a: XIV: 14.

implications remain a challenge and invitation until perhaps beyond the grave we arrive at the vision of pure existence.[1]

The explicit setting out of a proposition with a complete show of logic will often appear stilted and clumsy compared with the brevity and ellipsis of ordinary speech[2]: this is perhaps more noticeable in English than in medieval Latin. In conversation we try to avoid stiff-set attitudes. It must be confessed that the study of scholastic texts does not help simple unaffected intercourse. For any movement is gawky and ungracious when the bones show through. Consequently the logical patterns of sentences and paragraphs are not evident in an idiomatic style. This holds alike for ordinary exposition and for scientific treatment; the systematic and sustained argumentations of the *Summa Theologica*, which keeps as nearly as possible to explicitly logical forms, would be at least five times its present length, prolix, full of repetitions and elephantine sentences, were every judgement to be articulated and exposed with a full show of logic.

Logic cannot emulate the raciness of penny wise, pound foolish; perhaps more than other arts, it should be concealed—not however in verbiage, of that St Thomas is free. In any case there are many things that are best taken in your stride and not paused over; for if the intemperate are too intemperate, the temperate commonly insist overmuch on their temperance: paradoxes must be left in their brief and vivid truth, and many challenges must sound but once, as with the signal from the skipper to the King's harbourmaster, 'expected time of arrival 0745 if friendly aircraft stop attacking me,' or the diplomatic counsel, 'en politique il ne faut jamais dire jamais,' or the cry, 'O, call back yesterday, bid time return.' Nevertheless all judgements that are meant to form part of rational exposition should be capable of being broken up into their logical components and then reconstituted; the assembly of a long goods train would be impossible but for the sidings and switches of the shunting yards.

---

[1] *Summa Theologica*, 1a: XII: 1.
[2] Commentary, I *Perihermenias, lect.* 6.

CHAPTER XIV

METRONOME AND MELODY

THE dialectic of St Thomas cannot be appraised by concentrating on his logical apparatus. Restless and scattered thoughts converge to one centre[1]: reasoning is to understanding what time is to eternity[2] and as fragments to a single whole; its appetite is for rest and simple immediacy. While we listen therefore to the clip-clop of scholastic sounds we must also let ourselves be carried to this release. As we have said before logic is a means, not an end; perhaps, like empire-building, better absent-minded. Over-conscious logicality can be like forced jocularity, so before looking at their notional form, we may be well advised to pause over the divergence between the logical and the psychological qualities of propositions.[3] Let us start with the direct and simple style of the line:—*My blood so red for thee was shed.* How awkward is the translation into a formal proposition:—the effusion of my living blood (subject) is, in the past tense (copula), on your account (predicate); yet the underlying structure can be displayed only in some such fashion as that, though the original and construed propositions have a different psychological ring.

The variance between the measure and the pulse, the abstract logical pattern and the vital experience of thought, is like that between notional and real being. An object present to mind merely as a logical product does not sound the real and physical notes of being; for that matter, the rational perception of reality does not attest intimate contact and immediate vision.[4] From the beginning the *Summa Theologica* insists that '*to be* can mean either the real act of existing or just a propositional affirmation, whereby the mind credits *is* of a predicate with respect to a subject: in the first sense of the word we do not grasp the being of God; but in

---

[1] VI *de Trinitate*, I, 3rd question.
[2] *Summa Theologica*, 1a: X: 1, 4. 1a: LXXIX: 8.
[3] *Ibid.*, 2a–2ae: I: 2, 6.
[4] *Ibid.*, 1a: XLV: 4. 1a: XIII: 1, *ad* 2. Disputations, X *de Veritate*, 5. Disputations, *de Anima*, 20. *Summa Theologica*, 1a–2ae: III: 6.

the second sense of the word, we know that the following proposition formulated about him is true, namely that he exists: this we infer from his effects.'[1] Affirmation, then, falls short of possession; we can think of things without having them fully alive in our minds; if this be the case with the scientific examination of real things, with greater reason does it apply the logical scrutiny of notions and propositions. The logic of thinking differs from the meaning and substance of real knowledge as a skull differs from a human head.

Nevertheless verbal composition is the sign of identity[2] and the analytical passages of St Thomas do not lose sight of their true purpose, which is to assemble the elements in order to join them.[3] Between the lines must be read the hope that ratiocination will lead to union, *secundum totam essendi potestatem*.[4] Mental distinctions are the more impressive for being drawn reluctantly: over alacrity here is perhaps the peculiar weakness of the scholastic. The separations made by logic are not a case of *divide et impera*, of keeping things disunited in order the better to control them; they are applications of that general theological law of life, uttered in the sacrificial counsel that death precedes rebirth, requiring parts to be separated if they are to be recomposed, the fragments gathered in eternity where nothing is lost, a man to be born again. This spirit of a world restored breathes even through formal logic; and the meagre entity of logical coupling would draw us to the very substance of God, drily understated as He Who Is.[5]

Mere logic no more renders the confluence of thought than the level lines of the printed page, broken up by words and punctuation, represent the pitch, rhythm, melody, and accent of speech; moreover the movement of logic is not free and loping, but stiff and mechanical even to the point of jerkiness, like the man in the clock at Strassburg or the figures of an animated cartoon. It exhibits a succession of clauses rather than a continuous flow. How can you pick a piece from the stream or a portion from the tempest?

---

[1] *Summa Theologica*, 1a: III: 4, *ad* 2. 1a: XLVIII: 2, *ad* 2. Opusc. VIII, *de Ente et Essentia*, Ch. 1.

[2] *Summa Theologica*, 1a: XVI: 7. I *Contra Gentes*, 36.

[3] *Summa Theologica*, 1a: LVIII: 2, 3, 4. 1a: XIII: 12.

[4] I *Contra Gentes*, 28.

[5] *Summa Theologica*, 1a: XIII: 11.

For logic, then, mental activity is not a response to a moving need, but to an object displaying a pattern of set rational forms.[1]

This condition conforms to a deductive philosophy considered as a closed system, a sequence of related propositions, all expecting certitude, with assents not haunted by the fear of the contrary being true, and all dealing with natures rather than with facts. The philosophy of St Thomas is indeed deductive, but it is not shut in: it is based on an 'historical' experience, works from an induction, adds to didactic logic the play of dialectic, and expects a joyful seeing face to face. It is a philosophy not of ideas, but of existents; and must therefore be accommodated to contingents. Certitude may be found here, as when I am certain that I exist or when I unhesitatingly take my friend's word, yet the severely rational reason does not find the evidence so compelling as with an abstract truth.[2] Scholasticism has not always avoided the appearance of preferring paper calculations to experimental research. On one hand there is the ideal construction, on the other a constant improvisation; another reappearance of the old opposition, stated in early Greek philosophy by Parmenides and Heraclitus and echoed in our days by the contrast between the mathematical and the physical treatment of physics.

The quality of thinking in hard and fast terms rather than in shades and echoes gives a certain edge and bite to the language of the schools, and at the same time makes the style less suggestive and supple than later idioms where the structure of logic is more obscured and the purpose, like that of the romantic symphonies, is more to rouse a mood than to point a meaning. For this reason, logical fallacies are more blatant in Latin than in English; anyone

---

[1] The traditional working logic is occupied with pure categoricals, that is propositions which assert that one noun is or is not associated with another, more than with modals, that is propositions expressing the mode of association. (Opusc. XLII, de Propositionibus Modalibus.)

[2] On matters of belief such certitude is known as moral certitude: the term is also applied to practical judgements of conduct, where a high degree of probability in the abstract becomes a sufficient and safe rule in the concrete: more cannot be expected. (Summa Theologica, 2a–2ae: LXX: 2. 2a–2ae: XLVII: 9, ad 2). The modified assent to an uncertain truth is called opinion. Doubt is not an act, but a state of mind; a suspension of assent; positive when the pros balance the cons, negative when evidence is lacking either way. (Summa Theologica, 2a–2ae: II: 1. Disputations, XIV de Veritate, 1.)

who is suspicious of a passage may be advised to translate it, if not
into scholastic Latin at least into stiff and formal sentences. The
thinker who is not content to remain merely a logician is well
aware how stilted logic appears by comparison with the ease and
movement of thought, how small a place it holds when set in the
total needs of human life. Yet he knows, too, that correct measure
is required for rational tranquillity and beauty too; logic sets the
key and tempo without which a melody must falter into unrelated
sounds.

The difference, therefore, between the logic and the psychology of a proposition should not be unexpected. Logic can dis-
sect a statement into subject, copula, and predicate, and submit
these parts again to more detailed analysis; but from a psychological point of view the statement, despite the complexity of the
logical parts, may express the single and undivided perception of a
single whole through every living cell of the percipient,[1] and, like
the façade of Notre Dame of Paris, be taken as the sum of its
elements only by formal artifice.[2] Many authors have moved away
from the doctrine that complex states are pieced together like a
mosaic from simple perceptions and affections; their trend now is
to insist that no single situation can be adequately analysed into
its elements. When I conceive *black cat*, I do more than add the
concept *black* to the concept *cat*, nor do I merely continue a sum of
addition when I introduce the concept *good luck*: taken together
they make up a single appreciation, a unique *mise-en-scéne*; *black
cat brings good luck*, is a judgement virtually containing many concepts, yet actually betokening a whole and undivided perception
of an object against a background of magic. The effect is gram-
matically and logically cumulative, but affectively simple, as in
Burke's description of Hyder Ali, 'a menacing meteor, compound-
ing all the materials of fury, havoc, and desolation in one black
cloud.'

---

[1] *Summa Theologica*, 1a–2ae: CXIII: 7, *ad* 2. 1a: LVIII: 2. 1a: LXXV: 3, *ad* 3.
1a: LXXXV: 5.

[2] Logical complexity can go with psychological simplicity, a fact to remember
for its theoretical as well as for its practical truth. People who choose their
words carefully are frequently single hearted, perhaps some of the differences
between friends come from not recognizing the candour of a qualified and
stammering statement that seeks to correct the false harmonics of a flat
declaration.

Logic, however, does not merge itself into this drive to single-ness, but stands aside and divides the situation into bits and pieces. If the statement about black cats is a preliminary to exposition, then must it be capable of logical articulation in some such pro-position as, black cat is an effective sign of good luck, or words to that effect. The interest is not in psychological processes for their own sake, but in their use as instruments of correct and com-municable knowledge. Here again we must observe that logic does not treat of objective physical reality nor render an account of conscious and affective states—'be still the hautboys, and the flute be dumb.'

Verba philosophorum sunt formalia, the speech of a scientist is regulated and formal; a certain literalness is expected in exact ex-position, and some suspicion will greet figures of speech, or the jubilance of Reuter's correspondent who wrote after Alamein, 'the claims made in the air communiqué were more than true—they were an understatement.' There is a sobriety about logic, which, if lacking enchantment, is yet not devoid of its own proper elegance, or even pawky humour, an unpretentiousness about the dressing and the drill, for there have been victorious armies, like the men of Saratoga, that were ragamuffins on parade.

Truths do not flow into our mind like crustaceans into the wide and ready jaws of a basking whale. They have to be pursued and selected. An effort of judgement is required; and only then, when the reason affirms or denies, is a position reached that can be called correct or incorrect, true or false.[1] The mind is open to the con-ception of many ideas, some of them strange and remote, but all in a sense are exempt from control or criticism; they are like the first motions of sensuality before there is any question of delibera-tion. Even definition is only of an essence, the aristotelean imper-fect, *what it was for it to be,* the mind must make a further advance to reach an existent. Apprehension takes a meaning, *respicit ipsam naturam rei,* but judgement states a being, *respicit ipsum esse rei*[2]; and it is then, when the mind adopts an attitude and commits itself, that the passage is made from ideal essence into real existence[3] and the tests for truth and logical coherence are applied.

---

[1] *Summa Theologica,* 1a: XVI: 2. Disputations, I *de Veritate,* 3.
[2] *Summa Theologica,* 1a: III: 4, ad 2.
[3] V *de Trinitate,* 3.

How often we pass judgements is another matter; for lengthy periods we are like passengers in the train watching the country-side go past. A complicated and ornamented idea may look like a judgement; a statement may be a physical discharge with little real meaning. Slogans are to judgements what bogy words are to ideas: an emotion is roused and let loose but nothing of rational significance is communicated:—throne and altar; a life for the Czar!; the people's justice; down with the priests; let him be crucified; how scandalous; that is heresy; these reactions, auto-matic or exciting, are not always rational judgements. In any case, feelings have to be cooled and purified before they can be treated by logic.

That until a judgement is passed the reason cannot either be approved as true or condemned as false is a touchstone in episte-mology. Imagine a statement that reveals hallucination; yet re-flection shows that the error of the composition does not invali-date the elements from which it is formed.[1] I say there is a pink snake coiled round the tea-cosy the doctor wears on his head: I am mistaken; but in the world there is pink and snake and tea-cosy and doctor: the mixture is fantastic, but the ingre-dients are real enough; and I diverge from reality, not so much in my perception of a curious conjunction, but in affirming that the apparition is a fact by my bedside. My state of mind is at fault, not in expressing a complex notion, which you also express as you read these lines, but in making affirmative judge-ment, the pink snake is coiled and the doctor is wearing a tea-cosy and all of them are here.[2] The terms are sound, but their composi-tion is wrong; the data may be passed, but the elaboration has gone wrong. This applies not only to such extreme instances, but also to all cases of error, where accurate information from the sources may be fed to the centres of collation, but there misinterpreted.

Let us repeat that the truth or falsehood of a proposition in sober fact or well-established theory is no concern of formal logic; yet its criticism obeys the same beat as that of epistemology, the final verdict is not passed on notions until they are assembled in the form of a judgement. Some notions are bare, others are dressed to attract attention—enlightened self-interest, prudence to

---

[1] *Summa Theologica*, 1a: XVII: 2, 3. Disputations, I *de Veritate*, 10, 11, 12.
[2] *Summa Theologica*, 1a: LXXXV: 6.

the pitch of heroism—others give you pause, as when a popular daily hails a 'gloves-off radio speech,' but while noting the logical form, the time for acceptance or rejection is not until after the attempted build-up.[1]

'Bongs!' I exclaim aloud.—My companion may suspect that I have mixed my consonants or am not dealing with the practical conduct of life, but the logician in him will wait until I say something more.—'Bongs,' I continue, 'are incandescent, and so are gas mantles, and therefore,' I conclude, 'bongs are gas mantles.' He now knows that he need not bother his head about what bongs may be, except from curiosity, because I have broken the rules of logic and have certainly not shown that they are gas mantles: on the face of it my conclusion does not follow, and the concluding judgement is therefore incorrect. Were I merely to muse, ' Bongs, incandescent 'm, gas mantles 'm.' I would not commit myself, though such wavering reveries sometimes do duty for judgement and even for argument. But I adopt a position when I introduce the copula and proclaim a judgement, bongs are incandescent, or, gas mantles are incandescent. This example takes a proposition that is incorrect considered as a conclusion; but there are others faulty to start with, when, for instance, an abstract term is predicated of a concrete subject: Yeasto is Health! it is unnecessary to be a dietician to know the sense is defective. Or again the use of an incomplete term, the country is slowly: slowly what? However a complete term is sometimes supposed, as in such statements as, slowly does it, tuck it under, look out!

---

[1] *Summa Theologica*, 1a: LVIII: 5.

CHAPTER XV

QUALITY AND QUANTITY

SOME statements that cannot be cast in the mould of quantity can yet be scientific and exact; commensuration, to use St Thomas's term, is not always rigid for there are plastic likenesses and living adaptations. In every affirmation lies an identity subtler than the plain correspondence expressed when a kilometre is said to be five-eighths of a mile or twopence-halfpenny the cost of a letter by inland postage; even in those cases, beneath the adjustment of amounts, the mind is moving in a world beyond quantity and dealing with evidence irreducible to mathematics. The relationship between terms set up by the logical copula of a proposition cannot fairly be contracted to relationships denoted by the symbols for equals, plus, minus, and so forth. *Is* is more embracing and comprehensive than *equals*, and the composition effected in a proposition represents the unison of the mind with notes of nature; the diversity of terms is fused into one thing.[1] The heart of reality, even material reality, is not mathematical, though to display a general scheme of mathematical relationships may be useful and beautiful. Mathematics draws on other disciplines for the evidence of its presuppositions and implications. Matter itself is intelligible without quantity, for which reason St Thomas criticizes the pythagorean doctrine that things are constituted by numbers.[2]

Now traditional logic studies the sense of propositions that would respond to such unquantified objects. For the sake of clearness and brevity and also for the convenient exhibition of form in a symbolic system, much as a physical problem may be explained by making a mechanical model, a mathematical notation may be adopted, as when numeral terms may be taken to indicate, not a material division of quantity, but a formal contrast of diverse forms, and may imply, not a multitude of units, but a manifold of perfection in purely spiritual reality.[3] Nevertheless the affirma-

---

[1] *Summa Theologica*, 1a: XIII: 12.
[2] V *de Trinitate*, 3.   [3] *Summa Theologica*, 1a: XXX: 3.

tion or negation of identity between subject and predicate cannot adequately be translated by quantitative proportions and functions.

Equality is a consequence of quantity, which is a category of dimensions.[1] Logic into the bargain throws in things that have no size. It is true that they may be given a quantitative reading for the sake of practical control and to supply the imagination with material. But the mind can transcend these figures and still remain strictly scientific. That it may escape into poetry or religion or sensibility is more generally admitted than that science itself is not committed to a mathematical method,[2] yet this appears from its employment of distributive ideas, which are beyond the reach of mathematics.[3] Apart from the analogies that may enter and be

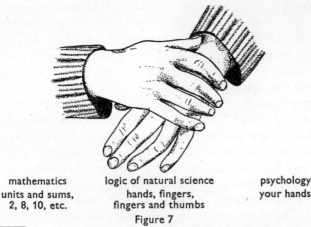

mathematics	logic of natural science	psychology
units and sums,	hands, fingers,	your hands
2, 8, 10, etc.	fingers and thumbs	

Figure 7

[1] Commentary, II *Ethics*, lect. 6. *Summa Theologica*, 1a: XLII: 1.

[2] The proposition that men are mortal does not mean that men = mortals, for this is not true anyhow, if only because many mortal things are not human; that is, the number of human units is not equivalent to the number of mortal units. Nor can the proposition be set right when corrected to read, men + x = mortal, x standing for an unknown quantity to be neglected. Apart from the psychological misreading, there is a logical rupture; the subject of the proposition, namely men, has been changed from a distributive to a collective sense. The original meaning was that each-and-every man is mortal, now changed to all-men-in-the-bulk.

[3] Mathematics works with singular and collective notions. The former represent units, 1, 2, 3 . . . etc.; we need not decide whether 3, for instance, represents a singular mathematical idea, or 3 singular ideas, namely 1, 1, 1, or a collective idea, namely 1 + 1 + 1. Collective ideas are sum totals, products, and so forth. (Cf. *Summa Theologica*, 1a: XXXI: 1, *ad* 2.) *Cf.* Figure 7.

welcomed, their sense cannot be limited to forms and relations of quantity. They are as elastic as water, and as non-compressible. *Humanity* is not a sum total, produced by the addition of many units; it does not promise a community so much as a society, an intercourse between many entire substances. The proportions of quantities cannot cover such exchanges, which are parts of a situation the classical mathematics cannot entertain. Science itself has to cope with imponderables, with 'points of three dimensions and superficies of three.' When he is forging a blade a smith is not merely engaged in metallurgy,[1] and similarly natural science and philosophy are not merely exercises in applied mathematics.[2] Men are mortal, money is a medium of exchange, happiness is the purpose of activity, all such propositions—and they include the propositions implicit in the striking of equations—set out to establish an identity between subject and predicate that cannot be measured by figures. They suppose a flexible and subtle communication of identities in kind between diverse things over and above the equivalence of distinct units affirmed by arithmetic. The expression of this intercourse supposes the qualitative union of minds and things.[3] Only in one sense, and that not the highest, is a tobacco pipe said to be worth a guinea; the ordinary judgements of the mind break out from quantities and are taken into a continuous flow of quality and substance, they are assimilated into a spiritual tissue, not checked in as though by a cash register: there is a freedom even in numeral terms, and twelve and 12 and XII and a dozen are a parable of this spiritual ease.

For all their display of self-sufficient evidence, equations take for granted that very qualitative perception of reality which logic attempts to structurize. One difficulty of trying to set mathematics and logic apart is here suggested; for existential mathematics cannot be treated purely, it is never exempt from logic and philosophy. When we say that $2 + 7 = 9$, do we suppose that, if pressed, we can demonstrate the assertion with match-sticks or do we imply that it is evident in itself without the test of experience? No matter, for in either case we take for granted some such principle as the following, the contrary of a

---

[1] *Summa Theologica*, 1a: LXXXIV: 8.

[2] *Ibid.*, 1a: LXXXV: 1, *ad* 2.

[3] Disputations, I *de Veritate*, 3.

necessary truth is impossible, which principle neither derives from mathematics nor is capable of mathematical proof.

We are sailing into waters too wide and deep for mathematician and logician alike. They are for the metaphysician to navigate. It is enough to observe that the symbol = is not the same as the logical copula *est*. Asked to instance a chain of logical reasoning, many would fall back on their memories of Euclid, partly because geometry, but not logic, is in the general curriculum for schools, partly because a certain spareness of thought is there disclosed, and partly because mathematics, as St Thomas notes, is less fluid and offers certitude more imaginable than does philosophy.[1] A pythagorean strain has always persisted in western thought. Yet geometry itself depends on logic, though its severity gives it an appearance more purely logical than that of other sciences. Logic, and dialectic still less, is not limited to mathematical modes. Though dealing with the proportions between numbers, points, lines, figures, and solids, it also reaches more widely to arrange dimensionless qualities and substances. A humbler and no less decisive test is that science must also treat with existents. It is this junction with reality that mathematics cannot touch. Here are two apples. Can we be scientific only about the twoness, or can real appleness come into science? A mathematical transcription may appear to explain apple, but the problem has been but thrust further back, and the 'physical' still remains unresolved. The humane influence of Boethius always ran strongly in the stream of scholasticism, and the sensibility of quality was respected. The outward style may have been formal, but the spirit was baroque rather than palladian, the result a building of movement, not of repose.

Some exponents of the technique of mathematical or symbolic logic have spoken as though the old traditional logic were obsolete, bad rhetoric masquerading as science, while its defenders, limiting mathematics to arguments proceeding on a purely quantitative basis, have echoed Hobbes in effect, who pooh-poohed a page of algebraic symbols with the remark that it looked as if a hen had been scratching there. But in truth the two disciplines, while as distinct as a tree and a pylon, are

---

[1] VI *de Trinitate*, 1. 2nd question. *Summa Theologica*, 1a: I: 5, *ad* 1.

complementary. If accurately stated their results do not clash. Mathematical logic cannot operate without some of the philosophical assumptions that traditional logic alone is able to match; while the traditional logic on its side should respect the convenience of this special symbolism for the exhibition of pure logical form and relations[1] and for working with the concepts of mathematical physics. It is a legitimate extension of the methods employed by Aristotle and an instrument of the liaison between the special sciences. A precious rule of criticism should be respected; let data be explained in their own proper terms. Criticism should proceed from within a subject. Music should not be defined by colour, nor life by non-biological concepts, nor identities by equations, nor quantities by qualities, nor literature by history, nor scholastic theology slighted for not providing the loving recognition of the divine presence.

---

[1] Albertus Magnus (*Perihermenias*, Tract. I, *cap.* 2) holds the method valid for the syllogism. Judgements, however, are more intractable.

Chapter XVI

TYPES OF JUDGEMENT

HAVING roughed in some of the surroundings, let us now look at the logical construction of judgements and propositions. Like other projects they may be complete, *judicium perfectum*, or incomplete, *judicium imperfectum*. An incomplete judgement has no status in logic except as a compound notion; it hums and haws, and arrives nowhere; you see it's an er er. It is not confined to halting speech, but may be found in fluent but rambling utterances. A long drawn out paragraph may disguise the absence of a predicate, and perhaps of a copula into the bargain. An um-ah manner may affect a wisdom that is not present, but grudging speech is less logically discouraging than is the chatter of unconnected words. Until a subject is capped by a predicate there is no judgement; an accumulation of subjects is no substitute. One merit of the scholastic method is the clear display of the vaulting of judgement and argument on the pillars of terms; an unfinished arch is more evident in the architecture of the period than in the disguised structures of later styles.

Complete judgements have a recognizable subject and predicate. They may be brief, just three words, such as Henry Ford's dictum that history is bunk, or they may stretch out to greater length. The arguments of early scholasticism are usually built up with short propositions. Here the logic is more accessible than in ornate and intricate and extended styles. Most propositions are composed of complex terms—what sedg'd brooks are Thames's tributaries—and sometimes in their course they gather so many qualifications that they run to the length of a paragraph. Meandering propositions are controlled with difficulty.[1] Complicated

---

[1] The following example is taken almost at random from a piece of philosophical reviewing:

'The central contention, from this standpoint, is that metaphysics as such, whatever may be the extent of the ramifications which it may legitimately throw out towards the domains of aesthetics, morals or religion, must be viewed in detachment, in a dry light, as an extrapolation of the cognitive reason which cannot

terms and sentences are sometimes used to disguise what would be repugnant in simple appearance; the pretentious enactments of the lawyers and excuses of the clergy, says Macaulay, do not sound so well when put in petty terms.

Complete judgements may be cast in the form of a statement, or a question, or a command, or a plea. 'Whoa! Buttercup!' and 'RSVP' are virtually complete judgements; 'Go away with you,' and 'Please prove your antecedent' are explicitly complete. Though they enter into the etiquette of logical intercourse, commands and pleas are expressions of the practical, not the speculative reason, for they are used to exact or recommend a certain course of action. Statements, *enuntiationes* or *enuntiabilia*,[1] which explicate objects in the indicative mood,[2] are the scientist's and philosopher's propositions of predilection. Exclamatory and other subjectless propositions, such as 'Huzza!' or 'How odd' or 'What weather,' are tantamount to complete judgements, but in formal exposition the propositions employed for preference take the form of *a* is *b*.

Apart from rousing interest, as in the opening words of *Barchester Towers*, 'Who will be the new bishop?' queries are almost as important as statements. The art of asking proper questions is scarcely less difficult and disciplined than the art of answering them. To every science there are appropriate questions, just as there are special traps.[3] A well-framed and pertinent enquiry often goes more than half-way to meet the reply; it has been said of Aristotle that he generally asked the right questions, whatever the answers may be. Who does not know the embarrassment of being expected to answer without being addressed with a proper question? The rambling recital of cosmic grievances ending with a

be expected to touch the material or even the spiritual concerns of mankind, and which, debarred *in limine* from discovering the why of what we find in the world, must confine itself to acting as a heuristic principle of explanation capable of sustaining the precise weight of what we find.'

The sentence needs to be stripped down to the bare statement that metaphysics imposes a mental pattern on our experience. Long sentences sometimes have the trick of giving with one hand and taking with the other. Leading articles that do not wish to commit themselves adopt a delphic style.

[1] *Summa Theologica*, 1a: XIII: 12. 2a–2ae: 1: 2.
[2] Commentary, I *Perihermenias*, lect. 1, 6, 7.
[3] Ibid., I *Posterior Analytics*, lect. 21, 22.

pause, and there you are, expected to justify God's ways with man.[1]

Some questions are simple and without guile; others, known as leading questions, are in effect charged with statement. For questions are frequently more than simple interrogations; 'Hey, Johnny Cope, are you waukin' yet?' and 'Cui bono?' They may contain an argument, 'What shall it profit a man if he gain the whole world and suffer the loss of his own soul?' or a threat, 'And shall Trelawny die?' Sentences that begin, 'Do you think . . .?' as in, 'Do you think the Germans are the only ones to have horrible concentration camps?' are frequently rhetorical and intended to inform your interlocutor that you hold the contrary view. A series of mounting questions is an artistic device that can produce a powerful effect—for where is Bohun? where's Mowbray? where's Mortimer? nay, which is more and most of all, where is Plantagenet?

Let us now consider the various types of statements that may be used in exposition. They may be categoric or conditional in their manner, affirmative or positive in their form, necessary or contingent in their matter.

A statement may be flat and downright, or guarded by conditions. If the connection between subject and predicate is unqualified then the statement is categorical; if however it depends on an expressed condition then the statement is conditional or hypothetical.[2] Some people are temperamentally suspicious of categoricals, yet ultimately these offer the only firm foothold and, epistemologically considered, all conditionals have to be taken

---

[1] On the eve of Waterloo, asked by Uxbridge what his plan was, Wellington countered with the question: 'Who will attack the first to-morrow, I or Buonaparte?'—'Buonaparte.'—'Well,' said the Duke, 'Buonaparte has not given me any idea of his projects, and as my plans will depend on his, how can you expect me to tell you what mine are?'

[2] Not restricted to propositions containing an *if clause*. Under hypotheticals are also classed disjunctive propositions which say that x is either y or z, and conjunctive propositions which say that x cannot be both y and z. These details must be left to a treatise on formal logic; as also the treatment of modal propositions and the rules for the conversion of propositions from one type to another.

back to them.[1] It is possible to jump claims with an air of moderation, and to assume too much under the mask of diffidence: the supposition can be gratuitous, and, as St Thomas notes,[2] though he very rarely uses *per impossibile* argument, the statement may be true even though it reposes on an impossibility—were a man a donkey he would be irrational.

Unlike Newman, who wrote in a letter to Froude that '*if* is a great philosopher, as well as peacemaker,' the scholastics in the main course of their working logic keep to categoricals, and the broad argument of St Thomas can be mastered without recourse to hypotheticals. Yet sometimes these latter offer a convenient springboard, as with the principle of John Ireton; 'If every man has the right to political power, every man must have the right to property.' But often they are difficult and exasperating to deal with, since they imply a compressed argument. 'If you think that, sir, you cannot be serious; but I know that you are not frivolous, and therefore, etc.'—that in its way is an argument, but the whole point lies in the first proposition, and it is a distraction to have to prove, or even to deny, that you are not frivolous.

In this place may be mentioned that complex form of conditional argument known as the dilemma, which may be resolved into two or more hypothetical statements. A famous example is Morton's Fork, the argument used by the minister who was raising money for Henry VII; 'if they be sparing, they must needs have because they laid up; if spenders, they must needs have because it was seen in their port and manner of living.' Though contrasts are not seldom encountered, and also, though less frequently, that kind of argument known as the *reductio ad absurdum*, authentic dilemmas are very sparingly used in scholastic writing. The effect of a well-pointed dilemma can be very telling, like Nelson's and Collingwood's two columns bearing down on the ragged crescent of French and Spanish ships at Trafalgar. Yet the manœuvres of such arguments are too involved for direct and expository dialectics, and, contrary to the popular view, the classical texts of scholasticism are usually content with the rudimentary figures and a simple logical style.

---

[1] Commentary, I *Perihermenias, lect.* 1.
[2] I *Contra Gentes*, 13.

Next, in considering affirmative and negative statements,[1] two useful bearings can be taken. First, that the predicate of an affirmative proposition is always a particular and restricted notion, unless clearly stated otherwise. Second, that the predicate of a negative proposition is a general and unrestricted notion. Consequently the extension of the predicate is indicated by the affirmative or negative form of the proposition. The extension of the subject is frequently left indefinite[2] and the context usually supplies whether all or some are meant; cause is prior to effect, signifies every cause; food is necessary for life, signifies some food. It is the predicate, however, that strikes the significant note of a judgement.

Take the affirmative proposition, birds are winged: here the predicate, winged, must be taken in the restricted sense of meaning some, not all, winged animals. The point is important, for as will be seen in dealing with the sweep of arguments a not infrequent fallacy lies in giving an unrestricted meaning to the predicate of an affirmative proposition: the police track down crimes— and sins are crimes—and therefore the police track down sins, or should do so in a Christian state.

This governing rule of affirmative propositions is not taken to apply to perfect definitions, where the predicate so exactly hits off the subject that both terms are synonymous and interchangeable: but definitions are not judgements strictly speaking, and we may take it that the terms of affirmative judgements cannot be transposed without error. If, as the puritan said, pleasure is a sin, we cannot switch him over to mean that sin is a pleasure. Europe is the Faith, that is a judgement of philosophical history that may command the respect of many who would repudiate the proposition that the Faith is Europe. In common argument subject and predicate are not rarely taken as convertible terms. Because it is supposed that fascist-minded people are critical of Russia, it is inferred that all people critical of Russia are fascist-minded; because religion is a virtue, it is inferred that all virtue is religious. This inversion is among the most frequent causes of bungled argument.

Take the proposition, birds are not viviparous: here the meaning of the predicate is unrestricted and the sense of the proposition

---

[1] Commentary, I *Peribermenias*, I: lect. 8, 9, 10. [2] *Ibid.*, II: lect. 1.

is that no animals that bring forth their young alive are birds. Hence the usefulness of negative propositions. The advantages of negation in notions has already been referred to, the same decisive abruptness is characteristic of negation in propositions. A negative form may produce a firmer effect than can be obtained by positive but particular statements. The divinity is not in any sense corporeal, the divinity is in some sense spiritual—the negative states more than the positive; the former excludes pantheism, the latter does not. Despite their protestations of meagreness, the old Cistercians constructed masterpieces of Gothic architecture; contemporary theologians belonging to the tradition of the *theologia negativa*, diffident about the power of the human reason to formulate positive judgements that would truthfully reflect the nature of God, nevertheless managed to build from their negative judgements an edifice more imposing than they intended. The systematic study of mysticism also suggests that there may be more light in the dark night than in the bright notions of the manuals, more life in the purgative way than in the easy acceptance of what immediate circumstances provide. This of course supposes that the enquiry has something to go on: there is no advance through flat denials, for while negation may be more sweeping than affirmation it is not so liberal; an affirmative statement implies the negation of its opposite, but the reverse is not true, a negative statement does not imply the affirmation of its opposite: if a thing is white it is not black, but if it is not white it does not follow that it is black.[1]

---

[1] *Summa Theologica*, 1a–2ae: C: 7, *ad* 1.

CHAPTER XVII

NECESSITY AND FACT

AVOIDING the problem of how universal and essential meanings are embodied in individual and existential substances, we have still to meet the difficulty of attributing predicates to subjects in a manner binding for every time and place. The difficulty does not apply so much when judgements are apparently limited to merely mental and ideal associations as when they claim to represent the world about us. Here we are faced with the major distinction between necessary and contingent propositions which runs throughout the dialectic of St Thomas.[1] At one extreme is the statement that two and three make five, at the other that summer is dry and winter rainy.[2] For to speak only of sequences, some are inevitable while others are not, however frequent or customary these last may be. Accordingly a difference in the manner of predication is suggested, for it is one thing to reflect that human nature is fallible and another to condemn a man for such and such a lapse; one thing to draw up an ideal scheme of moral relationships and another to form a shrewd judgement about what is prudently practicable.[3] The difference is recognized by logic, which develops the purely mental implications; the source of the difference lies in the real world, where essential meanings run alongside incidental applications, or rather spring from them. Consequently a distinction must be drawn between abstract idealization and concrete realization, between types and events, between the philosopher and the journalist and between the logic of the disinterested reason and the existential dialectic of physical science and history. 'I remember,' writes Sterne, 'the grave and learned Bevoriskus, in his commentary upon the generations from Adam, very naturally breaks off in the middle of a note to give an account to the world of a couple of sparrows upon the outer edge of his

---

[1] Commentary, I *Perihermenias, lect.* 13.

[2] Opusc. XVII, *de Sortibus,* 1.

[3] *Summa Theologica,* 1a: LXXIX: 3. 1a–2ae: XIX: 3, 5, 6. Disputations XVII *de Veritate,* 1, 2, 3. *Quodlibet* III: 26, 27

window, which had incommoded him all the time he wrote, and, at last had entirely taken him off from his genealogy.' There are philosophers unlike Bevoriskus, who do not attend to the facts that flutter outside their study as, without experience of the contingent, they expand their principles in a system of pure meanings and attempt a necessity in an ideal construction. St Thomas is not among their number, though he insists on a necessity in truth irreducible to what we happen to perceive; his abstract forms acknowledge their source in concrete things.

Propositions are said to be necessary when they do not depend on external experience for their formal verification. Yet like the science of metaphysics which considers them in their purity, they are occasioned by the experience of events and abstracted from singular facts. The judgement as to the existence of anything must start from a historical experience, though the necessary meaning is not entirely to be resolved into the corresponding events and facts. Induction precedes deduction in the order of recognition. Propositions are said to be contingent when their truth is established by the observed course of events or by our own positive enactment.

The predicate of a necessary, or *per se*, proposition is regarded as belonging to or following from the nature of the subject. The judgement is passed without reference to extrinsic factors, from an inspection, cursory or prolonged as the case may be, of the subject of the proposition, and the statement bears an inner necessity; necessity, says St Thomas, is a mode of truth, and is in the mind, and ultimately in the mind of God.[1] The scrutiny of the meaning of terms provides the evidence. Take, for example, the following; secondary causes entail a first cause, laughter indicates intelligence, activity is for a purpose, the whole is greater than any of its parts. Their warrant, more or less instant, lies in the force of the very ideas operating according to the invariable laws of thought; they are autarchic, in the sense that they are independent of imports from the world of experienced outside facts; the predicate follows inevitably once the nature of the subject has been analysed, whether or not that subject has been posited as an existing reality, for they are statements about triangularity and humanity rather

---

[1] *Summa Theologica*, 1a: XVI: 7, 8. 1a: XIV: 2, 13.

than about existing triangular objects and historical men and women. At the risk of being misunderstood, let us say that these judgements are essential, rather than existential; or, in modern terminology, judgements of value, rather than judgements of fact.

To avert misunderstanding, let us repeat that necessary propositions are not the products of an effort of pure thought and that the metaphysics of St Thomas which contains them is not an ideal system suspended, like Mahomet's coffin, in mid-air with no support from the ground. For the analysis of ideally conceived terms can never arrive at the judgement that things exist, unless the elements of the topic under consideration are already known to be in existence, which knowledge requires a union of the mind with the world through the senses.[1] St Thomas elaborates a series of necessary propositions which are explications of and inferences from natures, but the argument throughout is firmly secured to the world of ordinary experience. His sheet anchor is that human thought does not rise from an intuition of pure meaning but from an abstraction of meaning in the material world.[2] There are many problems here. The region of facts always remains the North-West Frontier of philosophy, but there is no prosperity unless that be manned. St Thomas starts from human living and reaches out to its meaning; ontologism is absent, his purest speculation is not within a closed system, but is open to influences from below, as well as from above the reason.

A necessary proposition may be either immediately or mediately evident. The former is a self-evident proposition, *propositio per se nota*, when the predicate is so close to the subject that no intermediate term is required to manifest the connection; in other words, no proof is demanded, nor could it be furnished. Such are the primary grounds of thought underlying our thinking, the indemonstrable first principles[3] or standards of reference, in which all rational knowledge is evaluated. They neither altogether derive from our experience of fact nor in

---

[1] Commentary, III *de Anima*, *lect.* 10. *Summa Theologica* 1a: LXXXIV: 2, 3, 4, 5, 6.

[2] It is this, for instance, that makes all the difference between the argument St Thomas uses in the *quarta via* and the anselmic argument.

[3] Commentary, IV *Metaphysics*, *lect.* 6. Commentary, I *Posterior Analytics*, *lect.* 5, 6.

themselves produce an enlargement of our experience. They are not regarded as pelican principles which feed their young, for they have none. We cannot seriously doubt their truth, and yet we cannot directly demonstrate them. This, however, is from abundance, and not from lack of evidence; they are so primary that there is no deeper judgement to prove them from, for only derivative propositions, or conclusions, can be proved. The principle of contradiction—to be and not to be in the same way at the same time is impossible—is implicit in all our thinking: though it may be denied in so many words the very denial assumes its truth.[1] Nor is a direct demonstration possible since the attempt would suppose what is to be proved, and so incur the fallacy of the vicious circle. At most an indirect proof can be attempted, by showing that its denial is absurd,[2] an example of a *reductio ad absurdum*, which in some ways is to demonstration what a cartoon is to a portrait.

The self-evidence of a proposition may be hidden away, *propositio per se nota quoad se tantum*, in that the reality represented by the subject and predicate may be immediately and directly identical, without this appearing to some, or indeed in some cases to all human minds in their present state. Though axiomatic to the men who framed the Declaration of Independence, others may not endorse their conviction, 'We hold the truth to be self-evident that all men are created equal'; and there are principles certainly more profound and probably more valid where the mind does not enjoy an intuition in which the terms are allowed to speak for themselves. For the human reason is still half-enclosed in darkness, we are like owls or bats in sunlight, and can do little more than blink at the most evident truth of all, namely that God is.[3] The identity of the essence and existence of the first being is the most necessary and evident of all philosophical truths in reality, yet to our minds, his existence is not an evidently self-evident principle, a *propositio per se nota quoad se et quoad nos*, but an inference of natural theology[4]; the proposition, that God exists, comes under the second class of necessary propositions, those namely that are mediately evident.

Such propositions are made manifest by the medium of demonstration; they are conclusions, not vouched for by themselves,

---

[1] Commentary, XI *Metaphysics, lect.* 5.
[2] *Ibid.*, IV *Metaphysics, lect.* 7, 17.
[3] I *Contra Gentes,* 10. [4] *Summa Theologica,* 1a: II: 2, ad 1.

but by their principles or premisses; their subject and predicate are joined by a middle term. Examples of necessary propositions that are rigorously developed from other necessary propositions are, the square on the hypotenuse of a right-angled triangle is equal to the squares on the other two sides, an act of freewill presupposes deliberation, from God naught can be hid. We may note here that the conclusions of one science may serve as the principles of another.[1]

The classical application of the distinction between necessary principles and necessary conclusions appears in the controversy over St Anselm's so-called demonstration for the existence of God, the famous anselmic argument.[2] Take God as the subject of a sentence, he urged, and you must immediately affirm existence as a necessary predicate. Why? Because existence is contained in the very form of the meaning of the term God, which signifies to everybody who makes use of it, that than which nothing greater can be conceived. Now the greatest possible being must be conceived of as existing outside the mind, for did you not conceive it so, you could have the conception of a greater. A live mouse is better than a dead lion; an object you represent to yourself as really and actually existing is so much the greater than anything you consider to be a creation of your mind or a figment of your fancy. The reader may be left to decide for himself whether he is convinced; ordinary commonsense may not be much impressed, but the argument baffles philosophical refutation more readily than might at first be expected and has attracted minds of the calibre of Descartes, Leibniz, and Lepidi. The judgement passed on it by a religious philosophy working with psychological and historical sympathy will not be the same as that of a stringent rationalism examining it in isolation. St Thomas himself rejects this *jeu d'esprit* as an unexplained leap from thoughts to things. For though the nature of God is identical with his existence the idea we form of that nature is not extra-mentally valid unless

---

[1] Immediately evident propositions are called axioms or *dignitates*, also *propositiones maximae*; propositions that are immediately evident to experts alone are called *positiones*; propositions that must be assumed by a particular science, though they may be proved by a higher science, are called *suppositiones*. Commentary, I *Posterior Analytics*, lect. 5. In modern usage axiom has less dignity, meaning simply a rule adopted for the sake of argument.

[2] *Summa Theologica*, Ia: II: 1, objection 2. I *Contra Gentes*, 10. Disputations, X *de Veritate*, 12.

founded on a contact with existing reality, which for us in our present state is our material environment.[1] Our thoughts cannot make things, nor can the mind proclaim the existence of anything from its own inner resources without drawing on outside help.

Necessary propositions are sometimes called analytic propositions, because they demand assent from the mere examination of their terms without reference to outside truths, and they are contrasted with synthetic propositions, in which the predicate does not appear to develop the subject from within but to be added to it from without, the predication does not result from an analysis of the terms but from a build-up produced by our experience. To these we must now attend.

There is no denying that chance happenings are often more engaging than necessary consequences and that empirical conclusions are more exciting than deductions. Furthermore, the propositions that express such conjunctions seem, certainly to those of a positive and roving habit of mind, to add more to our knowledge than do propositions that are merely explicative. Moreover they determine the course of events; had Cleopatra's nose been shorter, said Pascal, the face of the world would have been changed. We cannot discuss here the value of waywardness and surprise: 'We'll keep it dark, sir,' the marine orderly has just said, 'as dark as a glow-worm.' But for the genius of analogy, metaphysics seems to leave these things on one side. In its regular routes it appears as a sober and consequential science, concerned with effects rather than with events, with the ordered propriety of objects and not with their disconcerting occurrences. But some defence of contingent propositions must preface our treatment of them, for in pure philosophy their status is rather lowly.

In contingent propositions the predicate happens to apply to the subject; the connection is not formed by the very force of the notions in themselves, *per se*, but by another factor, *per accidens*, namely our experience of the way of the world, of the constant recurrences and repetitions of similar phenomena, as well as of more startling observations. Snow is white; horses get up forefeet first, but cows get up forefeet last; you see Cotswold villages in South Lincolnshire, and I have just been speaking to a ruthless submarine

---

[1] *Summa Theologica*, Ia: II: I.

hunter whose dearest ambition is to be a curator of a museum of antique pottery. The opposite is conceivable in all these cases; without entering into spectographic chemistry let us say that snow could be green, and without violence to the necessities of nature that horses and cows could exchange their manner of rising. It would be another kind of world, but it is a possible world.

Hence contingent propositions are not binding on our minds by the inner necessity of their terms; 'experience,' said Hobbes, 'concludeth nothing universally'; they are not necessarily true in this sense, though we may rightly take them as unquestionably true, and in most cases it would be silly to doubt them. But their very meaning does not impose itself on the mind, which assents to them, not by their luminous self-evidence, but by its experience of facts. The learner of a foreign language is faced by a set of contingent propositions demanding much memory work, for the vocabulary and grammatical rules appear to be arbitrary, though later he may discover their interior logic; yet on the whole the process remains one of continually taking in fresh elements from outside. In this it is like an experimental science which works with facts and contingent propositions, and unlike a philosophical science which develops the meaning of principles.

Such arbitrary propositions—the word is used in no pejorative sense, for a gift is arbitrary—are said to be contingently true, *per accidens*. They happen so; of course once they have happened they have acquired a certain necessity, and are the matter for fatalism.[1] This happening may be constant and frequent, so much so that it can safely be expected to repeat itself always in the future; or it may be unexpected and rare. Its truth may be as steady as the rules for British foreign policy laid down in Sir Eyre Crowe's memorandum, or it may be *ad hoc* and only once, as when four hands of cards are dealt each containing a complete suit. But so long as a proposition is formulated without insight into a reason but solely from the force of events, then must it be classed as contingent and not necessary. Let us remind ourselves that we are making a distinction in logic, for in their psychological completeness most of our statements will be a fusion of necessity and contingency.

Labradors love water, steamrollers have the white horse of Kent on their smokebox door, men are born in original sin, Thomas

---

[1] *Summa Theologica*, 1a: XIV: 13. 1a: CXVI: 2, 3, 4.

Aquinas was a Christian, all these are contingent propositions. Often they contain generalizations so frequently true that they can be treated as unalterable general propositions. Some are based on the experience of the sequences of natural phenomena which admit of no exception in everyday life, they are necessary on the hypothesis that the world works in the way with which we are familiar,[1] and are said to be hypothetically necessary.[2] No return from the grave; an axehead sinks in water; fevers do not instantly abate at a word; to prefer solemnity to truth is a common failing of the devout.

They are arrived at by the process of induction, that is from an assembly of instances, not by insight into nature and meaning. They may be numerous, marmalade is stickier than jam; or comparatively rare, babies cannot spit straight; or they may require an effort of imagination, you cannot nail a jellyfish to the wall. Serious or frivolous, they go to make up the stock-in-trade of our workaday thinking; and yet philosophy seems to regard them as so much mental small-talk, for they are about incidents, events, facts, happenings. With these metaphysics has no direct concern, for it is at pains to frame necessary propositions out of a contingent world, to see the general and unchanging setting for the shifting throng of events. Its statements claim to be true in themselves, opposite statements are unthinkable; for strict metaphysics cannot tolerate the possibility of alternatives and there are no miracles in its proper field; a metaphysical doctrine that could be false is a metaphysical doctrine that is certainly false. Consequently pure rationalism does not deal with contingent propositions except in passing.

Nevertheless the metaphysics of St Thomas is not a purely ideal construction,[3] an ontology of notions, for its origin is an abstraction made from sensible data[4]. This junction of pure thought and contingent experience is a matter of much speculative

---

[1] *Summa Theologica*, 1a: CV: 6. Disputations, VI *de Pòtentia*, 1. II *Contra Gentes*, 25-30.

[2] *Summa Theologica*, 1a: LXXXII: 1. Commentary, V *Metaphysics*, *lect.* 6.

[3] *Summa Theologica*, 1a: LXXXIV: 1.

[4] Called by Aristotle an induction—but the term is not used in the scholastic sense of a product of inductive reasoning. Cf. Commentary, II *Posterior Analytics*, *lect.* 20.

difficulty into which we cannot enter now, yet to neglect that
the meeting is claimed would be to miss the point of St Thomas'
criticism of the arguments for the existence of God which start
from the scrutiny of mental essences.[1] In philosophy we may hope
to prove God from the world, but not the world from God. He
insists that we must work from the things about us. To deny this
junction is to deprive his thought of its realism, as the common
reader understands the word, and, by implication, to reduce his
Christian theology to an uneasy mixture of mental categories and
historical acts of God. The thinkers of the middle ages were well
acquainted with the problem; many took the easier line of philosophical idealism while reserving existential judgements to their
religious convictions, but Scotus ranges himself with St Thomas in
showing solicitude for the scientific status of facts.

Mathematics carries a necessity similar to that of metaphysics,
indeed more evident in that its convictions are more clear-cut, if
not so deep. The essences of triangles and circles are such that
they cannot be otherwise; a world where circles are square is unthinkable, though of course a world where nothing in fact is perfectly circular and no lines are really straight is easily entertained,
and indeed may exist, for all mathematics cares. That is a matter
for the physical scientist and his findings impair neither the theo-
retic validity nor the practical profit of mathematics, for circularity
and straightness would still have to be applied as standards. Similarly, metaphysics could not allow the principle of contradiction
to be contradicted, nor moral theory admit a case where lying
would be right or the end justify a bad means, whatever the excuses of conduct accommodating itself to the pressure of circumstances. The principles and conclusions of necessary sciences derive from the unchangeable meaning of natures, and are not open
to revision in the name of convenience. Practical improvizations
are not so severe and simple as the binding laws of theory; and it
may be remarked on matters of contingent interest that people can
hold apparently irreconcilable opinions. The Japanese Government in the midst of waging a bitter war against the United States
expresses its condolences on the death of the President; private
persons not rarely find themselves in two minds and committed to

---

[1] *Summa Theologica*, 1a: II: 1, 2.

divergent courses of action; a husband finds that he cannot live happily either with or without his wife. A poetical liturgy sings of a *felix culpa*, without shock to a sense of proportion. Facts are not easily marshalled into a single unitary scheme, and a critical mind will proceed gently before classing such paradoxes as contradictory or illogical.

The distinction between necessary and contingent propositions will recur in the treatment of deductive and inductive reasoning; it presages, as may have been noticed, the important difference between finding reasons and establishing facts. Interpretation and certification are both important, and neither should be allowed to suppress the other; nor should they be confused. Whenever there is an attempt to provide an explanation of the way things behave or have certain properties attaching to them, then the processes of philosophy are involved, or are at least imitated, for then there is an implied claim to be working with the natures and the inner necessities of objects, though whether these be the things we think they are is another question. But when different sets of facts are codified together, as happens in the experimental sciences, then we are not taken beyond contingent propositions. We are offered, not reasons, but readings, notwithstanding the impressive results of the arrangement and calculation, which may include the discovery of new sets of facts.

This difference will be developed in the account of the relations between philosophy and the experimental science. An elaborate and detailed examination of a fact and its translation into scientific terms will have the effect of temporarily quieting the mind, its association with other facts similarly described will increase the effect, especially when the formulation of a scientific law is achieved. The procedure, though useful and indeed indispensable, does not offer an explanation; in fact it may serve to postpone an explanation. A fresh and supervening process, either of inventing a hypothesis or finding a theory, must be instituted if there is to be an attempt to meet the inborn bent of the mind towards reasons. 'Sir,' said Dr Johnson, 'there is more knowledge of the heart in one letter of Richardson than in all *Tom Jones* . . . there was as great a difference between them as between a man who knows how a watch is made and a man who can tell the hour by looking upon the dial plate.'

CHAPTER XVIII

TREE OF PORPHYRY

THE account of the essential or accidental connection between the terms of propositions paves the way to the five predicables, or the five modes of attributing a predicate to a subject according to the scheme of Porphyry.[1] Would that we could apply Andrew Marvell's lines to the scholastic logic:

> But only with the Roses playes;
> And then does tell
> What Colour best becomes them, and what Smell.

But the treatment is more pressed and dried, a catalogue of five mental ways of attribution, namely genus, specific difference, species, property, and accident—of which the last marks the nearest a logic of pure ideas can reach to the world of variable and informal facts.[2] Flowing or flawed realities can be included in the scheme only when they are attracted to their nearest fixed and integral terms.[3]

Some old text-books picture the Tree of Porphyry, not unlike a Jesse window in an English parish church, with species sprouting out of genera, all arranged in order, as in a family tree. The scheme presumes that different things are rooted in the same reality and that some are not so different but they can cluster on the same boughs, branches, or twigs, according to their closeness. The classifications are common arrangements for the method of division and sub-division employed by the scientific treatment of any topic, and may be observed in the picture of the Geological Column, and in the arrangement of the *Summa Theologica*, where every question and every treatise and the whole work altogether may be schematized by the orderly and separate treatment of the special determinations of generic topics, though inevitably from the very

---

[1] A Greek logician of the early Christian centuries, whose *Isagoge*, or Introduction to the Categories of Aristotle, was often quoted by the medievals.

[2] Man is an animal—genus: rational—specific difference: rational animal—species: with a sense of humour—property: usually wears clothes—accident.

[3] *Summa Theologica*, Ia: III: 5.

nature of the case the divisions are not applied with the same exclusiveness as are the classifications of botany or zoology.

Take birds, for instance; they all have a common likeness, not possessed by daffodils, bluebottles, crabs and foxes. Let us, for the moment, call *bird* their genus. Now birds differ greatly among themselves, from tomtits to herons, from cuckoos to hawks, from little stints to coots and so forth. Let us call the operating factor their specific difference; here again we need not ask whether tom-tittery and heronishness and so forth are real or not; enough for the logician that the human mind adopts such categories for classification. Since he is concerned with the mental pattern of our thinking, he will investigate and discuss the qualities of a generic predicate—that's a bird, or a specific predicate—that's a thrush.

Birds are divided into different orders, which are divided into different families, and so again into sub-families and species. The classification is often detailed and complicated, and the identification of the different species, such as the spotted sandpiper, has been the occasion for a display of temper. There are not just millions of flying feathered vertebrates, but also classes of them, about twenty thousand. Waders can be grouped together, and doves, and wagtails and game-birds and so on; and among the waders, together with woodcock and curlew and snipe and plover, will be found the sandpiper—relatively long legs, four toes, hind toe elevated, two or three anterior toes united at the base. But even sandpipers, on this common base, exhibit special characteristics; some are 'lively, restless, and loquacious,' says Edmund Sandars, others are very shy and wary, others rather silent and rather tame; and so sandpipers, in their turn, have been grouped into different classes, the common sandpiper, the green sandpiper, the spotted sandpiper, and others.

As the divisions become more detailed and specific, so they also become more difficult to spot in fact; and the classification itself must grow more diffident, for the objects dealt with must be approached by careful induction, and not from preconceptions. It is often very difficult to determine what is and what is not a distinct species, and to assign the specific characteristics. Nevertheless, scientific workers arrive at approximate agreement, sufficient at any rate to recognize a freak, or a departure from a specific standard.

Now this must be noticed, the difference between the kinds of sandpiper comes from a factor extrinsic to the common concept of sandpiper; let us say, for the purpose of one illustration, from the concepts of green and spotted. All classification by genus and species conforms to this rule. If this new note is not a sport but a constant, and if it is not superficial but profound—the natural scientist must provide the tests—then some of the conditions for the constitution of a species are present. Otherwise the variations are less than specific, as with blue and brown eyes in men, or with the characteristics of natural curiosities. The classifications and divisions may attain the elaborate and classical perfection of Linnaeus or they may be more rough-and-ready, but though the terminology may vary they are all rigged according to the same plan.

First, a notion may belong to a subject as its genus. Such a generic notion indicates an essential and necessary part of a thing's nature, but it is not yet so differentiated but that it can apply to things of another nature. A generic idea represents an element common to different kinds; thus animal is a generic idea with respect to things so different as mayflies and men. That is a sweeping example, a wide class, or what is called a *genus supremum*: mammal which includes buffaloes and men, is an example of a narrower class, which may be limited to a *genus infimum*.[1] As St Thomas notes, a mule is not like a horse or a donkey in its species, but in its proximate genus.[2]

Secondly, supervening to the genus there is a distinguishing factor, of which the expressive notion is called the specific difference, *differentia specifica*. Difference implies a common ground[3]— a point of importance for dialectic—and is not such a strong word as diversity, which conveys no community between two objects. A specific difference is a part of the nature of a thing, indeed is that part which formalizes it as a specific kind of thing[4]; and, as we have said, it comes from outside the idea of the genus, for there is nothing in the genus as such to make it evolve the characteristics of one species or eliminate the characteristics of another.[5]

---

[1] *Summa Theologica*, 1a: III: 5. I *Contra Gentes*, 25.
[2] Disputations, III *de Potentia*, 8, *ad* 16.
[3] *Summa Theologica*, 1a: III: 8, *ad* 3. I *Contra Gentes*, 17.
[4] *Summa Theologica*, 1a: L: 2, *ad* 1. 1a: L: 4.
[5] I *Contra Gentes*, 14.

In many questions it is important to appreciate when the entrance of a fresh factor produces a new kind of situation, not only in matters of natural science, but also in affairs of conduct, as with the difference between homicide and murder; and when the difference is one of degree, as, for instance, with the difference between the R.A.F. block buster and the atomic bomb; size, of course, can sometimes change the situation in justice, as in the difference between a murderous attack with an ineffective or a lethal weapon.

Thirdly, as the result of the addition of specific difference to genus, the idea of the species appears, which sufficiently defines the nature of the subject. Whether in fact we can ever succeed in formulating concepts that not inadequately correspond to real natures is another question: according to the teaching of St Thomas we can, though he makes no extravagant claims. We may at least seize the exclusive and peculiar position an object holds in a rational scheme of real relationships; and that, if not the veritable quiddity which fascinated the scholastics of the decadence, is a great gain. The business of logic is merely to legislate on the status of the notion of species and of specific predicate, not to evaluate its claims to reality; to accept the forms of definitions, but not to question their force.[1] The science of reality works with more assurance when it leaves the substance of things and turns to the two supplementary notions of logical property and logical accident.

In the fourth place comes logical property, *proprium*, which is conceived, not as a part of the nature of the subject, but as necessarily deriving from it, *per se fluens*. In its severest sense, a property is what we call a peculiarity or special characteristic. The stock instance for the scholastics is sense of humour, or *risibile*, with respect to man or pleasure with respect to happiness. The former is not an essential constituent of human nature, but a necessary emanation of a boundless mind and heart, released through the imagination and kindly emotions, at the spectacle of the human scene. But other characteristics, necessarily emanating from a subject but not exclusively confined to its kind, are also termed properties, thus to be ticklish is a human property, though a nervous

---

[1] *Summa Theologica*, 1a–2ae: XVIII: 7.

system is the foundation of the same property in other animals as well.

Much scientific work at classification can scarcely expect to go beyond the tabulation of real properties. We are more diffident than the later medievals were about the power of the reason to lay hold on the natures of things; our world is more nebulous and sliding shadowed than theirs; we have not the same conviction of purpose at work, nor do we take the largest and brightest features of a thing as the most important. Still, properties serve well enough; could we but agree that man is an animal with a sense of humour, the theoretical gain would be considerable, and the practical gain even greater; similarly if we could agree that the good should be pleasurable.

In the fifth place comes a notion that is attributed to a subject not as a necessary property, but as a happening, a predication *per accidens*; as a dialect is to a language, or a personal trick to speech. This is called a logical, or predicable accident. Clothes do not make a man, and to be clothed is not one of his necessary attributes. Logical accidents hold the humblest place in the dialectic of philosophy, and logic scarcely deals with them except to notice that they are off the beat of what is inevitable, necessary, and proper. Accidental notions are the predicates of contingent propositions. What a welter of them there is in real life. And which are the more important notes in any statement about your interests, those that fall under the headings of necessity or those the logician must treat as logical accidents? History abounds in them; Saul sets out to seek his father's asses, and founds a kingdom instead; Photius feels misunderstood, and the Princess Charlotte dies through medical blundering. Yet theoretical science neglects such chances for the essential implications and proper consequences of objects.

Classification by the five predicables is not ambitious; Porphyry's is not the Tree of Knowledge, but something to climb. The predicables are limited to general ideas, and even so to univocal generalizations, and then only in their mental mode. For to begin with, singular things as such elude the classification,[1] which covers types and the proprieties, not persons and incidents; signposts of predication are set up to guide the right ordering of

---

[1] Disputations, IX *de Potentia*, 2, *ad* 11.

thought, but what is individual and accidental is just pointed at,[1] and since it comprises the greater part of human history, a very detailed world-plan must not be expected. Our consciousness teems with incidents, and logic will do little more than help us recognize them as such.

Secondly, leaving accidents aside, three of the four predicables, namely genus, specific difference, and species, fit univocal notions alone.[2] Analogical ideas, the noblest ideas of all, are not engaged, they are not fixed and steady, hence they cannot be fitted into genus and species, nor are they differenced from outside by a supervening difference.[3] Beauty, which is an analogical perfection, is not an addition to the entity of a thing nor a cosmetic, but a flowering from within.[4] So also with all the perfections of being; no difference can arise outside reality to difference it.[5] But a genus in the strict sense of the word,[6] is univocal in its various species; for purposes of scientific classification animal applies equally and in the same sense to buffaloes and to men; that we are better animals may be true, but this rises from other considerations. The specific difference is extraneous to the genus, thus rational is a notion extrinsic to the notion of animal and is not developed from it; and the species which results is also univocal to all its members. Genus is potential to all its species. But when, as in metaphysics, being as such is the object of study, outside which there is nothing, then such a principle of differentiation cannot be introduced. Being is implicit in every difference. We are skirting the fringes of the problem of the One and Many and can well leave it undisclosed, except to remark again that the subtle and pervasive notions proper to metaphysics are not univocal: being is not a genus or species,[7] nor is pure being a kind of thing[8]; existence is not a uniform actuality nor are truth, goodness, and beauty definable by logical analysis into their essential parts.

---

[1] IV de Trinitate, 2.

[2] I Contra Gentes, 32.

[3] Opusc. VIII, de Ente et Essentia, Ch. 3, 4. Summa Theologica, 1a–2ae: LII: 2.

[4] Summa Theologica, 1a: V: 4, ad 1. 1a–2ae: XXVIII: 1, ad 3. 2a–2ae: CXLV: 2.

[5] Disputations, I de Veritate, 1. III de Potentia, 16, ad 4.

[6] The term genus is used to mean species, e.g. genus humanum, and sometimes more loosely applies to any general heading.

[7] I Contra Gentes, 25.

[8] Summa Theologica, 1a: III: 5.

Thirdly, these five predicables represent five different modes of predicating, not five different modes of existing. They are the creatures of logic,[1] and must be taken as precise notions, not as ideas coupled with reality: rationality as a specific difference does not exist as such save in the mind of the scientist. The predicables are the five modes of being a predicate, not the modes of being. The scholastic classification of the latter is another matter; these are the ten categories, or ten predicaments, *decem praedicamenta*, namely substance and the nine varieties of real accidents, of which quality, relation, and quantity are the most important. The treatment of them belongs to natural philosophy and metaphysics, and not to logic.

The logical purpose of propositions is to enter into the pattern of correct argument. Every judgement is social, like the man who makes it; not at its best when standing alone. Yet before finding company, judgements may be ready for discovery when they define and when they divide. I open two books almost at random, and read, first in the one, 'Ah make the most of what we yet may spend,' and in the other, 'The inns are as bad as the roads are good.'

---

[1] Opusc. VIII, *de Ente et Essentia*, Ch. 3, 4.

CHAPTER XIX

DEFINITION

INFINITE is a term of reproach in an early usage, standing for what is shapeless, indefinite, and unclarified by form.[1] Aristotle praises Anaxagoras, the antique Greek philosopher—'who kept sober, while others spoke wildly'—for being the first to set the intelligence separating forms in the general swirl.[2] The old classical thinkers, including those who exalt the surge of life, display this desire for definition which still survives among the traditions we have received from the Greek and Roman world. To define, lay down a boundary, deliminate, mark well, set limits to, here is the first and necessary act if a discussion is to get under way. One meaning must be isolated and other meanings excluded.[3] In the library I look for a work of clear exposition and open G. M. Trevelyan's *History of England* and read: 'The English Civil War was not the collapse of an outworn society in a chaos of class hatred and greed, but a contest for political and religious ideals that divided every rank in a land socially sound and economically prosperous.' There, briefly, the stage is set.

Definition is to discourse what firm resolution is to conduct. The constant rule of the *Summa Theologica* is to open a question with a definition, a sentence explaining a term and separating its meaning from that of other terms. As Hobbes said, 'the light of human minds is perspicuous words by exact definitions first snuffed and purged from ambiguities.' This practice has the merit of preventing equivocation, and sometimes of forestalling controversy; moreover the question is hedged in, for ordered enquiry must be dominated by the sense of the limited objective and debate must be kept from straying all over the place. Furthermore, definition sharpens and sustains the perception of what is significant throughout the distractions of circumstances; a liberal democrat

---

[1] *Summa Theologica*, 1a: VII: 1. I *Contra Gentes* 69. Disputations, I *de Potentia* 2.

[2] *Summa Theologica*, 1a: XLVII: 1.

[3] *Ibid.*, 1a: XXIII: 7.

will hold steady to his condemnation of rigged elections whether they are run by a dictatorship or a swindle democracy.

But definition itself must be defined: it is a proposition that gives an unambiguous and exclusive meaning to a term or thing. Many scholastic arguments are in fact scarcely more than sustained definitions of the terms of a thesis; but that is great praise: though it throws but a narrow beam, better a lamp to light his feet than a stick to beat him on his way. Few of us mind having things explained to us, but to be argued at, that is another affair. Who has not suffered the trial of being mistaken for a hostile critic by people with a touchy and expostulatory turn of mind when previously there was no intention of gainsaying them? The tone of the *Summa Theologica* is rarely polemical. Skim through the articles and you will find many that merely define the sense of the terms of the discussion, draw a primary distinction, then perhaps a secondary distinction, and quietly indicate the conclusion appropriate to each member; the punch, if that is not too strong a word, is kept until the replies to the objections.[1]

Definition is the first objective of dialectic and the first condition of mutual advance in debate. Yet it is initial, not final; and even a later scholastic, who may have hunted definitions as if he were a terrier after rats, cannot be allowed to deserve the taunt of Butler's lines,

> He knew *what's what*, and that's as high
> As *Metaphysick* wit can fly.

For logic it is the explication of an exact motion, the statement of what's what, *quid sit*, the expression of a quiddity. Accordingly most treatises on the traditional logic place this making clear of meaning under the heading of notions, and treat the logic of definition before the logic of judgement. St Thomas speaks of definition as the culmination of simple apprehension,[2] the first logical act of the reason. It is true that a pure definition is the

---

[1] Examples from the *Summa Theologica*. Is death inborn in man? (1a–2ae: LXXXV: 6). Is God's existence demonstrable? (1a: II: 2). Is this the best of all possible worlds? (1a: XXV: 6). How is good the cause of evil? (1a: XLIX: 1). Does pleasure lie at the heart of happiness? (1a–2ae: III: 4). Are all men ruled by the same natural law? (1a–2ae: XCIV: 4).

[2] *Summa Theologica*, 1a–2ae: XC: 1, *ad* 2.

elucidation of a meaning and, unlike judgement, does not amount
to an affirmation of existence,[1] nor does it enlarge our knowledge,
since subject and predicate are convertible and synonymous; nevertheless our treatment of definition has been postponed until the
present, partly because it is expressed in the form of a proposition
and not of a term, partly because in practice it tends to become a
judgement and more than an elucidatory concept; indeed Aristotle
refers to some definitions as quasi-demonstrations[2]; for example,
'thunder is the noise of fire being quenched in the clouds' is a
formula that exhibits the cause of a thing's existence. Seldom do
we hit off a situation so exactly that the definition offered and the
object exactly coincide in our consciousness; we know what we
mean but cannot accurately and completely render our meaning.

The mind may try for the bull's-eye and not always succeed.
Then there are flashes of form—memory is what you forget with
—that escape the rules of exposition. To steer between decision
and diffidence is a difficult art. Fools rush in where angels fear to
tread; but rational animals are neither one nor the other; neither
angels, who can manage without definitions, nor must they needs
rush in, though they must assuredly tread: their minds are pedes-
trian, advancing from point to point, covering the ground a bit at
a time; yet because they are rational, and no more than rational,
and because their intuitions are intermittent, desultory, and informal, they must attempt to define even the mysteries, though
well aware that the deepest and most simple things are not subject
to such articulation. Otherwise they could neither think nor talk
about them, but only exclaim Ah! ah! ah! with Jeremy the Prophet.
Not that successful definitions are always flat; sometimes there is
a spice in their truth, as whenWilliam Cecil told his son that 'gen-
tility is naught else but ancient riches,' and sometimes a dance
behind the dead terms, as when God is called *actus purus*.

Definitions are not all equally ambitious nor are their subjects
equally responsive. Therefore we must consider the different types
of definition. They may be divided, first into nominal and real
definitions, and secondly, real definitions may be divided into
descriptive and essential definitions.

Nominal definition, the first to crop up, sufficiently indicates

---

[1] Aristotle, II *Posterior Analytics*, 1, 89b.   [2] *Ibid.*, II, 10, 93b–94.

what the term in question stands for. By this statement of the meaning of the name subsequent discussion can avoid the cruder types of equivocation. 'Here is an account of the race,' says the radio broadcaster, and then completes the nominal definition, 'at Newmarket this afternoon'; you know he is going to talk about horses, not eugenics. Or like Squeers: 'We go upon the practical mode of teaching. C-l-e-a-n, clean, verb active, to make bright, to scour. W-i-n, win, d-e-r, winder, a casement.' The *quinque viae*, the five ways of theism,[1] though deeper knowledge may come later, are originally about the meaning of the term *God*, the unchanging principle of motion, the first cause, the ground of necessity, the purest thing, the universal planner; *et hoc dicimus Deum* is the common refrain of all the conclusions.

Such are nominal definitions, dictionary pieces, that serve to tidy the field of discussion. Good will does not supply their absence in contemporary religious and social exposition. When technicalities are engaged, as in legal, mathematical, and logical questions, the nominal and real definitions will often coincide, the meaning of the term and the meaning of the thing being the same. Fix such phrases as contempt of court, felony, misprision of justice, square root, logarithm, syllogism, vicious circle, and you have enclosed all the entity that is to be found there. Were the mind content with such clippings, our power of definition would not be despised; but our ambitions are greater and we demand definitions of objects fuller and more real in a world not completely explicable.[2]

Real definition gets to closer grips with the nature of the thing signified by the term. The mind can address itself to this business with modesty and confidence. Aristotle and St Thomas begin their *Metaphysics* by insisting that the pursuit of causes is the quality of wisdom: the architectonic are nobler than the merely executive

---

[1] *Summa Theologica*, 1a: II: 3.

[2] Nominal definition is not precisely the same as etymology, though the two are connected: the etymology of a word is given by tracing its history in language and exposing its pedigree; in this the nominal definition will appear; *hope*, you say, is a word deriving from the Norse and meaning an inlet of the sea in the Orkneys; here both the etymology and the nominal definition of the term rule out the psychological and moral attitude of mind and attitude of will also called hope. *Summa Theologica*, 1a: XIII: 2, *ad* 2. 2a–2ae: XCII: 1, *ad* 2. Disputations, IX *de Potentia*, 3, *ad* 1.

arts, and the performance of jobs is enhanced by an insight into their reasons.[1] A wise captain keeps his crew informed to the limits of security as to the purpose of any operation they are engaged on and so keeps them in good heart. At this point a digression on the four causes will help us to appreciate the scholastic approach to our environment; for though individuality remains mysterious and indefinable, individuals exist in natures and types, not only as things, but as kinds of things, and these we may hope to define by seeking their real and positive general principles, in other words their causes.

Four great classes of cause are enumerated[2]: first, the final cause, the end, purpose or *finis*, which meets the question, why? *propter quid?*[3]; second, the efficient cause or agent, *agens*, the active principle of production, which meets the question, whence and how? *a quo?*[4] Both of these two causes stand outside the effect or object under consideration, and accordingly they are sometimes termed the extrinsic causes. The remaining two causes are within the object and are termed the intrinsic causes; namely third, the material cause or underlying subject, which receives a specific stamp of reality and meets the question, in what? *in quo?*[5] and fourth, the formal cause or specific principle, which meets the question what, *quid?*[6] These causes are but summarily indicated here; the full treatment of their existence, nature, and divisions belongs to metaphysics.

Let us now take an example of definition by the application of these four categories.[7] We start far back with an etymology and nominal definition. You enquire, 'What is a multiple pom-pom?' and I reply with the etymology; 'Multiple, a word from the Latin *multum* meaning many, pom-pom, probably onomatopoeia from the noise it makes, though that is more like a giant and explosive typewriter,' and then with the nominal definition 'the term does not stand for the red blobs on a French matelot's cap, but for a piece of artillery, sometimes called a Chicago piano by the war

[1] Commentary, I *Metaphysics, lect.* 1, 2. VII: *lect.* 17.
[2] *Ibid.,* V: *lect.* 2, 3.
[3] *Summa Theologica,* 1a: XLIV: 4. 1a–2ae: I: 2. 1a: CV: 5. 2a–2ae: XXVII: 4.
[4] *Ibid.,* 1a: XXV: 1. 1a: XLIV: 1, 2.
[5] *Ibid.,* 1a: IV: 1. Opusc. II, *de Principiis Naturae.*
[6] *Summa Theologica,* 1a: CV: 5.
[7] *Ibid.,* 2a–2ae: XXVII: 3. Commentary, II *Posterior Analytics, lect.* 9.

correspondents.' Then I attempt to supply a real definition by applying the concepts of the four causes: first by showing the final cause, which includes the end and the means; 'its purpose is to destroy aircraft and small torpedo craft by bringing to bear a rapid and heavy concentration of many explosives or armour-piercing shells:' secondly by indicating the efficient cause; 'it was made by the designers, technicians and machinists of the great armament firm of Vickers:' thirdly the material cause, 'of steel and other high-grade metals:' fourthly the formal cause, 'and it consists of such and such an arrangement of four or eight barrels and a breech loading mechanism on a rotating mounting.' So you are left with a pretty fair general idea of a multiple pom-pom. The procedure, which may be more or less clumsy, can be recommended in the case of other objects that call for explanation.

The final and efficient causes lie outside the thing to be defined, for which reason a definition which looks to them, a genetic or causal[1] rather than an analytic explanation, will be extrinsic; yet the word *nature* comes from *nascitura*,[2] and if we are in at the birth of a thing we are acquainted with more than its name. On many issues, and those the most ultimate, we are offered no more than extrinsic suggestions, as when it is said that things are diverse and dissimilar in order to shadow forth the pure and simple perfection of God,[3] and in science the proofs must often proceed from extrinsic causes.[4] That peace is the effect of charity[5] is an example of definition by an active principle; that clocks are for telling the time, of definition by purpose. Both are included in the opening of the simple catechism:Who made you?—God made me. —Why did God make you?—God made me to know him and love him and serve him in this world and to be happy with him for ever in the next. The purpose indicated may be very secondary, and to this extent the definition will lose in depth though it may gain in shine. Not a few belong to the same class as the reply of the boy in

---

[1] Cause without qualification usually stands for efficient cause; less frequently for final cause; rarely, unless so stated, for material and formal cause. An effect is the dependent of an efficient cause.
[2] *Summa Theologica*, 3a: II: 1.
[3] *Compendium Theologiae*, Ch. 72.
[4] VI *de Trinitate*, 1.
[5] *Summa Theologica*, 2a–2ae: XXIX: 4.

the religious instruction class; 'sacraments,' he said, 'are for getting you off purgatory.'

The definition of things according to their end, or by teleology as it is called, is a feature of aristotelean and scholastic science,[1] twisted sometimes and prolonged in an extravagant fashion, especially when the direction of a thing's inner drive, or internal finality, its burden of private appetite, is lost in the spectacle of a general scheme of external finality[2] or in the account of its rôle of subservience and interaction with other things in a more or less arbitrarily conceived system. Why mosquitoes? To train us to keep our tempers. Some of the purposes assigned in medieval science are as far-fetched as that. I am reminded of old Tom Beazeley's teleology in *Jacob Faithful*: 'Water, indeed! The only use of water I know, is to mix your grog with, and float vessels up and down the world. Why was the sea made salt, but to prevent our drinking too much water?' The distinction between internal finality and external finality is of major importance; the former lies in a thing's activity to its proper end, in accordance with the law that its specific nature impels a thing to some condition, while the latter is the co-ordination of that activity with the activities of others in a balanced design.[3] Impressed by the apparent chaos around them, men preying on men and bugs preying on all, many have been led to conclude that there is no purpose anywhere; they argue from the lack of order between many things to the lack of direction in each: but in reality there is no lack of purpose but too much purpose; not feebleness, but exuberance wrecks the plan we expect.

After the middle ages the definition of things by final causes fell more and more into disfavour; this was partly in reaction against the fanciful ascriptions of some of the scholastics, partly in distrust of such 'metaphysical' concepts as appetites and prefixed goals and conscious designs,[4] which were displaced by the advance of empirical thinking. History itself came to be read, not liturgically, but in the pressure of events; man was the product of his changing environment, Egypt worshipped the cat because it

---

[1] *Summa Theologica*, 1a: XCI: 3, *ad* 3.
[2] *Ibid.*, 1a: LXV: 2.
[3] Disputations, XXII *de Veritate*, 1.
[4] *Summa Theologica*, 1a–2ae: XLVII: 2, *ad* 3.

was the granary of the ancient world, soil erosion explained the spread of Islam from Arabia. Whereas scholastics had inserted events into a large-scale theological drama and were certainly deficient in the scientific methods of history as we understand them, things now came to be defined more and more by how they come about and by what were the factors of construction. Money is wealth, water is the product of oxygen and hydrogen, a wish is the result of organic pressure, birds fly because they have wings, they do not have wings because they must fly. At least something of the old logic survived in this harking back for a principle of repeated sequences, even when it was pictured as a mechanical force; there was an expectation that an antecedent could be found for consequents, that a law was at work, though it may not have amounted to causality in the philosophical sense of the word. But that confidence has now declined, even in physical science, with the growing sense of impredictability, and also in political judgements, where gossip has been substituted for evidence and our public men and journalists are curiously illiterate about reading the forces working to produce a social situation, particularly in foreign affairs; they talk like men keenly interested in the present and in the indefinite and freely evolving future, but without knowledge of the past. But to understand the world we must know its history, which is another way of saying that we must appreciate the value of genetic definitions.

With the development of biology and the greater modesty of mechanistic interpretations there are indications that a sense of final causality is coming into its own again; there is a lessening disinclination to recognize that the activity of living things is shaped and explained by reference to an end. In the examination of an animal reaction to a given situation the explanation by efficient causes lights on the mechanism of production, nerves, reflexes, muscles, glands, and the like. But the biologist will also consider the activity as a response to a need, the need being for an appropriate end: he will cautiously avoid making an entity of such an end or purpose, nevertheless he will constantly be invoking the analogical concept of a final cause. Without going back to the stock purposes dear to the natural philosophers before the *Novum Organum* and without holding that all the purposes of the world are planned for man's convenience, or endorsing the biblical and ethical interpretations of backwood fundamentalism, or claiming a prophetical spirit, we may accept a stream of purpose at work about us and try to canalize it in our definitions. At any rate the grasp of some such general meaning means that we are not at the mercy of one limited technique, as when the real significance of sea-power is appreciated, and not limited to one weapon, such as a warship. Definition by final causes is a salient feature of the scholastic method, and dominates the specification of activity by its formal object.[1]

Moving causes do not enter into the essence of a thing.[2] But we may concentrate on the object in itself after considering its extrinsic causes, and seek to formulate an intrinsic definition by stating its material and formal causes, and chiefly the latter. Of what is it made? And what is the form of its constitution? What in brief, is its very nature? Success is not hardly won when we are dealing with artificial things, such as multiple pom-poms and synthetic foodstuffs, or with mathematical and logical entities, such as highest common denominators or disjunctive propositions; nor are we baffled when we attempt to describe natural things, such as centipedes and salmon, by their accidental characteristics.[3] But to reach the heart of things, to penetrate the mystery of matter, and to enjoy insight into the forms that determine it, that is beyond our power to achieve with complete success. Beauty is more easily described by its effects than by its components.[4] We are at ease with such artefacts as railway systems, chess problems, torpedoes, or with legal entities, such as civil rights or the bye-laws of the Thames Conservancy Board; but natural substances are more teasing, too variable to be fixed, too complete and whole for a formula, and, like Charles James Fox, too big for definition. We are able awkwardly to locate a thing without managing to define its truth; many things we know sufficiently for recognition— I know a horse when I see one—and concerning some perhaps we fancy we know more than most; others we can elaborate in scientific terms and are even able to reconstruct them, chlorophyll for example; but this is certain, that we do not see the complete

---

[1] *Summa Theologica*, 1a: I: 7.   1a–2ae: LIV: 2.   1a–2ae: LX: 5.
[2] *Ibid.*, 2a–2ae: CLXXX: 2, *ad* 2.
[3] Commentary, I *de Anima*, *lect.* I.
[4] *Summa Theologica*, 1a: V: 4, *ad* 1.   1a–2ae: XXVII: 1, *ad* 3.   1a: XXXIX: 8.

essence of a material thing at a stroke. We touch here on a perennial issue, between wild nature and law, *phusis* and *nomos*, which
the trained mind tends to settle in favour of the latter.

The formal cause is the specific factor that we seek to capture,
the mind is a hunter of forms, *venator formarum*. The material
cause must be respected, for St Thomas follows Aristotle in insisting on the inclusion of a reference to matter in any definition
of a material thing.[1] Despite their tendency to formalization,
both stress the importance of context and subject. Yet form is the
significant element, and matter by itself is indeterminate. How
much we should distrust judgements based solely on the stuff of
things and without regard to their formal significance is brought
home to us by the readiness of the socialist press to applaud everybody that rises against the propertied classes and of the religious
press to support all parties that have a church connection. For
similar persuasions political murder and brigandage are differently
appreciated according to the side that perpetrates them.

Deep down in the human mind there is an aspiration to discover the inner forms of things that will be content with nothing
less. Here is one fascination of purely logical analysis, and a temptation to desert physical things and avoid all truck with existents,
agents, and ends.[2] Hence the need of capping logic with dialectic. St Thomas notices that the physical sciences must often
cast about outside the object of their study; this running to and
fro from one thing to another, *discurrendo*, and treating with extrinsic causes is proper to ratiocination, more restless than the
mathematical scrutiny of form and the metaphysical contemplation of meaning.[3] Some material factors wholly escape us, others
are but dimly known.[4] The sciences must envy the calm of
mathematics and metaphysics because, not always with success,
they are all seeking form. Now some of the scholastics were sanguine that the human reason could fairly easily find the formal
causes and force its way into the essences of material things. But

---

[1] V *de Trinitate,* 2. Definition of a material type abstracts from singular
material conditions, *materia signata,* but not from general matter, *materia com-
munis, materia non signata.*

[2] Commentary, VII *Metaphysics, lect.* 7.

[3] VI *de Trinitate,* 1. 1st question.

[4] Opusc. XIII, *Compendium Theologiae,* Ch. 104.

in effect their quiddities became little more than laboured conceits, and in their multiplication of abstract aptitudes and satisfactions and 'frequency of insignificant speech' they lost sight of
the need for observation and experimental verification. The world
bristles with difficulties. Metaphysics is not a short cut through
physics; the facile fabrication of a form is no substitute for the
meticulous methods of scientific registration.

The streaming thoughts of a master tend to congeal in his disciples: looking back on his definitions and arguments on his deathbed St Thomas said they were like men of straw; so also Karl
Marx shortly before his death observed, 'Anyhow I am not a
Marxist'; and John Wilkes ended a condemnation with 'in fact,
sir, he was, which I never was, a Wilkite.' Henry James was surprised to discover that Tennyson was not a tennysonian, and in
this sense it may be doubted whether Plato was a platonist, or St
Thomas a thomist, if that means one who believes that an augustan
peace has been established in thought. At any rate his philosophy
remains an intellectual adventure. He opens doors, rather than
shuts them. But there was a period when many scholastics grew
complacent and lacked the stimulus of a discontented agnosticism.
Deep problems lurked in their controversies, but they seemed intent on points of logical detail; they had come to play with words
and had ceased to wrestle with things. The catalogue might be
enlarged, but the system was final. Forms were the counters they
used, and there was little attempt to make them meet the new
facts that were being discovered. Not without justice were they
attacked by the scientists from the seventeenth century onwards;
but these, in their turn, or some of them, grew equally dogmatic
and uncritical and produced forms of their own, though they did
not call them essences. They left their method of open-minded
empirical enquiry and began to philosophize instead. Their judgements were no less flat, though perhaps their temper was less considerate and responsible. There are no natures, they said, things
are but complicated machines, make a model and you will understand them. They had a gentlemanly respect for feeling and
qualities, so long as these were kept private, or at most left to the
religious or artistic temperament; but from the strictly scientific
point of view they held that all that was not tractable by mechanics
and mathematics was fairytale.

Since that period of a special mood of rationalism, confident but limited, we have learnt more caution and are more critical in our belief in apparatus, possibly more open to admit that there is a strictly scientific approach to other objects besides quantities. Nothing can justify the flight from reason, not even the excesses of the rationalists; what was needed was a liberation of the reason from an admittedly useful technique converted into a cramping philosophy, and the recovery of the idea that scientific truth is not restricted to mechanical and mathematical forms. Even the new diffidence about scientific dogmatism should not refuse to see that the reason can at least work like a system of radiolocation and can pinpoint an object. On examination it will be found that the object has been plotted in a series of intelligible relationships. There would be no science of any sort unless there were a justifiable hope of finding reasons, that is essence and natures, in this minimum sense,[1] and of aiming at true conclusions in a defined framework. That they are not complete is true, but an insertion has been made, there is explanation up to a point, the mind has begun to think of essences, and, as Madame du Deffand said in ironic marvel at the miracle of St Denys, it is the first step that counts.

Without claiming to have exhausted the secrets of plant life we can lay down in general its notes of difference from merely mineral layers and where it falls short of animal vitality. Much may escape analysis, some ascriptions are unsteady, such terms as fir and pine have been loosely used. Animal growths can scarcely be discerned from seaweed in the grasses that foul the hull of ships. Notwithstanding these difficulties the broad statement of what constitutes the difference between plants and animals still remains. Then consider animals, we are not entirely unaware of the specific differences between them, of the profound differences, for instance, between cats and birds, and between cats and dogs, though there are gaps to be filled in, and the delimitation of a true species is sometimes attended with great difficulty, since domesticated cats are not alone in having habits inimical to true breeding and the fixture of types.

The actual definition of objects is the task of the natural

---

[1] V *de Trinitate*, V: 2.

sciences and philosophy, not of logic; though logic is expected to rehearse the conditions and types of definition; and this would largely be a waste of time unless the characteristics of real definition could be realized. Popular terms are frequently descriptive, or become so by association; daddy long legs, snapdragon, toadstool, buttercup, yaffle, jellyfish, butcher bird, glow-worm, seem to be lifted above the pedantry of nomenclature. As Dr Johnson noticed; 'Some things may be made darker by definition. I see a *cow*. I define her, *Animal quadrupes ruminans cornutum*. But a goat ruminates, and a cow may have no horns. *Cow* is plainer.' He was being crotchety and illogical, but one can sympathize with his sentiment.

On the supposition that the mind knows real kinds, we can admit that there are workable definitions that are intrinsic to their subjects. Many are no more than descriptive and no more undress nature than does the definition of Gothic as the pointed style of architecture expose its structure; for essential differences are largely unknown to us but must be signified by derivative and accidental differences[1]; laughter is a convulsive and noisy agitation excited by the ludicrous, man is a featherless biped, God is the simple cumulus of all perfections,[2] eternity is the entire and all at once perfect possession of endless life.[3] It is a ruling principle for St Thomas that appearances are not masks of reality, but revelations; but in using them to determine the underlying nature he prefers the terms *designation* or *notification* to *definition*.[4] But there are cases where definition may be granted to denote, if only in general terms, the essential specification of an object.[5]

The perfect type of definition according to logic is that which assigns the lowest genus of a thing and states its ultimate difference, from which it follows that univocal natures alone offer much satisfaction to the strictly definitory approach. The four following may be taken as representative definitions, useful for our thought and more than nominal in their bearing; man is a rational

---

[1] Opusc. VII, *de Ente et Essentia*, Ch. 6. *Summa Theologica*, 1a: XXIX: 1, *ad* 3.
[2] *Summa Theologica*, 1a: IV: 2.
[3] *Ibid.*, 1a: X: 1.
[4] Commentary, I *de Anima*, *lect.* 1. Disputations, X *de Veritate*, 1, *ad* 6. *Summa Theologica*, 1a: LXXVII: 1, *ad* 7. 1a–2ae: XLIX: 2, *ad* 3.
[5] *Summa Theologica*, 1a–2ae: III: 2, *ad* 2.

animal, a cause is a positive principle on which another real being depends, logic is the art and science of thinking correctly, virtue is a good habit.[1]

Behind the movement to definition is the passion for meaning and typification, the instinctive assurance that, besides the contingent play of individual incidents, there are objective kinds or natures in the world with settled implications. By this test in the arena of human conduct we recognize a man of principle; and it is present in the classical moral theory that there are objective kinds of action, some right, some wrong, some indifferent in themselves, moral forms which are the proper object of moral science. An action wrong in itself is not justified however urgent or compassionate the motive,[2] and this condemns alike the forging of the False Decretals and killing for mercy. On the stubborn rock of definition the most sweeping advantage must break. Before disaster overtook us from the cult of sheer energy, whether as a racial protest or in the name of a State claiming to be above all law and uncontrolled by rational forms, men tended to acquiesce in actions that were demanded for the benefit of the group, perhaps out of inability to deal with the very size of the political and economic problems involved. Moreover the more sensitive had trained themselves to cultivate individual appreciation and be sympathetic with exceptions. These became romantic precedents and the classical laws of kinds an outworn convention. Where is the real case for divorce, contraception, euthanasia, adultery, unless in an intense regard for individual expression blind to the general definitions of law? But there are signs of a recovery of the sense of the limited objective, which is one form of the modesty required to recognize the laws that govern us; a new awareness of the importance of means in morality, a conviction that some actions are not tolerable whatever the overriding motive or the impulsion of our rulers, that we must respect the natures of things and foster a personal sanity, an immediate candour, kindliness and restraint, and must condemn all causes that offer violence to these values, however wide and unmanageable may be the corporate forces. All this is but an application to social morality of the aristotelean conviction that about us there are real kinds which we must discover

---

[1] *Summa Theologica,* 1a–2ae: LVI: 4.
[2] *Ibid.,* 1a–2ae: XIX: 2. 1a–2ae: XX: 1.

and respect, kinds of things and kinds of action.[1] Moral judgements
are best confined to these actions considered in themselves and
need not extend to private motives; to the *finis operis* of human
conduct and not to the *finis operantis*.[2] This also is the guiding rule
in English law, which judges the intentions of a criminal from the
natural consequences of his action and does not probe into his
private sinfulness.

Essential definitions can be furnished only for things that can
be strictly defined, namely material objects in which the genus and
the specific difference, or at any rate a quasi-genus and quasi-
difference can be distinguished. The Tree of Porphyry is planted
in the ground, and genera and species are conditions of corporeal
being; with other beings the terms may be illustrated and sufficiently defined but there is no question of assigning a strictly
essential definition.[3] Furthermore, only types or classes of
material objects can be so defined; individuals may be pointed at,
a definition attached to their general nature, but their singular
being remains secret. These bounds having been set to definition,
three traits are required in a good specimen, namely that it should
be exclusive, elucidatory, and fresh.

The predicate should apply exclusively to the subject to be
defined and to no other, otherwise the subject is not disentangled
from everything else and the definition fails in its purpose. In
other words, subject and predicate should be convertible and
interchangeable terms, or conterminous, that is, one should be
neither wider nor narrower than the other. Temperance is a
moral virtue that maintains the measure of reason in the con-
cupiscible appetite; will is the appetite for good proposed by the
intelligence; in these cases subject and predicate are as convertible
as in the proposition, equilateral triangles are equi-angular triangles, the statement does not grow, but cannot be budged.
Definitions do not themselves advance knowledge, for which
reason they are not full-blown judgements; their rôle is to make an
idea clear and establish the conditions in which judgements and
arguments can be developed. Strong drink is a mocker, temperance is a virtue, God is a spirit, human liberty is the absence of

[1] *Summa Theologica*, 1a–2ae: XVIII: 1, 5.
[2] *Ibid.*, 1a–2ae: XVIII: 2. Disputations, II *de Malo*, 2, 3, 4.
[3] Commentary, VII *Metaphysics*, *lect.* 3.

compulsion, none of these are definitions because the predicate is not limited to the subject.

The second quality of a good definition is that the predicate should clarify and not obscure the subject: unlike the definition of change proposed by a man of science, a peridhoretical synechy of pamparallagmatic and harroteroporoneumatical differentiations and integrations. Moreover it should be brief and positive, unlike the parliamentary explanations of legislation which labour into obscurity, and perhaps are meant to. Circumlocutions about deep and ultimate realities are inevitable, the style of von Hügel can scarcely be improved on; such subjects cannot be brightly defined in an explanatory sense since there is nothing to define them by. Apart from religious mysteries, the attempts to designate such ideas as being or good cannot have the assurance with which the reason can tackle secondary and univocal natures. Nevertheless they are failures, unless they make the subject clearer. 'Mr. Dangle,' his wife complained, 'here are two very civil gentlemen trying to make themselves understood, and I don't know which is the interpreter.' It cannot be said that scientists and philosophers generally, nor theologians, have been so gentle and considerate with the Mrs. Dangles.

The third quality of a successful definition is that it avoids tautology and the predicate does not repeat the term to be defined. Business is business; the chief difference between men and women is sex; sleep is the inability to stay awake; such examples do little to make their subject clearer. But many alleged tautologies in fact bear the note of necessity, and we are given something to go on when fatigue, for instance, is defined objectively as a diminished functional capacity and subjectively as a general feeling of lassitude immediately referred to the muscles and combined with a desire for sleep. Asked to define something, what is the clash of colour? and there is a likelihood that the Brains Trust will introduce into the answer the very notion they have been asked to clear up, and talk about the clash of light rays. The definer must watch this tendency, just as he must watch his arguments lest they become vicious circles.

An example of this common repetition is found in a coffee-house scene in *Roderick Random*. The company was discussing the art of war, and the general pronounces: 'I'll tell you what an épaulement is. I never saw an épaulement but once, and that was at the siege of Namur; in a council of war, Monsieur Cohorn, the famous engineer, affirmed that the place could not be taken. "Yes," said the Prince of Vaudemont, "it may be taken by an épaulement." This was immediately put into execution, and, in twenty-four hours, Maréschal Boufflers was fain to capitulate.' Here he made a full stop; and the old gentleman repeated the question, 'But pray what is an épaulement?' How that querulous tone still echoes after discussion.

For scholastics the weather report on most problems was 'visibility good'; yet though they conducted their debates with a dry pertinacity that avoided emotional suggestion and literary richness, the greater spirits among them were alive to the limitations of their method; they lived close to a mystery and did not act as if they could enclose and seal things in a specific notion and label and deliver them with a superscription. Yet they recognized that definition was the first condition of rational dialogue and would always begin by settling their terms. For most terms are differently echoed in the sensibility of different people; communication is secure only when they agree on the same meaning; logic lies behind the warmth and cordiality that is truly human.

Yet for all the stress they laid on the importance of definition the scholastics always made very clear the self-denying ordinance to which we have already referred, namely the impotence of rational definition to capture the singular.[1] Now since the thomists among them also held that every complete substance in the world is a singular and individual thing, they were not likely to expand their rigorous and protracted method of logic into a supreme and all-embracing doctrine[2]; that was reserved for the later centuries of subjective idealism. Their dialectic was a method of explaining facts according to the structure of mental necessity, not of spinning facts out of the mind's inner resources; they neither began nor ended by thinking that appearances are deceptive; their movement is epitomized in the five proofs for the existence of God,[3] all of which start from observation of physical reality; the mind accepts and interprets what is given, but

---

[1] V de Trinitate, 2, ad 4.
[2] Summa Theologica, 1a: I: 2, ad 2. I Contra Gentes, 63–71.
[3] Summa Theologica, 1a: II: 3.

does not project a scheme all its own and call that the stuff of reality.

Then again, it is one thing to frame everything of rational interest in a logical scheme and quite another to imagine that logic provides the explanation. The scholastics attempted the former, but not the latter. Science using logic, they held, could deal with natures, types, kinds; and scientific definitions could be extended into explanations of such objects, which though real, are not things; for real things are not types, but individualized types, they are *rationes in materia*. To speak of the way of rational knowledge, and not of the obscure way of sympathy, *compassio* or *connaturalitas*,[1] the individual can be reached only by an enumeration of general notes which gestures in his direction. He is not defined essentially, but described: 'There was a man in the land of Hus whose name was Job.'

This limitation is particularly observed in moral judgements; priggishness and moral indignation are hard to find in the writings of St Thomas; his moral science does not deal with personalities, but with types of human conduct. These are finely analysed with psychological delicacy before they are approved, allowed or condemned; but the area of personal motives and imputability is known only to God who searches the heart, while those whose office it is to judge here can reach no more than a *prudens aestimatio*, an approximate and provisional conclusion.[2]

The ballerina dances away from definition like the Lady into Fox; but she has human nature, and of that the scientific reason can hope to settle the meaning and purpose, well aware that a pure rational animal would be a metaphysical monster were it to appear. Definition is not merely restricted to types and natures, but, as we have already observed, is at ease only with natures that are univocal, that is with natures lying relatively near the surface of being, not with the heart of things, so various and analogical. Whether or not rational definition can achieve real validity is a question for natural and critical philosophy to settle; all that logic can do is to decide the notional form, divisions, and qualities

---

[1] *Summa Theologica*, 2a–2ae: II: 3, *ad* 2. 2a–2ae: XLV: 2. 1a: I: 6, *ad* 3.

[2] *Ibid.*, 1a–2ae: XCI: 3, *ad* 3. 1a–2ae: XCVI: 1, *ad* 3. 2a–2ae: XLVII: 9, *ad* 2. 2a–2ae: LXX: 2. Commentary, I *Ethics*, *lect.* 3.

of definition. The psychological requirements of a good definition are no whit less important: it should arrest the attention and keep our interest. What is an island? The dictionary says, a portion of land surrounded by water. But entire continents are that, and who thinks of the Americas as an island? We must visualize the sea all round; and here the schoolboy's definition is more vivid, a portion of the sea with no water in it.

Chapter XX

DIVISION

AFTER definition, a proposition advances into explanation when a division is called, setting out the different parts of a subject. Three conditions are present, a whole, parts, and a common basis. To shape a lecture a list of headings is drawn up and the subject divided among them. A division is executed by stating a common topic and exhibiting its different varieties; this leads to a closer definition of the subject. It is ordinarily expressed in a disjunctive proposition; to-day is either Sunday or a weekday; created being is either substance or accident; a human virtue is either cognitive or appetitive, if it is cognitive it is either intellective or sensitive, if it is appetitive it is either volitional or emotional. *Les trois façons de conter l'amour—l'ironique, la romanesque, la libertine.* Division is also the basis of that lofty manner of argument that proceeds, while on the one hand *abc* yet on the other hand *xyz,* of which examples will be found when moderates and respectabilities patronize such subjects as genius, the supernatural, and the demi-monde.

In a physical division of a whole, as of a human body into head, limbs, trunk, each member is less than the whole; but the term *division* is also used by analogy of any distribution of a general object, where sometimes it may happen that each part possesses and is more than the whole; a negro is more than a man, a lyric is more than a poem, marriage is more than a sacrament.[1] Logic

---

[1] There are divisions corresponding to the various kinds of composite wholes, and their types may be noted. First, potential and logical wholes; universal ideas, which may be univocal with respect to their parts, such as the genus *pea* with respect to its many botanical varieties, or analogical, such as *being* with respect to the multiplicity of things. Secondly, actual wholes, which may be composed of essential parts, such as man with respect to body and soul, or of entitative parts, such as created being with respect to essence and existence, or of integral parts, which may be either homogeneous, as in the case of the molecules of water, or heterogeneous, as with the numbers of an organic body. Thirdly, there is an actual whole which is composed of different abilities, thus man is a *totum potestativum* containing many faculties of operation. *Summa Theologica,* 1a: LXXVII: 1, *ad* 1.

takes division as the distribution of a topic into relevant and exclusive parts, governed by rules[1] which may be noted with profit,
for when faced with dilemmas and alternatives, it is well to test the
division from which they are mounted. Mankind, according to an
eighteenth-century epigram, is divided into men, women, and
Herveys; the macaroni may have admired the wit, but logicians
cannot accept the propriety of the division.

The first, and most important, distinction to be drawn is that
between contingent and necessary divisions. Contingent divisions
are like the contingent propositions of which they are an example;
they deal with events, facts, and the way things work out; they
are based on the happening, not on the strict inner necessity of the
topic. For historic facts are not to be deduced from pure ideas.
Political divisions are of this character; Rangers and Celtic, Guelph
and Ghibelline, Federal and Confederate, Cavalier and Round-
head; so also are the divisions of the periods of architecture and
of literary vogues. Such divisions could have been otherwise, and
sometimes the different parts shade into one another and even
exchange their meaning in the course of time; a revolution succeeds and the agitators then form a vested interest, while the old
parties plot a counter-revolution and may offer a more advanced
social programme. Nor are such divisions so complete and final
but that people with a cross-bench mind may hesitate to accept the
alternative and refuse to make an issue, perhaps because they hold
a third and higher position that is not stated; as when a man who
reverences the old tradition of Europe and yet would also promote
its development finds that he cannot cast in his lot with the
parties either of the Right or the Left.

Usually the opposed parts of such divisions are contraries
which admit of intermediate stages.[2] Nevertheless common usage
does not exact a complete enumeration of parts: for example, the
following divisions are just, though in fact they are contingent,
inductive, and incomplete: there are two kinds of English duck,
surface feeders and divers; fields are of two kinds, those you walk
straight across and those you walk round the edges of, and the
latter either contain growing crops or a bull; theories of knowledge
are either nominalist or idealist.

----

[1] *Summa Theologica*, Ia–2ae: XVIII: 7.   [2] *Ibid.*, Ia–2ae: C: 7, *ad* I.

If however a topic is divided into contradictory parts then a strict necessity is struck, however trivial or idle the occasion: mankind can be divided into those who support Aston Villa and those who do not, the field either contains a bull or it does not.

Is, or is not, the two great ends of fate.

The validity of a contradictory division is inescapable, and if in many cases the usefulness may be questioned, yet the necessary truth exhibited attracted the powerful and subtle mind of Suarez as a possible clue in explaining the certain foreknowledge of free and indeterminate future events. For all its air of finality a contradictory opposition is a piece of logical cautiousness; there is nothing more clear-cut and decisive, and yet at the same time so safe.

A necessary division, like a necessary proposition, issues from the very nature of the subject[1]; it does not depend on what happens to be so, but on what must be so and not otherwise. There are different levels of necessity: the ecclesiastico-legal necessity of the division of religious into those of amateur and those of professional status; the artistic and psychological necessity of the division between classical and romantic; the biological necessity of the division of animals into male and female; the moral necessity of the division of particular human acts into right and wrong; the logical necessity of the division of an argument into two propositions and three notions; the mathematical necessity of the division of abstract quantity into points, lines, figures, and solids; the metaphysical necessity of the division of being into cause and caused, and of created being into substance and accident.

The scholastics appear to overload some contingent divisions with necessity; this was particularly the case with certain theological and time-honoured distinctions; their reverence for antiquity exceeded their powers or perhaps their tastes for literary criticism, and by their deductive cast of mind they were bent on assigning reasons, if only probable ones, arguments *ex convenientia* or *suasiones*, for the divisions of physical and historical phenomena. At times there is an extravagant flourish about such rationalizations, not that they were meant to be taken very solemnly.

---

[1] *Summa Theologica*, 1a–2ae: XCV: 4.

St Thomas himself, with his immense respect for his predecessors
and characteristic kindliness of interpretation, sometimes appears
to read into a definition or division more than the original author
could have intended. Yet though he adopts the phraseology he
seldom allows it to clog his own freedom of analysis. He uses the
terms of St Augustine, for instance, but beneath the sincere de-
ference an argument is developed that is entirely his own. Despite
surface appearances to the contrary, which can mislead the incon-
siderate, the thomist doctrine of sexuality and sin is not augus-
tinian.[1] That is perhaps the major instance where his theological
thought must not be merged in that of his predecessors nor his
words allowed to screen his meaning. To come to philosophy,
the same ruling applies to his relationship with Aristotle, from
whom he takes terms and arguments and yet infuses a new meaning. Thus his metaphysics must be freed from the physics of
Aristotle though the terminology is similar, as in the argument
from motion to its quiet source,[2] in the doctrine of creation[3] and
of divine providence.[4] But to return to the question of division,
there are many instances where St Thomas seeks to canonize a
traditional enumeration, many articles which begin, whether such
or such a subject is suitably divided,[5] and then proceed to a sympathetic search for the necessity, and sometimes to a sympathetic
reconciliation of the apparently contrary arrangements of illus-
trious authorities.[6] Yet he is always aware of the differences
between a recommendation and a proof.[7]

Divisions may be good or bad; the test in formal logic is largely
one of elegance or clumsiness, in material logic of regard for the
nature of the subject and absence of strain or violence. There are
three tests for a good division; that it should have a common root,
that the branches should be complete, and that they should not
cross.

---

[1] *Summa Theologica*, 1a–2ae: XXX. 1a–2ae: LXXXII: 3.
[2] I *Contra Gentes*, 13.
[3] *Ibid.*, II: 15–30.
[4] *Ibid.*, III: 64–97. *Summa Theologica*, 1a: CIII.
[5] *Summa Theologica*, 2a–2ae: XLVIII.
[6] *Ibid.*, 1a–2ae: LXI: 3, 5.
[7] Eleven emotions: *ibid.*, 1a–2ae: XXV: 3. Five senses: *ibid.*, 1a: LXXIV: 3.
For the comparison between wine and women. *Quodlibet* XII, 20. Zoological
divisions: *Summa Theologica*, 1a: LXXVIII: 1.

By the first test a division should be based on the same consideration throughout the same generic subject or topic, *idem fundamentum*. On this account the following division fails: military aircraft can be divided into fighters, biplanes, and those with air-cooled engines; the foundation of the division has been changed. Yet a shift of subject is allowable in a compressed statement, as when Eric Gill said he was out to recreate that blissful state wherein everybody shall be an artist, none shall know it, and only the best accredited philosophers shall write about it. The following objection against the existence of God, put very strongly by St Thomas,[1] makes the mistake of dividing supreme evil against supreme good as though they were on the same plane: if of two contraries one is illimitable, then the other is out of existence: but the term God means a being infinitely good: if, therefore, he existed there would be no evil: but in the world there is evil: therefore he does not exist. An extension of this fallacy is found, more frequently in theory than in practice, whenever the creator is divided against his creation and both terms treated as though they signified mutually exclusive realities in a common frame of reference, whereas the creator is beyond all the categories and not within the same scheme of comparison; creatures can neither add to nor detract from his excellence; God alone is no less than God plus the universe; and consequently his being does not invade and destroy the beings he creates. Love of him does not subtract from love of others, to attend to him does not mean emptying out everything else. He is a jealous God; zealous, expounds Dionysius, for see how ardently he sustains and cherishes; one body by its presence in a place must extrude another, but he is everywhere, giving very being and place itself to things; by his presence are other things present.[2]

The second test requires a good division to be complete. There was an old judge who remarked that for his first ten years on the bench he worried whether his judgements were right; for his second ten years he knew they were right; and for the last ten years he hadn't cared a damn whether they were right or wrong: that is an interesting case, but establishes no complete survey of ripening judicial functions. We can take the following examples

---

[1] *Summa Theologica*, 1a: II: 3, objection 1.   [2] *Ibid.*, 1a: VIII: 2.

as complete divisions; human actions are right, wrong, or neutral in themselves; the object of activity is either a means or an end; causes are final, efficient, material, or formal; field sports are for fur, feather, and fin. As we have noticed, a complete division is easy when contradictory notions are employed; in dealing with contrary notions it is more difficult to know when the entire field is covered and an important part has not been missed, especially in contingent matters; it is like trying to anticipate all the ways the cat may jump.

The logical impropriety of incomplete enumeration has led to many miscalculations in human affairs, as when before Waterloo Napoleon never seemed to allow for the loyalty of Blücher to Wellington or that the old marshal would fight again after the hammering at Ligny. Yet enumeration that is not exhaustive in dealing with facts will pass muster when it is put forward tentatively, as will be seen with reference to incomplete yet sufficient induction. The topic is sufficiently expanded when we say that there are three orders of Grecian architecture, the doric, the ionic, and the corinthian—the strong, the elegant, and the rich. Or when we say, though the division fails by the first test, that English painters are water-colourists, portrait painters, or illustrators of a mood. Incomplete logical antithesis is never to be accepted except as a figure of speech: there are two kinds of men, those who do the right things for the wrong reasons, and those who do the wrong things for the right reasons; for in practice and in theory there are others who do the right things for the right reasons, others who do the wrong things for the wrong reasons, and yet others who do the right or wrong things for no reason at all.

The third test for a good definition is that the parts should be mutually exclusive and not overlap. The division should be by opposite reasons, rather than by a diversity of things.[1] Therefore the following divisions fail: there are good Christians and bad Christians and clergymen; trees are either deciduous or coniferous —for larches are both. The pattern of the *Summa Theologica* proceeds according to the logic of contrasting and exclusive parts; the ramifications are complicated but there is no useless repetition; cross-references abound, but the divisions are not

---

[1] *Summa Theologica*, 1a: V: 6, *ad* 3.

tangled; there is no substitution of one member for another, and each section is worked out with no intrusion from another.[1]

A quiet and careful thinker will treat divisions with great respect. He will be particularly careful in the use of alternatives and be critical of the either-ors of forthright partizanship. Not every difference, says Aristotle, precludes identity, for a division is always on a common basis.[2] Real truths do not fit so easily into the antitheses of logic. Violent oppositions are alien to the philosophical spirit of St Thomas. Our knowledge of eternity comes to us from time[3]; matter is for form[4]; sense for the betterment of reason[5]; law is for freedom[6]; and nature for something higher than itself.[7] Yet a well-balanced and sufficient division conveys at once the details and contrasts of a situation within the limits of a sentence. 'He held his battalion (1st Battalion, The Loyal Regiment) together for twenty days of incessant fighting under bomb and shell fire, without losing a yard of ground to the enemy which was not regained by counter-attack or vacated with orders given by higher command.'

Moreover, division starts that type of argument known as the dilemma, of which a celebrated example is Aristotle's defence of philosophy; 'You say that you must philosophize, then you must philosophize: you say that you must not philosophize, then to support your contention, you must still philosophize.' Finally we may note the native habit of writing in an antithetical style which while apparently presenting both sides of a question decides in the end for neither, for the question is left single under the appearance of division, as in the inscription on the obelisk at Naseby, which warns us that the battle left 'a useful lesson to British kings never to exceed the bounds of their just prerogative and to British subjects never to swerve from the allegiance due to their legitimate monarch.'

---

[1] For careful division and subdivision consult the short but characteristic Opusc. IV, *de Aeternitate Mundi contra murmurantes*. Also *Summa Theologica*, 1a–2ae: LXI: 2, for four cardinal virtues.

[2] *Posterior Analytics*, II, 13, 97a.

[3] *Summa Theologica*, 1a: X: 1.

[4] *Ibid.*, 1a: LXXVII: 1, 5.

[5] *Ibid.*, 1a: LXXXIV: 6. 1a: LXXXVI: 1.

[6] *Ibid.*, 1a–2ae: CVI: 3. 1a–2ae: CVII: 1.

[7] *Ibid.*, 1a: XII: 1. 1a–2ae: III: 8.

THE *est* of a proposition is some response to the *esse* of being. For the reasoning reason here is the root of life. Cut this out and all judgements and subsequent activities would be as brittle as dead twigs. Nourishment is drawn from the conjunction with existence, which lies too deep for logic and is but half-uncovered by critical metaphysics. When the mind develops ratiocinations the processes, though apparently more complicated, present less of a problem. Their measures are contained in logical forms and may even be figured according to the schemes of mathematical logic. An argument draws its strength from the force of the original premisses, but once they are accepted, if only as postulates, the mode of progression is a subject which logic is perfectly able to tackle. This certainly applies to arguments which expand what is already contained in the premisses. In the case of more venturesome arguments which may produce statements that are not conclusions to be resolved into their principles but fresh judgements merely occasioned by them, a supplementary dialectic will be required, able to work with probability and co-operate with the imagination, the activity of a lively *ratio particularis*, so important a part of the method of the sciences.

Reasoning, and its verbal expression in argument, is the third stage now to be considered. A proposition attains logical majority when joined with other propositions. For as ideas wax into judgements so do judgements into ratiocinations. A judgement is born, not in solitude, but in a medley of other judgements, which by attraction and repulsion are constantly producing new and fresh judgements. There is a dynamism in every mental act, even the most abstract, bearing it onwards; there are commas, but scarcely any full-stops in thought. A simple observation is quickly taken for a preference; the poor you have always with you, these words were used a century ago to justify the existence of a lowly and needy proletariat. A group of terms prompts a train of reasoning. There comes to my memory the inn-sign, Friendship Inn—Free

House; also the three-word condemnation, ignorant, indolent, insolent. Ideas and judgements are arguments in embryo.

Arguments are to propositions what propositions are to terms, for as a proposition is the mating of terms so an argument is the mating of two propositions. A third proposition, the conclusion, *conclusio* or *consequens*, springs from the inherent productivity or consequence, *consequentia*, of the two when united; it is the follow-through of the joint force of two mutually interacting antecedents, called the premisses; the release of that movement by which logic ceases to be just the jerky contact of terms and comes alive with the curve of a delightful place kick, and more importance. The conclusion is conditioned by the premisses, as in pronunciation a letter is modulated by the preceding letters, *s* by *d* and *t* in *cads* and *cats*, and *d* by *th* and *ss* in *breathed* and *kissed,* and its evidence wholly derives from the evidence of the premisses.

We speak of a line of thought, the thread of discourse, and spinning a yarn. Care is needed to keep the thread and yarn unbroken. Logic ensures the consecutive development of the process. Notions should enter in proper sequence. A child is taught its figures in order from 1 to 10, not higgledly-piggledy from 9 to 3, from 7 to 4.

> 'Tis ours to live in structures which demand
> The aid of scaffolding to make them stand:

so logic is not concerned with the texture and psychological echoes of ratiocination, but with its scaffolding; not with the richness or poverty, but with the bare pattern of discourse. Let us pause for some observations on the limitations of reasoned knowledge, the impossibility of attempting to demonstrate everything, and the difference between the logic and psychology of argument.

CHAPTER XXI

SENSE AND SENSIBILITY

HYPOCRISY pays tribute to virtue and honour is rendered to reasoning even by those who would slight it. Gorgias the Sophist said, first that reality does not exist, secondly that if it does then it cannot be known, and finally that if it can be known then it cannot be communicated. Such a rearguard action of scepticism may be fought with the instruments of reason; in fact many anti-rationalists have commanded a very pointed and rational style. In an account of the scholastic dialectic, which flourished at a period when confidence in the powers of the human reason ran high, the prejudice against the reason must be considered, and respectfully to begin with, as manifesting a discontent similar to the revolt against merely conventional religion. By our nature we desire a complete and immediate grasp of the things that attract us; love wells from knowledge and sets up a pressure for more.[1] And all that the reason seems to offer is a set of explanations, almost a set of excuses: reality is held at arm's length the better to be examined. We would be swift and direct and natural; our reasoning makes us laborious and roundabout and artificial. Plato refers to the ancient feud between philosophy and poetry; St Thomas admits that cogitation is not contemplation[2] and accepts the fact almost as a handicap.[3]

Other fashions have set in after periods when severely rational methods were apparently allowed to be exclusive and all-embracing. The pendulum of philosophy swings to extremes, from Descartes to Fichte, from reason to instinct, from classical to romantic. The arts oscillate in sympathy between the symmetrical and the picturesque, Beethoven and Berlioz succeed Bach and Handel, the Lake poets follow Pope, St Pancras answers Kings Cross. The ebb and flow of intellectualism is mirrored in the life

---

[1] *Summa Theologica*, 1a: XX: 1, *ad* 3. 1a: LXIV: 1. 2a–2ae: XLVII: 1, *ad* 1. 1a: LXXXIX: 4. 1a–2ae: XXVIII: 1, 2.

[2] *Ibid.*, 1a: XXXIV: 1, *ad* 2.

[3] *Ibid.*, 2a–2ae: XLIX: 5, *ad* 2. III *Contra Gentes*, 37, 38, 39.

of the individual. Who is content with the attempt to be strictly reasonable? The more apparently successful the attempt the deeper the disquiet, and the more impetuous the drive to escape into poetry and enigmas which proffer no explanation.

> Ask not of the Muse that she disclose
> The meaning of the riddle of her might.

Whatever the cause, many would not take the accusation of lacking logic greatly to heart. Nevertheless whatever may be the gain in spontaneity and the biographical interest of an impromptu of surprises and personal idiosyncrasies, whatever the revelation of the rare and the immediate profit from an accommodating adjustment to the shifts of affairs, ordered social converse declines in proportion to the surrender of logic. All values then become personal, all standards subjective: types are left for things, and the lapse is easy from Kierkegaard to Buchman. The sense of the singular instance easily becomes the cult of the unique. We may threaten, and cajole, and please, and frolic, and sulk: but how can we instruct and be instructed, and how discuss and communicate? And, more menacing, how can we enjoy freedom under a common law? It will be found that richness itself requires the austerity and economy of close reasoning.

Scientific and philosophical speech are the first to suffer when there is no common grammar, instrument, and background of thought. Presently a whole culture begins to decay, as in Europe where there remain but the remnants of a civilization based on the rule of rational law.[1] Though invaded by the forces of appetite and irresponsibility, almost unconsciously we retain some of the old values of order. Some capital still remains to be spent. Many are prepared to die for causes of which they are unable to state the reasons. Though rational intelligence endures, more indestructible than mass moods and the precarious balances of totalitarian communities, yet it must suffer from the pathetic and vulgar effects of the philosophical despair over the reason prompted by an excessive rationalism: instead of the humanity of the old popular songs we have the drivel of Ah wanna take the sennimen'le vuh of you Beeuh-tiffle baby Ahm shore crazy 'bout you! instead of weighing

---

[1] *Summa Theologica*, 1a–2ae: XC: 1. XCIII: 1.

the alternatives of policy we are conditioned by propaganda, which bears the same relation to argument that exclamation does to meaning, or slogan to judgement.

Now rational discipline steels us to steady argument, a job to be done, without a quiver either of repulsion or of pride. It would have us abstain even from the ring of words, whether they be ugly or glorious—and my mind turns as I write to our screen of the Eighth Flotilla, *Faulknor, Fame, Foresight, Fearless, Foxhound, Fortune, Firedrake, Forester*, and *Fury*, what gaiety and sacrifice and efficiency the names summon up!—and, forgetting temporarily their implications bend exclusively to the severity of the argument. We need have no illusions, and seek neither a floral dance nor a couch; a rational philosophy can know beforehand that the discontent with logical processes is partly justified, and that the method will not take the mind as far as it would go. Yet if on that account we refused to start with reasoning we should be like a traveller from London who would not take the Great North Road because it does not go all the way to Thurso.

There are tracts strange to the respectable reason. The world is born a bastard, or more happily a love-child, and is only subsequently legitimized into rational society. There is mind in the begetting, but not a reasoning mind; even the civic reason stirs from a desire deeper than logical consciousness, groaning with creation, yearning for a rest surpassing the movement to conclusions.[1] A scholastic philosopher past the flush of his tourneys in the schools, though he may still admire the exacting analyses of a Cajetan, will confess that it is not enough to be reasonable and self-regarding. For all his sustained logic the historical setting of his religion is enough to remind him of that, and the folly of the gospel is a constant challenge. There must be love in the mind, not only in the bowels, if knowing is to be living, if we are not to

> . . . knock at dusty doors to find
> Her beauty dusty in the mind.

But still we must be logical and still insist on the arid outlines of the syllogism and the categories of being. For what else can we do? The very rejection of the reason is dull and meaningless

[1] *Summa Theologica*, 1a: LVIII: 3.

unless it be done by the reason; there is no tragedy at a low level of mentality. What we must certainly avoid is the temptation to attribute to intellect or mind as such the limitations and labours of a present human condition, of identifying ratiocination with the pure act of knowledge or even of taking the assimilated cells of rational knowledge for the ligaments that bind them together. For knowing is the highest activity of life, not merely the preparation for it.[1]

St Thomas was an intellectualist, that is, he held that the principle and end of human happiness is an act of knowledge[2]; the core of reality is intelligible and even not unreasonable. But he also recognized that reasoning is but an interim activity of a mind at present in the lowest of all possible intellectual states, more a mind in the making than a mind achieved, holding in the world of intelligences the position of matter in the world of things,[3] engaged in an environment discovered in bits and pieces, not yet enjoying the simple vision of everything in all, working its way gradually from discovery to discovery, and rarely at rest in this process or discursus.[4]

The rules of logic are wholly subordinate to that vital process; our discourse is conducted on the imperturbable and infallible bass figures of logic which themselves do not convey the melody. Though the intricacies of logic may be as interesting as the mechanics of a fugue, their inherent purpose is to produce correct conclusions, and their overriding purpose to produce true conclusions, only that the mind may be opened to a simple and immediate vision at the end. Logic is so much engineering, and good gothic engineering it is in St Thomas, a framework of pillars, buttresses and ribs for the imaginative pinnacles and decoration of other men, a symmetry and restraint supporting a living dialectic.

Though logic be a transport in the modern and not in the eighteenth century sense, its unconscious aspiration is to find poetry, as the unconscious aspiration of deliberate activity is to find ecstasy, which, as Cowley wrote drowns all *what*, or *how*, or *where*. But heaven helps those who help themselves, except for

---

[1] *Summa Theologica*, 1a: XVIII: 3.
[2] *Ibid.*, 1a–2ae: III: 4. 1a–2ae: XVI: 4. 1a: XXVI: 2.
[3] *Ibid.*, 1a: LXXIX: 2. 1a: LXXXV: 3, 5. I *Contra Gentes*, 57.
[4] *Summa Theologica*, 1a: LVIII: 3. 1a: XIV: 7.

the touch of good fortune, which cannot be relied on without presumption.[1] Reasoning is meant to be orderly and sustained, not desultory and intermittent. The mind that shirks set discipline drifts into chattering, as the will that avoids the responsible choice of good peters out into waste: at least that would be the prospect but for the mercy of God.[2] There is a fundamental modesty about logic, a content with moderate things, a respect for the irony of creatureliness, a submission to the precept that we must begin at the beginning. It is not a matter of inspiration, but of hard work. We must resist the persuasion that feeling is all. In Europe, and notably in his own country, the movement of sensibility, swollen by the genius of Goethe, has almost obliterated the clear and limiting outlines of the classical order. Despite his reputation as a liberal democrat he and his followers have brought on the eclipse of reason and more dangerously than Maurras threatened the conception of liberty under a rational law. Set up the idol of the hero, and the shadow of the bully falls across social life; break the bounds of logic and appetite takes charge. The more-than-man becomes the less-than-man. Charles Churchill in *The Rosciad* recites his character:

> . . . beyond the modesty of obedience.
> —With truly tragic stalk,
> He flies, he creeps—A Hero should not walk.

His is the conviction that contracts have no binding force when they interfere with immediate interest, and that promiscuous gratification is the right of those strong enough to take it, mounting to a tremendous mass narcissism that must be broken if Europe is to remain a family of nations. Logic is the thin end of the wedge.

[1] *Summa Theologica*, 1a–2ae: LXVIII: 1, 2.
[2] *Ibid.*, 2a–2ae: XLV: 2.

CHAPTER XXII

REASONING BACK

THE old myth that the earth is supported by a giant, who stands upon a tortoise, set on an elephant, and the elephant's legs go all the way down, may serve as the text for our second pause. The process of reasoning backwards cannot be carried on indefinitely. It is unreasonable to expect the reason to reason to everything. A start must be made from somewhere, ultimately from principles which cannot themselves be proved, as movement is set off by a perfectly immobile principle.[1] All argumentative instruction, says the first sentence of the *Posterior Analytics*, proceeds from pre-existing knowledge. If we set ourselves to prove everything we push reasoning too far and will end by proving nothing, *qui nimis probat nihil probat*. A truth is demonstrated by appealing to another truth; we cannot go back and back, always asking *quis custodiet ipsos custodes?* for eventually we shall find truths that look after themselves. Neither definition nor demonstration allows of infinite regress[2]; the mind eventually comes to a stop, not at a blank wall, but at a truth so self-assured that proof can neither be needed nor supplied.

Behind such an indemonstrable first principle no rational infiltration is possible. It is not, strictly speaking, a postulate, for that is a conditional and particular supposition or an arbitrary decision made to get thought moving, while a universal first truth pervades our thinking from the start, as the principle of gravity is present in all the canons of architectural construction. We may remark here that presumptions may be of different kinds.[3] A particular enquiry must take some things for granted, but we cannot say, let us for purposes of argument assume the first principles of thought, for they precede the very act of assumption. Consequently metaphysics makes no postulates from which to draw a succession of

---

[1] *Summa Theologica*, 1a: II: 3.
[2] Commentary, I *Posterior Analytics*, lect. 31–35.
[3] *Ibid.*, IV *Metaphysics*, lect. 6.

theorems. It is the office of dialectic to find postulates at a lower level.

A first principle may be considered a commonplace or a truism, perhaps even a platitude, nor need the philosopher wince at the epithets of tautological and dogmatic; his are not 'the sad tautologies of lavish passion,' and anyhow he lays no claim to be discovering new facts. For long periods the proposition may seem flat, then come moments when the meaning is seen with a new sense of shock: being is the object of mind, joy is the end of knowledge. Yet, to speak generally, first principles are not agents of discovery, or, in the scholastic phrase, principles of invention, but principles of reduction, bases to fall back on; contractions, not expansions, of enquiry.[1]

Every departmental science has proper and particular first principles on which to base its own special enquiries. No attempt is made to prove them, they are taken as axioms, *dignitates*, worthy of credence.[2] Mathematics, for instance, does not prove the existence of quantity and number. The principles of a subordinate science are accepted from another and higher science, of which, in a sense, they are the conclusions, thus moral philosophy takes over from psychology and metaphysics the first principle that man is a rational animal capable of reaching complete happiness. Some sciences stand on their own feet, others are carried by another: all work under the vault of metaphysical first principles. If the principles of a particular and subordinate science are called into question, then appeal must be made to a higher science. Suppositions derive from higher truths, and a particular science can neither criticize nor defend itself[3]; ethics itself cannot demonstrate that happiness is available or that duty is binding, it has no secret or private light.[4]

The sciences should be arranged in order like an army or a fleet; they may work as an independent command or a detached ship for a special operation. But always their own proper autonomy within their own limits is to be respected, there should be no attempt at a despotic control by a higher science—no attempt at a theological

[1] Commentary, II *Metaphysics*, lect. 1.
[2] III *de Trinitate*, 1.
[3] *Summa Theologica*, 1a: I: 2.
[4] *Ibid.*, 1a: LXXIX: 12, 13.

physics or a metaphysical economics—but together they should form a society under the rule of wisdom, or proto-philosophy.[1]

Metaphysics, the highest and most universal science, derives from no other science. There is no court to which it can appeal, though of course the metaphysician himself will always find comfort in the corroboration of the other sciences. When doubts are thrown on his principles, then their proper defence can be conducted by nothing else but metaphysics, and then only if the critic be prepared to accept some standard of truth: if he will accept nothing and he professes to be a universal sceptic, nothing remains but to expose the hollowness of his dogmatism. No debate is possible unless he puts his head out.[2] Yet no claim is advanced that first principles may be directly and positively demonstrated.

The first principles of philosophy are the ultimate conditions of thought, not means to the enlargement of knowledge; though resolved in them, other truths cannot be deduced from them by any method of construction.[3] They are explicitly engaged by critical metaphysics, or epistemology, which scrutinizes their validity, rejects universal doubt, and leaves the way clear for the arguments of philosophy.[4] They are the ultimate laws of rational thought, underneath is the mystery of pure being and pure knowledge, not the holy and supernatural mystery which may indeed be hinted at, but the philosophical mystery flushed by all profound searchings into reality. This is not chaotic incoherence, but the paradox of

---

[1] *Prologue to the Commentary on the Metaphysics*. The *locus classicus* for the ranking of the sciences is to be found in Opusc. XVI, *de Trinitate, Question V*. The superior science is termed the *scientia subalternans*, the inferior science the *scientia subalternata*. In practical issues, such subalternation will involve direction: since war is an instrument of policy and policy itself a means to the good life, military science is subordinate to political science and political science should be subordinate to moral science. In theoretical matters there is an important distinction: one science may form part of a more general science, as a species is part of a genus, thus rational psychology, *scientia de animali*, is contained in natural philosophy, despite the special and additional data it must study; or again, one science may derive its very principles from another science, as the rules of perspective are taken from geometry. This last is subordination in the strict sense of the term, *subalternatio propria*. *Loc. cit.*, V: 1, *ad* 5. Disputations, I *de Potentia*, 4.

[2] *Summa Theologica*, 1a: I: 8. 1a: II: 1, obj. 3.

[3] Commentary, IV *Metaphysics, lect.* 6. I *Ethics, lect.* 3. Opusc. XIV, *de Divinis Nominibus*, I: *lect.* 2.

[4] *Summa Theologica*, 1a: LXXIX: 8.

truth pushed beyond the smugly rational amenities ; dark to the reason by an excess, not a deficiency, of form.

The business of logic, which does not begin with wonder nor end in awe, and is even less ultimate than morals,[1] is not meditation on these depths, but the conduct of transactions in the existing mental system. It is the middleman, the business man, and like him no more to be trusted as our master. All that need be noted at present is that while one process of reasoning may be set in motion by another and previous process, the series of demonstrations cannot be carried back indefinitely. To expect reasoning to stretch endlessly backwards is like saying that the elephant's legs are so long that they reach all the way down: to expect it to stretch infinitely onwards is the beginning of a nightmare. Everything may indeed be approached in a reasonable spirit, but not everything is the proper subject for direct demonstration.

---
[1] III *Contra Gentes*, 34, 35.

CHAPTER XXIII

PATTERN IN MOVEMENT

THE different approaches made by logic and by psychology to mental processes and states have already been mentioned. As with judgements so with reasonings; the logical structure may be a collocation where the psychological response is flowing and irreducible. Of this we can no more successfully divide the bits than we can unscramble an omelette; yet logic is able to take a whole to pieces and then reconstruct it from the parts. The analysis, however, is mental and does not claim to correspond exactly with the psychological components of the activity. Even simple objects are stated in composition, as when a point is defined as that which has no parts.[1] A logical hiatus is not meant to impede the literary scansion.

A complicated mental process may flash like lightning: Mozart and Nelson could take in a lengthy development at one hearing or one glance, the mounting of a symphony or the deployment of a fleet. This does not apply to genius only, but in some measure to the sober progress of all reasoning. The logical pattern and procedure, an allotment of different parts, though present and operative, may not be consciously recorded. Though the charge is separately loaded there is but one explosion. The mind sees the truth of a conclusion entirely included and demanded by the premisses and has but one idea of it, not three.[2] Cogitation rises to meditation, and meditation to contemplation.[3] Assent is more direct and simple than its translation into logic suggests; our understanding of a sentence is not just our registration of the letters of which it is composed. Logical analysis takes real knowledge as the aggregation of its parts, which it rarely is in psychological fact.

QUI ANTE DIEM PERIIT

SED MILES

SED PRO PATRIA

---

[1] *Summa Theologica*, 1a: LXXXV: 8.
[2] *Ibid.*, 1a: LVIII: 2.   [3] *Ibid.*, 2a–2ae: CLXXX: 3, *ad* 1.

This is not merely a group of words from an epitaph to a Norfolk soldier, still less a group of letters. Grammar does not make the quiet pride and resignation; nor does logic produce the truth and force of argument.

Our lips may lag behind our running thoughts, we may jumble our words when everything is clear and urgent. Portmanteau terms enter at a stage beyond didactics. An over-conscious and articulate logic may seem to clot a flowing conviction. In a sense, the more convinced we are the more difficult we find it to enter into logical explanations. Logic may be long when the psychology of an argument is short: Lord Beveridge's statement, 'If the world is safe for small nations, it will be safe for all nations,' is a compressed argument that does not require to be picked to pieces. And contrariwise, logic may be short where the psychological force of the argument is drawn out.[1]

Logic, then, has to be lifted out of the psychological context. The core of rational meaning has been separated from a stimulating image, the significance of a judgement from the emotional echoes, and as numbers are counted in the ringing chimes so logical form is separated from the continuous flow of mental and organic responses to environment. The treatment is episodic. In taking argument to bits we do not imply, therefore, that reasoning is little more than the assemblage of logical parts. They are moving parts; even in machinery, an artificial unity without the flowing current and singleness of an organism or a valid argument, the parts cannot be understood without noting their interaction and appreciating their purpose when placed together. Yet they must be known in separation before the machine can be assembled. And

---

[1] As in the passage from William Cobbett on the Valley of the Avon: 'It seemed to me that one way, and that not, perhaps, the least striking, of exposing the folly, the stupidity, the inanity, the presumption, the insufferable emptiness and insolence and barbarity, of those numerous wretches who now have the audacity to propose to *transport* the people of England, upon the principle of the monster Malthus, who has furnished the unfeeling oligarchs and their toad-eaters with the pretence that *man has a natural propensity to breed faster than food can be found for the increase*; it seemed to me that one way of exposing this mixture of madness and blasphemy was to take a look, now that the harvest is in, at the produce, the mouths, the condition, and the changes that have taken place, in a spot like this, which God has favoured with every good that he has to bestow upon man.' The argument could be proposed in fewer and briefer propositions.

so logic isolates a solo argument from the rich orchestration of the human argumentative process. The argument is then stripped down to elements which are scarcely attended to when the mind is enjoying its knowledge. Discourse is not built up in layers, but is a continuous process, of which the psychological repetitions and associations and spurts without punctuation can be reproduced by a stretch of words in apparently irrelevant sequence; the attempt has been made by James Joyce and Gertrude Stein, but will not be expected from the conventional forms of exposition. Yet under the tide there is obedience to the mental shapes of intelligibility; and logic, which is the special study of these, is at least as near to psychological reality as a geological map is to the face of England.

Dialectic listens even to the historical references, but logic is like a man who is indifferent to whether *Ein' feste Burg* or the *Coffee House Cantata* is being performed, for both reveal the technical excellence of Bach. But then it is not meant to buzz in a vacuum; it is like the virtue of prudence which can thrive only in and through the activity of the other virtues.[1] Logic works in and through the evidence supplied by the other sciences; it is neutral to truth as the edge of a knife is indifferent to saving surgery or to murder. To allow more to logic would be to convert real philosophy into something like a country run as a Police-State.

Mental correctness, *ratiocinatio recta,* is distinct from mental fullness, and yet it is geared to reality.[2] Logic alone, however, cannot show why conclusions are guaranteed by their premisses; that is its axiom, the working postulate accepted from the critical sciences of reality. In general we can say that the impulse to be reasonably human will make us trust the connections relied on by logic. A correct conclusion shares in the objective truth of its principles, though, as already noted, a correct conclusion does not necessarily share in their falsehood if they happen to be false. If

---

[1] *Summa Theologica,* 1a–2ae: XLVII: 6.

[2] By correct inference, from true principles a true conclusion always follows. By correct inference from false principles a false conclusion will usually follow, though sometimes it will happen to be true. By incorrect inference from either true or false principles the statement which results, which does not merit the title of a conclusion, may happen not to be false, but has no standing and security. Given two propositions that are true, the only third proposition that can be drawn from them will itself be true; a statement that follows from them incorrectly is not thereby untrue, but unproved.

however they escape error, that is but a lucky chance that cannot be relied on to occur again. Probably in most cases when a true enough statement emerges from false principles the process of reasoning is incorrect, as when the prosperity of the wicked in this life is urged as an argument for the existence of hell hereafter.

But thinking intends to produce such chance and incidental effects no more than a doodler aims to produce a beautiful work of art: his figures may be beautiful, but he is not thereby an artist. An ending to a train of thought may happen to be true, but it is not thereby properly demonstrated and binding. All the sciences deal with what is *per se*, the *per accidens* is left to chroniclers and diarists; the deductive sciences deal with effects, not events; on looking back their consequences are seen to have been inevitable, not guesswork. Scientific sequences tend to follow certain patterns and to avoid certain defined irregularities; a logical training leaves the mind scored with the lines, like the great high roads on the map of Roman England, and unlike the chart of a watercourse losing itself in a swamp. We speak of the drift of an argument, but for science and philosophy it should have a controlled current. Correctness of thought is the first aim of logic, a correctness directed to truth; and to this may be added a certain elegance and economy of style, the observance of the proper pauses and courtesy towards antagonists, the brief distinction and ample explanation.

The movement of a systematic science or philosophy, or indeed of any ordered body of conviction, advances in a phalanx of many arguments. For purposes of examination, however, the scale of the dialectic must be reduced and one argument singled out and treated as a unit. In doing this we sound the warning again that the logical structure does not display the psychological situation of an argument. As a proposition is composed of two terms so an argument is composed of two propositions called premisses, from which a third proposition, called the conclusion or consequent follows. The conclusion, though wholly dependent on the premisses, contains the effect of the argument; the sting is in the tail, but the tail curves over the body. It is a mistake to think of the conclusion first and the premisses afterwards, to erect the conclusion in the place of the premisses. People who rationalize a dream and who propose a demonstration for a conviction they already hold for non-rational reasons are not allowing the premisses to do their work,

7

but are arguing for a preconceived idea from the same preconceived idea, a fallacy found alike in obscurantist and modernist thought.

For two propositions to be authentic premisses and to produce a conclusion they must touch one another, or rather more, they must mutually share in some common term; ultimately this implies identity in a distributive nature. Nothing follows from two unrelated statements:—the Amazon is the longest South American river—Jupiter is the morning star—so what? The universe is so vast; the world is but a speck of dust—and yet you seriously ask me to believe that God so loved the world as to send his only begotten son? Many arguments are like that; the chasm may be hidden by mist formed from unprecipitated particles of sympathy or hostility, but it is there. Valid positive arguments have no breaks, but are joined together by the middle term.

This is the common term shared by both premisses. It is the very keystone of the argument, locking the two extremes together. It is the link in Mr. Jingle's style and the bed of Mr. Jorrocks's— 'where the M.F.H. dines he sleeps, and where the M.F.H. sleeps he breakfasts.' The correspondence of two terms with a common third term brings them together, and the argument moves on the analogy that two things equal to a third are themselves equal to one another. But it is only an analogy, for the union partakes of the identity of meaning, and is more than an equality of quantities; the fundamental principle is more akin to the saying that what is sauce to the goose is sauce to the gander.

The middle term is the centre of the argument, the term on which the attention should be riveted. In most of the articles of the *Summa Theologica* it is possible to underline one term on which the process revolves. Thus in the four articles in which St Thomas builds up the essential nature of law,[1] a reasonable ordinance for the common good issued by public authority and effectively promulgated, the fundamental concept is the primacy of the mind in the happiness of society.

The point of an argument lies in the predicate of its conclusion, which is called the major term or extreme; the premiss in which it is found is called the major premiss. The subject of the con-

---

[1] *Summa Theologica,* 1a–2ae: XC: 1, 2, 3, 4.

clusion is called the minor term, and the premiss containing it is called the minor premiss.[1] We may note in passing three features of formal debate. First, that the proposition contested is usually the minor premiss—please prove your minor premiss, that is the most frequent request in disputation. Secondly, the unrestricted extension of the middle term. Thirdly, that the terms used are broad enough to bear different senses; it is the function of scholastic distinction to separate them and so refine the argument.

---

[1] A typical argument may be set out as follows:

middle term is major term—major premiss
but, minor term is middle term—minor premiss
therefore, minor term is major term—conclusion.

For example:—to sell what does not exist is wrong—but, usury is to sell what does not exist—therefore, usury is wrong. *Summa Theologica*, 2a–2ae: LXXVIII: 1.

CHAPTER XXIV

PROOF AND EQUATION

THE truth that two plus three equals five is enclosed in numbers, but that two apples and three oranges are five pieces of fruit ranges largely outside. Must we surrender the claim to be scientific when we pass the boundaries of quantity? Can objects of sensibility be translated into a medium that is not mathematical? The anatomy of didactic logic is cleanly separated from the sensible qualities of its subject, even so the structure is not wholly mathematical. Though the principle at work is not unlike the axiom that two things when equal to a third are themselves equal to one another, the comparison needs the proviso that philosophical propositions and proofs attempt to state more than a correspondence of quantities. Logic, and dialectic still more, governs a style of exposition unlike that of quantitative mathematics; its movement is more free, supple, and analogical than the comparatively restricted, unbending, and univocal calculation of numbers. As metaphysics is implicit in mathematics, but is not there committed, so logic is contained in the validity of mathematical demonstration; it can also ride on the curled clouds, and define where accuracy, *acribologia*, cannot be demanded.[1]

Animals are mortal, men are animals, therefore men are mortal: clearly the argument should not be read to mean, animals = mortal, men = animals, men = mortal, for men are not equivalent to mortal things, if only because of perishing jackdaws, codfish, and oak-trees. Can we recast it as an equation of quantities by substituting *included among* for equals, so that the amended translation reads, animals are included among the number of mortal things, men are included in the number of animals, and therefore men are included among the number of mortal things? To urge that this bears little resemblance to what we feel we mean is a double-edged weapon, for the mathematician will retort that

---

[1] Commentary, II *Metaphysics, lect.* 5.

the transposition of argument into the forms of the traditional logic is artificial in any case. Who naturally argues in set syllogisms? Our experience of proof is of a series of reflections that proceed more or less after this fashion: men now . . . mortal? yes . . . why? 'm because they're animals. The conclusion jumps to the mind before the reason is professed.

The root reason why some arguments cannot be reduced to figures of quantity lies in the nature and application of distributive ideas. We have already noticed their difference from collective ideas. In the argument cited all the terms are taken distributively: for by saying that man is animal we mean that whatever can be predicated of animal can also be predicated of man; a man *is* an animal; an identity of nature is affirmed. A distributive notion carries a general nature that is applicable to many things, and wholly to each and every case.[1] It is like the widow's cruse, never exhausted; not given in driblets, wholly dealt out, but never diminished; communicated without detriment, sharing in that society of knowledge—and love—where, unlike other generations, there is gain without loss and growth without decay; for knower and lover becomes another without ceding his identity.[2]

A distributive whole, therefore, is quite unlike a pile of counters, or a lump sum, or anything of the sort, which is so much the less for anything expended. Moreover a distributive whole is as numerically multiple as its parts, whereas a collective whole covers many things only when they are run together and not considered in themselves; a bo'sun's mate is a member of the ship's complement and to that extent sinks his personal identity. Until the peculiar communication of distributive idea to each and all is marked, the special movement of logic in philosophy cannot be appreciated; the agility, pervasiveness, and power of sweet penetration whereby its operations differ in kind from the additions and comparisons performed by accountancy. The circulation of thought is not limited to systematic deduction from postulates in one straight line. Because of the elasticity of distributive and analogical ideas,[3] the discipline of philosophy has a spring in

---

1 Commentary, I *Posterior Analytics, lect.* 11.
2 *Summa Theologica,* 1a: XXVII: XXXI. 1a: XII: 2, *ad* 3.
3 *Ibid.,* 1a: IX: 1, *ad* 2.

its step like that of the Light Division in the Peninsular War, 'a grasshopper trilling at its heels,' *sapientia mobilior omnibus mobilibus,*[1] a quick and lively play irreducible to the finest adjustments and complications of quantities.[2]

Scientific calculations must often be set out like a page from Bradshaw, for when objects can be computed and measured by fixed or sliding scales, then the application of mathematics to non-mathematical material is most useful. Since the seventeenth century the method has been greatly extended and has justified itself by many practical successes, even with such apparently intractable material as that of psychology, where, for instance, co-efficients have been devised to register how different items of experience tend to go together. But even a scientist may find himself engrossed in measurement at the expense of observation. Thought itself should not be machined; the purpose of the natural scientist is to classify rather than to weigh: his forms cannot be treated as the units of thought as if they were like the solid atoms of Lucretius; he does not treat the deficiencies and privations of being exactly as minus quantities,[3] nor can the concept of extension meet the situation of first cause and secondary cause each acting as total causes of the same effect[4]; he works with moods of being, sullen and debonair, that cannot be reduced to fixed numerations, and with thoughts that pass dimensionless; he allows for the extras to quantity; his reasoning runs free and close-hauled; he seeks reasons rather than ratios; while as for the metaphysician he makes complete abstraction from number, size and shape: yet logic meanwhile keeps in company with all such movements.

A distributive notion, then, is not a lump total shared out to many in parts, but a meaning totally and completely possessed by each. Whether in point of fact the human mind can profitably work with such general ideas, and whether an insight into natures can be gained thereby, these are questions that lie outside logic in the domain of general and critical philosophy. We shall be in a better position to venture judgement after we have considered the

---

[1] *Wisdom,* vii, 24.

[2] Opusc. IX, *de Hebdomadibus,* Prologue.

[3] *Summa Theologica,* Ia: XLVIII: 1, 2, 3, 4. Ia: XLIX: 1. IV *de Trinitate,* 3.

[4] *Summa Theologica,* Ia: CV: 5. III *Contra Gentes,* 89. Disputations, III *de Potentia,* 7.

difference between scientific deduction and induction and touched
on John Stuart Mill's objection to the syllogism. At present it is
enough to notice the claim of philosophical science to deal with
distributive meanings. What is asserted about mortal things is
asserted also about men, not because the two ideas represent equivalent masses or areas, which, as we have seen, is not the case, but
because they enjoy an identical predication. This is arrived at
because a distributive meaning expresses a general nature, which
is not a sum resulting from the addition of units nor a general
pool of experiences. There is a spirituality about such statements
transcending quantitative adjustments. Their sense defies translation into numerical notation. Many of our mental processes do
not deal with quantities, even when numeration seems to be involved. Three of her four children come into the room, 'But
where's Caroline?' asks the mother: she has numbered them, but is
it the fourth she misses, or Caroline? Here is no rareness of abstraction, no strain of cerebration. There are African tribesmen owning
great herds of cattle who are reputed to be incapable of counting
into two figures, yet who know at once if a single beast is
missing.

Recourse to distributive ideas broaches the distinction between
deductive and inductive types of reasoning. Deduction works
from a general to a particular idea: it is rather like the calculation
of position in navigation from dead reckoning. Induction is the
reverse process of arriving at a generalization from particular cases:
rather like the calculation of position from observation. One
would expect pastoral people to precede cultivators, and hence we
might argue deductively that the primitive inhabitants of this
island were herdsmen; the confirmation of the principle by the
evidence of archaeology resorts to induction.[1]

Deductive reasoning is of two kinds, a priori and a posteriori.
The former works from the centre outwards from cause to effect,
the latter in the reverse direction from the periphery, from effects
to cause. A priori deduction starts from what is antecedent in
reality and arrives at a consequent, as when intelligence is shown to

[1] All deductive arguments suppose the rule that whatever is predicated of a
general nature may be predicated of every particular object possessing that
nature, which rule is referred to curtly as the dictum de omni, dictum de nullo, said
of all, said of each; said of none, said of not one.

be the root of freedom,[1] or when a doctor explains the symptoms
by the disease, or when it is said: a ship requiring assistance flies a
red St Andrew's cross—but the *Garcia Moreno* is a ship requiring
assistance—therefore she will be flying the red St Andrew's cross.
But more frequently we argue from the general to the particular by

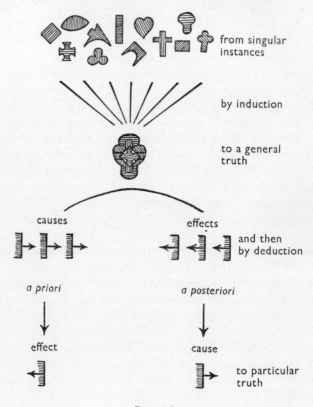

Figure 8

working from effect to cause, when, says St Thomas, the effect is
more manifest than its cause,[2] as when intelligence is inferred
from a sense of moral responsibility, or when a doctor diagnoses a
disease from the symptoms, or when it is said: a ship flying a red

---

[1] *Summa Theologica*, 1a: LXXXIII: 3, 4.   Commentary, III *Ethics, lect.* 11.
Cf. Figure 8.
[2] *Summa Theologica*, 1a: II: 2.

saltire is a ship requiring assistance—but the *Garcia Moreno* is flying
a red saltire—and therefore she is needing assistance. Such deduction is called *a posteriori*.

In both cases, the arguments proceed from a general knowledge
of the sea and shipping to the particular instance of the *Garcia
Moreno*. In the first case, of *a priori* reasoning, it is the expert who
has noticed the ship's condition and expects the appropriate signal,
arguing from cause to effect, the most comfortable of all demonstrations. These *a priori* arguments have been given a bad name;
they have been called more pretentious than profound, but their
type is the most commanding. And St Thomas cannot be criti-
cised if, without special pleading, he approaches every Christian
problem with the previous conviction that rationalism cannot con-
tradict faith nor nature be hostile to grace. For the beginner the
commonest deductive argument will work contrariwise, namely
from effect to cause: the apprentice will see the flying red saltire
before he mistrusts the wisp of steam abaft the hold. Such *a posteriori* arguments are prominent at the beginning of natural theology; here on the point of method St Thomas is not an initial
theist who descends to creatures, he looks first at our environment
and finds that it can be made reasonable only by the inference that
God exists, his philosophy does not begin from the first cause, but
arrives there; he starts from the clues, not in possession of the
secret; he makes a diagnosis rather than a prognosis.

In reverse to deduction is the course of induction, the inference of general truths from particular instances. This is not
rarely confused with the *a posteriori* style of deduction, because
both are ascending arguments and appear to search for principles.
Induction has the air of starting from effects and arriving at causes,
but we are more accurate when we say that it starts from events
and works to their formulation in a general law. Though similar
in some respects and interconnected, both types of argument must
be kept distinct from one another: the test of their difference
always remains this, all deduction is based on general meanings,
whether they be causes or effects, while induction is based on the
experience of singular instances. The following may serve as an
example: through all his long years at sea, the mate has observed
that ships requiring assistance hoist a red saltire—there are enough
cases here to formulate a general rule—therefore, ships requiring

7*

assistance always fly a red saltire. This inductive method is wide-spread in the experimental sciences and indeed is a necessary preliminary to philosophy.

It may be remarked at once that both approaches, the deductive and the inductive, are necessary and supplementary. Neither should supplant the other. Let the subject be Christian poetry; then we may declare deductively, poetry is born of conflict, and of all faiths Christianity is committed to the conflict at the heart of human experience, and therefore it is a religion which should be expected to express itself powerfully in poetry; or, inductively, we may run through the pages of the *Oxford Book of Christian Verse* and see how far this statement is warranted by the facts.

CHAPTER XXV

SYLLOGISM

MATHEMATICAL arguments excepted, the syllogism is traditionally taken as the classical expression of a deduction from two premisses. St Thomas treats it at length in his commentary on the *Posterior Analytics*. Our treatment is restricted to the categorical syllogism the most straightforward and the commonest according to thomist usage, which is based on categorical propositions: possession is nine points of the law, and I am in possession, and therefore, etc. An instrument more of demonstration than of discovery, it has all the finality of Henry VII's rejoinder with the doctrine of effective possession to the division of the Western Hemisphere between Spaniards and Portuguese made by Pope Alexander VI. A hypothetical syllogism starts from a condition: if you have eaten your cake you cannot keep it, but you have eaten your cake, and therefore, etc. Hypothetical propositions, as we have seen, tend to beg the question, or at least, and this is curious, to introduce distractions in their attempt to disembarrass the mind from affirmations about existents. St Thomas appeals to them infrequently. Various types of complex and modulated arguments may be included under the heading of the hypothetical syllogism. Following the development of symbolic logic in recent years, new formal structures of argument have been analyzed. There has been some inclination to cast the traditional logic in the rôle of Procrustes, slain by the Theseus of the new logic. But if the limitations we have defined are respected, and the scholastic logic is not made to stretch and lop the limbs of arguments that do not easily fit its bed, the validity and humanity of its method need not be impugned.

Arguments may be defective in the letter yet alive in the spirit, as in the sportsman's so-called syllogism: if there are trees there is a wood, and if there is a wood there are woodcock. Even as to the letter, the validity of a strictly deductive argument does not require the articulation in proper order of major premiss, minor premiss, and conclusion; though the proper form, if not currently demanded, should be carried, like a passport, and on occasion produced. In some cases it will be of advantage for debate to be conducted in strictly syllogistic style, so that fallacies may be detected readily and excluded as they occur.

Nothing but explicit syllogisms were admitted in formal scholastic disputation. That was the etiquette, which made for exact if somewhat pompous discussion. But after the formal debate and the reply to the objections couched in syllogistic form, *argumenta in forma*, the meeting was thrown open to informal objections, *argumenta extra formam*, and discussion became more ranging as the objections lost their first tight discipline. Nevertheless a good logician would still try to isolate the point in the most rambling statement, and to set out the argument formally in his own mind in order the better to deal with it. As a novice he had been coached 'to watch out for the middle term.' At first sight the method may appear clumsy and full of repetitions, yet we recall again the distinction between the mechanics of a thing and its spirit, and in effect it is an economical form of argument, the very repetitions, as with saying the rosary, being expected to quiet and fix the attention. The logic is designed for a methodic advance; the offensive is built up by establishing magazines at successive stages with all the solidity of a pattern-book operation. However in the realms of speculation as elsewhere an adventurous dialectic and the Wingates must also be employed, for deep penetration into problems, leaving areas to be cleared up behind them, and relying on air-dropped supplies for their maintenance.

Two recognized types of deductive argument not couched in explicitly syllogistic form are the aristotelean sorites and the enthymeme. The sorites, or heap, is an argument consisting of a series of more than three propositions in which the predicate of the first proposition becomes the subject of the following proposition, and so on until the conclusion is reached, where the last predicate is joined to the first subject. Clerical celibacy means the sacrifice of marriage—sacrifice of marriage means esteem for marriage—esteem for marriage means the promotion of marriage—the promotion of marriage sends up the birthrate—therefore

clerical celibacy sends up the birthrate. A good sorites has all the
fascination of a long and rapidly advancing column; if not so
clumpy and compact as a single syllogism, it thrusts out leanly and
swiftly, like the spear-head of a panzer division in the Polish
campaign of 1939.

Virtually several syllogisms are run together. Were the argument to be written out in full syllogistic form several additional
propositions would be demanded; not however any new terms.
The argument then becomes such that the conclusion of one syllogism is the premiss of the next: in this shape it is known as a
polysyllogism. This example from Francis Quarles is sufficiently
near to the style:—

> My soul, what's lighter than a feather? Wind.
> Than wind? The fire. And what than fire? The mind.
> What's lighter than the mind? A thought. Than thought?
> This bubble world. What than this bubble? Nought.

The second type is an abridged syllogism known as the enthymeme, which is to a full argument what a portmanteau word is to
a complete phrase. One of the premisses is suppressed; since you
have just come back from the Mediterranean, I take it that you
have been inoculated against typhoid; God is not in the categories
because he is pure being; the substance of the soul is spiritual
because it displays spiritual activity; love is not the form of joy
because it does not constitute the presence of its object. Such
elided syllogisms abound in the text of the *Summa Theologica*;
many, if not most, of our current proofs are in the form of an
enthymeme; in many ways the most agreeable type of argument
'candid and clear because the middle term is stressed and left
ringing.'

Some statements meant to be probative are more compressed
than enthymemes. *War Savings are Ships*: faced with that poster
many a naval man must have murmured, would they were. One
of the values of the unabridged syllogism is that it fills in all the
gaps; for sometimes conclusions cannot be perceived in their premisses; if, for instance, I argue that the doctrine that all men are
equal is tantamount to a denial of free will, I am properly expected
to show the connection, which does not appear immediately.
Many discussions in fact proceed in a series of swoops; they would

gain were they slowed down, and made to move in a series of short steps. Loose and slipshod thinking can pass unnoticed until it is made to regulate itself to a syllogistic advance. From a reputable review is lifted this brief statement of the position of absolute pacifism; 'it is based on the broad general principle that no end, however good, justifies the adoption of evil means, and, therefore, to resort to violence, either to preserve that which we value or to achieve it, cannot, in the long run, bring the desired result.'

Chapter XXVI

RULES, FIGURES, AND MOODS

'RULES, like crutches,' says Edward Young 'are a needful aid to the lame, tho' an impediment to the strong.' The eight regulations for syllogisms are most manifest when there is a limp in the argument, or at least a suspicion of one. The first four refer to the terms of a syllogism, the last four to the propositions; they are not exclusive, for one argument may contain several offences, and though they need not be remembered in detail, they bear out the general requirements of all argument. Most of the objections cited by St Thomas against his own theses observe them; their application to contemporary thoughtful writers may yield discouraging results.

The first rule is that one syllogism should not contain more than three terms. This is not a cramping limitation, which would make of reasoning a kind of three-legged sloth, who has no power of working his toes separately and is doomed to move suspended under the branches of a tree, a tree perhaps that is but the tree of Porphyry, if we are to believe some opponents of the traditional logic. The syllogism is more agile; its terms need not be, and rarely are, simple terms; they may be compound, such as the-English-middle-class-voter-in-a-rural-area-where-the-farming-is-mostly-arable. Terms inevitably gather qualifications as the argument gets under way and gathers speed: cause becomes efficient cause, efficient cause becomes secondary efficient cause, secondary efficient cause becomes secondary efficient instrumental cause, and this in its turn may be even further modified.[1] Similarly the middle term may be analogical so long as the liberty does not become license. Growth is legitimate on the base of the original three terms. But an argument with four terms is another affair; it is like a horse with four white legs, concerning which, according to the old country saw, the advice is 'do without him.' In effect, the presence of four terms indicates that two separate arguments are virtually at work, as in Aristotle's syllogism of the

---

[1] *Summa Theologica*, 1a: XLV: 5. 3a: LXII: 1, 4. Disputations *de Potentia*, III: 4.

incontinent man,[1] and these may or may not be connected: every
additional fresh term spells an additional argument.

The point of the rule becomes clear when we consider that
classical reasoning is essentially the comparison of two notions, the
extremes, through a common third. When four terms are present,
there is no common middle term but two diverse terms instead;
consequently no comparison can be instituted. It is surprising
how many alleged proofs in reality consist of four terms, or even
more, cemented together, not by logic, but by the prejudices,
tastes, inclinations or imagination of the proponent. Some English
nonsense stories have the logical irrelevance of four term arguments; there lies their effect, as in the case of the diner-out who
thrust both hands in the cabbage and plastered his hair with the
mess: 'Oh, Mr. Golightly,' enquired his hostess, 'what are you
doing?'—'Heavens,' he replied, 'I do beg your pardon, duchess, I
do indeed, what a stupid mistake, I thought it was spinach.'
Others develop a fantastic situation according to a thin and exacting logic, like the man who takes an umbrella to bed with him in
case it rains.

When they come to be examined many serious arguments as
well are found to use one term in two senses. In fact this fallacy
of double meaning is present in arguments that appear to have
some standing, but eventually have to be rejected. The scholastic
procedure is to look carefully at them; they are never blankly denied unless they are blatantly at fault; even then they are usually
treated with a rather deadly courtesy. Among the works of St
Thomas one alone can be said to be charged with temper, the *de
Unitate Intellectus* against the Parisian Averroists, which ends:
'If anyone would glory in the false name of science and would controvert what I have written here, let him not mutter in corners and
before adolescents who cannot judge of these difficult matters, but
let him write, if he dares, and he will find me ready, and others
who are better qualified, to resist his error or counsel his ignorance.'
It may be recalled that Siger of Brabant, the chief object of the
attack, kept his cordial admiration for the author.

The general practice is for one term of the objection to be subjected to a distinction, this term is then shown to be used in two

---

[1] *Ethics*, VII, 3, 1147a. *Summa Theologica*, 1a–2ae: LXXVII: 2, *ad* 4.

different senses in the premises, so constituting a four term argument. That is the mark of good discussion—never deny, seldom admit, often distinguish. A generous frame of mind contains the conviction that men are more right in what they affirm than in what they deny, recognizes truth in every serious argument, makes for the advancement of theory, and is the first to suffer in the hurly-burly of practical controversy. 'Mr Vavasour,' observed Disraeli, 'saw something good in everybody and everything, which is certainly amiable, and perhaps just, but disqualifies a man in some degree from the business of life, which requires for its conduct a certain amount of prejudice.' There are not a few occasions where St Thomas appears to credit an argument with more weight than it probably held in the mind of his antagonist: he offers a sufficient reply, and then goes on to develop a distinction which throws more light on the question: could there be a greater courtesy and responsibility of mental companionship?[1] From this process of distinction comes the tracery of disputation, as exact and branching as the architecture of the period, vaulted and buttressed, stressed and secure, different in spirit from the plaster torrent of the baroque or the learned and mannered surfaces of later periods.

The second rule of the syllogism is that terms in the conclusion should not bear a sense wider than that in the premises. Not rarely arguments are conducted in the hopeful frame of mind of expecting more from the conclusion than can ever be extracted from the principles, a kind of usury to be condemned in conversational as in commercial transactions. What is not put in cannot be pulled out. An argument is rejected as too sweeping when it goes beyond the terms of reference, as happens when a restricted notion in the premises becomes an unrestricted notion in the conclusion. For instance; coercion is detrimental to freedom—but coercion is the effect of law—therefore all law is detrimental to freedom: *law* is a restricted notion in the minor premiss, for the public application of pressure to maintain order is the effect of some laws; but in the conclusion law has swollen to an unrestricted notion. Such a fault is committed on a large scale by the denial of psychology on physiological principles, of morals on psychological principles and contrariwise, the denial of philosophy on

[1] Disputations, XXII *de Veritate*, 5, ad 3.

mechanical principles, of theology on empirical principles—'there is no such thing as the omnipotent, because words aren't things'— of personality on economic principles, of this world on other-worldly principles—in this respect the godly often give as good as they get from the ungodly in the counterfeit of logical argument.

This second rule is practical: for reasoning should be like an army, careful not to push beyond its lines of communication. Nor should we venture hopefully into argument, like an unarmed nation into war. When arguments go too far and too fast, they arrive at positions which cannot be sustained; as when from the well-founded principle that all law must be supported by the divine and natural law, a moralist goes on to conclude that the civil law should enforce under penalties all the precepts of morality; then virtue begins to look like a busy-body.

One feature of a good argument is to be content to prove one thing at a time. Otherwise debate degenerates into a mêlée; implications and anticipations are rapidly assumed, while the original point is lost sight of. Take for example the now dying reverberations to Paley's *Natural Theology*: from the admirable adaptation of means to ends which can be discerned in nature it is inferred that there must be an artificer who establishes its construction and directs its working: immediately we are faced with objections against the existence of a good and benevolent God from the fact that many evils flourish unchecked. But one thing at a time. Evil does not disprove the need for a designer; it raises the question whether the designer can be called good except in a strained sense of the term. Furthermore, we have to ask whether a good God is necessarily a being who has our interests at heart. Frequently the objector fixes on those evils which most offend human sensibility, for we are repelled by the thought of a worm which bores into and destroys a water-snail, 'a most beautiful creature with delicate spiral shell,' after which its larva is encysted on grass by the pond to be eaten by a sheep which then gets liver-rot. The debate has gone helter-skelter from design to evil, and from evil to human discomfort.

The third rule of the syllogism is that the middle term should not enter the conclusion, a precept for elegance rather than validity. If we reflect that the purpose of an argument is to unite two different notions through a common middle term, we shall agree that the presence of this go-between is no longer required in the conclusion. This is a well-planned world from one point of view—but there is evil in the world—therefore the evil in the world is well-planned from some point of view: when a middle term is thus discovered in the conclusion we may well suspect that the argument is inconclusive and has not advanced beyond the statement of the premisses.

The fourth rule of the syllogism is that the middle term should occur at least once as an unrestricted and general notion. The rule is indispensable and the failure to observe it introduces the fallacy of the undistributed middle, one of the most frequent in reasoning. Food is necessary for life—but chocolate is food—therefore chocolate is necessary for life. Or again; communists are a nuisance to big capitalists—but social reformers are also a nuisance to big capitalists—therefore social reformers are communists. Both arguments are wasp-waisted, for their middle terms, *food* in the first case, *nuisance to capitalists* in the second case, are restricted notions, meaning respectively some food and some of the nuisance. Neither conclusion is valid; nor does it even follow from the second that some social reformers are communists, or that some communists are social reformers. But observe what happens when the middle term is made unrestricted by turning one of the premisses into a negative proposition: communists endorse the marxist dialectic—but social democrats do not endorse the marxist dialectic—therefore social democrats are not communists. This is a correct argument for the middle term is now distributed, according to the rule which says that the predicate of a negative proposition should be taken in an unrestricted sense. The value of negation, already noted in notions and propositions, extends to arguments. There is a finality about it, sometimes an effect more disarming than convincing, as in the plea of the ordinary in *Jonathan Wild* who recommended his preference for punch as 'a liquor nowhere spoken against in the Scriptures.'

The foregoing four rules refer to the terms of the syllogism; the following four refer to the propositions; and the first of these, the fifth law of the syllogism, lays down that from two negative premisses no conclusion follows. In the logic we are considering a double denial does not produce an affirmative; there is no hope of constructing any conclusion from a purely negative attitude, any more than on the plane of social reform does it follow that to raze existing institutions to the ground, however much they have been abused, is to prepare for the erection of something very much better. The soul is not a gas—but the body is not the soul—therefore the body is a gas: that is an open fallacy, which would deceive nobody: but we are hoodwinked by other arguments which conform exactly to the same logical type, such as the argument that the social revolution is not on the side of vested interests, and the Catholic Church does not throw in its lot with the social revolution, and therefore the Catholic Church is on the side of vested interests. 'We're going to Padstow for our holidays this year; for Sidmouth was the place we didn't go to last year, and Bude the year before'; there is no connection between the propositions. We have seen that negative notions and propositions offer a useful method of investigation, but it is on condition that they go with positive notions and propositions. Rejection must be paired with affirmation; that is an imperative of life as well as of logic.

Unless an affirmative premiss is present in an argument there is an unprofitable and teasing situation like that in the milk-bar, when the man asked for a milk-shake. What sort of flavour would you like?' asked the girl. 'I think I'll have one without flavour,' was the reply. 'Well, what sort of flavour would you like it without?'—'Ah, that depends on what flavours you have.'—'We've got strawberry, orange, lemon, banana, vanilla and lime.'—'In that case,' said the man, 'I'll have mine without lemon.' The girl looked through her bottles of flavours, and found that the lemon was finished. 'I'm very sorry, sir,' said she, 'but I'm afraid we're out of lemon.' The man replied in a pet, 'If I can't have a drink without a lemon flavour, then I won't have a drink at all,' and stumped out. Notice that even the humour of that particular piece of nonsense depends on its reference to positive notions. A sheer and total negative and contradiction is unthinkable; and negative propositions by themselves are quite unworkable in argument.

The sixth law of the syllogism states that two affirmative premisses cannot engender a negative conclusion. Affirmation excludes nothing; love of one's country and pride in her traditions is not reason for contempt of foreigners. When we are out to make a contribution to a discussion restraint is needed to prevent us topping our conclusion with a sweeping negative. Not rarely we find ourselves adopting a negative, or having it thrust upon us; we wished to acclaim one excellence and are taken to exclude another, as if anything is enhanced because another is diminished. If we would insert into a hurly-burly some delicate considerations to the effect that the issue is not quite so simple we are liable to be treated like the man who interferes in a domestic brawl. If we would suggest a supplementary qualification to a disputant engrossed with his own rightness we shall be taken for an opponent. How many controversies are the clash of two particular positions which in truth do not engage one another at all? But there is an enviousness even in argument, and it is a natural temptation to conclude, the truth is there and everything else is false, or, what a man! nobody else can touch him.

The seventh law of the syllogism is that nothing follows from two particular premisses; it is a restatement of the fourth law. Just as a double negative is sterile—mulish not only in obstinacy—so also is a double particular. The force of deduction lies in arguing from the general to the particular and a syllogism is void unless one of the premisses is general. Yet the employment of two particular propositions is not uncommon; since her time, many have argued like the servant girl who accused Peter at the fire. In some cases the conclusion may be restated, but then it is but a shadow of its former confident self.

The eighth law prescribes that the conclusion should follow the weakest premiss. A negative proposition, if more brusque, is rightly considered to be weaker than an affirmative proposition, and a particular proposition, if more vivid, is weaker than a general proposition; weaker, that is, saying less.[1] Consequently if one of the premisses be negative, the conclusion should be negative; if one of the premisses be particular, then the conclusion should be a particular proposition. This is a most useful rule to remember; once a negative or particular streak enters an argument it must stay there. This provides one simple test for detecting logical fallacies; as you listen to a mounting argument, watch for the negative or

---

[1] Commentary, I *Posterior Analytics*, lect. 38, 39.

particular phrase or both, and then when they come settle back to receive a negative or particular conclusion, as the case may be. If, as often happens, the conclusion be affirmative and unlimited, then you are quite safe in assuming that it is not logically valid.

So much for the rules of the syllogism, which also apply in measure to all forms of reasoning. Let us now attend to what are called the figures and the moods of the syllogism. 'Of various admirals,' says a character in *Mansfield Park*, 'I could tell you a great deal; of them and their flags, and the gradation of their pay, and their bickerings and jealousies. But, in general, I can assure you that they are all passed over, and all very ill-used.' This may serve as our text in touching on the varieties of the syllogism.

The position taken up by the middle term in the premisses determines the figure, shape, or *schema* of a syllogism. Four combinations are possible, and hence syllogisms fall into four figures or postures; or rather three figures are accepted, while the fourth, in old-fashioned circles, is considered rather unmannerly.

In a syllogism of the first figure the middle term is the subject of the major premiss and the predicate of the minor premiss. Man is a social animal—contemplative nuns are men—therefore contemplative nuns are social animals. Syllogisms of this figure are straightforward, they have the widest range and do not suffer from the special limitations attending the other figures. But often they do not accord with the idiomatic sequence of words.[1] In a second figure syllogism, the middle term is the predicate of both premisses, and in consequence, to ensure that it is general and not restricted, one of the premisses will be negative, and so also will be the conclusion. Frivolous people are not thrifty—but Ayrshire housewives are thrifty—and therefore they are not frivolous. In a third figure syllogism, the middle term is the subject of both premisses, and consequently the major and minor terms will be restricted notions if the propositions are affirmative. Their con-

---

[1] We do not argue: colds need to be fed—but I have a cold—therefore I need to be fed: but, feed a cold—I have a cold—feed me. Our preference for an active verb over a passive verb tends to put argument into the second or third figure. Most arguments, of course, suppress a proposition; but when they are set out in full, it will be found that in many cases the turn of speech does not naturally seek the first figure.

clusion will be accordingly limited. The bedouin are nomadic—
the bedouin are semites—therefore some semites are nomadic.[1]

Finally, syllogisms may vary according to the strength of their
premisses, which may be general and affirmative, general and negative, particular and affirmative, and particular and negative, to
place them in descending order. The combination according to
these quantities and qualities decides what is known as the mood
of the syllogism. Sixty-four combinations are possible, of which
but nineteen are found on examination to be legitimate. These
are indicated by the doggerel verse beginning *Barbara Celarent*.[2]
The figures and moods of the syllogism are like the conventions of
contract bridge, you may know them thoroughly and yet be devoid
of card sense—or cards. This is no place for such arabesques of
argument, and we may echo Christopher Sly, 'therefore paucas pal-
labris, sessa!' The reader who is interested in juggling with the

---

[1] There is also the fourth figure syllogism, supposedly introduced by the
physician Galen, and called after him the galenic syllogism. It is not very well
regarded by the old-style logicians, who prefer instead what is called an indirect
first figure syllogism, that is a first figure syllogism with the premisses transposed.
Nevertheless the fourth figure, if an outsider, does represent the way we frequently think, the middle term being the predicate of the major premiss and the
subject of the minor premiss, and thus very clearly appearing and acting as a
middle term, joining the two extremes. It is reasonable to laugh at a joke—and
to laugh at a joke is to laugh at yourself—and therefore to laugh at yourself is
reasonable. The indirect first figure also transcribes the natural flow of speech,
the middle term of the major premiss being picked up immediately by the middle
term of the minor premiss. Men are beasts—and beasts must eat—and men
must eat.

[2] The old form of the gibberish lines was:—

> Barbara Celarent Darii Ferio: Baralipton
> Celantes Dabitis Fapesmo Frisesomorum:
> Cesare Camestres Festino Baroco: Darapti
> Felapto Disamis Datisi Bocardo Ferison.

The colons group the legitimate moods in the following order: first figure
direct, *Barbara* to *Ferio*; first figure indirect, *Baralipton* to *Frisesomorum* (the last
two syllables of this word are added merely for the sake of scansion); second
figure, *Cesare* to *Baroco*; third figure, *Darapti* to *Ferison*. The vowels of the above
words give the mood of the syllogism: *a* means a general affirmative proposition
(*Affirmo*); *e* a general negative proposition (*nEgo*); *i* an affirmative particular proposition (*affIrmo*); and *o* a negative particular proposition (*negO*). Thus a syllogism in *Barbara* is in the first figure and has propositions *a-a-a*: *Festino* is second
figure with propositions *e-i-o*; *Bocardo* is third figure with propositions *o-a-o*.

figures and the moods is referred to the appropriate text-books on the traditional logic. There comes a point where the cultivation of logic for its own sake becomes, as it were, the foppery of thought and verges on the vice of curiosity, when, says St Thomas,[1] the pursuit of triviality interferes with more serious and pressing studies: he cites St Jerome: 'Priests we have seen, the Gospels and the Prophets put away, reading comedies and singing the amorous words of country songs.' The comparison points the censure, not the occasion.

---

[1] *Summa Theologica*, 2a–2ae: CLXVII: 1.

Chapter XXVII

DEDUCTION

THE prison in Oxford, where Cranmer was imprisoned, and since demolished, was called Bocardo. The old moods of the syllogism have less interest, save to the curious and specialist reader. But the difference sometimes muffled in contemporary thinking, between deductive and inductive argument is to be remarked, and in deductive argument the difference between *a priori* and *a posteriori* processes.

Scholastic deduction assumes that the human mind can conceive some real natures through distributive ideas and pass valid judgements about them. Mere logic is satisfied with coherence, but dialectic assumes that beyond the succession of phenomena repeated in sensitive consciousness there is a world of meaning in which the mind can move at home. The difference between necessary and contingent propositions has already been touched on: the former state a connection between two terms not entirely the result of empirical observation nor the effect of their repeated association in our experience, but rising from the very nature of the ideas of which the terms are the vehicles. A whole is greater than any of its parts; the proposition may be treated empirically, as when I look at my typewriter and see that the part marked *back space* is less than the whole machine, the idea nevertheless of what is a whole is not a product of my sight of the typewriter nor of my experience of thousands of other wholes. General meanings are not to be resolved into the sensations that occasion or confirm them; an examplar is intrinsically independent of its examples.

The matter may be made clearer by another example: the square on the hypotenuse of a right-angled triangle equals the squares on the other two sides. Few can have tested that truth for themselves, it is difficult to see how it could be done; for myself, I am not certain that I have ever seen a perfect right-angled triangle; the figures that serve are probably out by a few degrees. The affirmation emerges from the mere analysis of the ideas. So also with

217

other necessary truths; there need be no appeal to the way that things happen in the world of material fact. Experience has prompted such judgements, but has neither caused nor can explain them. Furthermore their contrary is not merely unobservable but also unthinkable. The truth and necessity of several such propositions, the first principles of thought and our confidence in finding at least a limited reasonableness in things, precedes and conditions the human appreciation of facts. These presumptions are already at work, though not expressly recognized as such, as soon as we begin to arrange and classify the data of consciousness. There are, of course, other necessary propositions not so primary. They are the conclusions of deductive reasoning. That deliberation precedes choice is revealed by an analysis of the ideas, though confirmation may be had from psychological observation and experiment, which may be able to certify that a phenomenon called choice is always preceded by a phenomenon called deliberation.

But when we come to muster our experiences, we discover other propositions that show no such inner necessity, though they are held to be generally true. China tea is paler than Ceylon; cats purr when they are pleased; red light for danger. They are forced on us by experience and their opposite is not observed; but their truth is not necessary, so far as we can see, from the very nature of the ideas; it is contingent on the world being organized as it is at present; and their opposite is at least thinkable.[1]

The fabric of deductive reasoning is woven from necessary propositions; of inductive reasoning from contingent propositions. The division is not quite so simple as that, for the threads are not

---

[1] Since the days of Kant, necessary propositions have been frequently called *a priori* propositions because they possess an inner mental necessity preceding verification by experiment: we shall avoid the phrase, partly because of the controversies it rouses in the field of material logic, partly because St Thomas reserves the term *a priori* to arguments. They are also called analytic propositions because the predicate appears from an analysis of the subject; and for the same reason they are also called explicative propositions. Contingent propositions in their turn have been called *a posteriori* propositions because they are developed from experience. But with St Thomas we shall reserve *a posteriori* to arguments. They are also called synthetic propositions, because the predicate builds up or adds to the area of the subject; and for the same reason they are also called illative propositions. But to keep to the terminology of St Thomas, on one side there are necessary propositions, *propositiones per se,* and on the other side, contingent propositions, *propositiones per accidens.*

and should not be so separate that they cannot be knit together. Deduction should always be seeking the contingent world, and induction should always be seeking necessity. Purely ideal forms are sterile; philosophy can be carried on with mental categories alone no more than farming can manage with the exclusive use of artificials; facts are to the former what muck is to the latter. There must be a living experience, abstraction must not lose existents, and if ideas are to be fertile history must be worked in with deduction. The type of demonstration central to the dialectic of St Thomas is exemplified in the five proofs for the existence of God; these are called mixed demonstrations for they are a compost of necessary truths and empirical observations. From the existence of change the existence of the changeless is inferred; the process is categoric; so also with the other proofs. Were the argument confined to purely mental meanings it would be hypothetical; if there be a changing reality there must be an unchanging principle, but there is a changing reality, and therefore, etc. The main effort of this philosophy, however, is not to effect an analysis of concepts, nor as a synthesis does it stop at relating ideas within ideal systems. The graftings are always taken from physical reality. Nevertheless in logic we can start by setting reasons and explanations on one side and facts and events on the other, and allow that deduction is mainly occupied with the former, induction with the latter.

The propositions proper to deduction do not entirely depend on exact observation of the turn of events; they engage the meaning of forms rather than their incidence in fact; and though the activity of the particular reason,[1] or what may broadly be called in general terms the sense of fact is supposed, the ideas contained will be general meanings, not singular instances nor groups of singular instances. When, for instance, the idea of man is introduced, the designation is not Adam and Eve plus every other human individual, but rather a specific meaning note apart from circumstances, the general type of which the historical embodiments are neither the preoccupation nor for a period the embarrassment of the deductive thinker.

At this place we must stop to glance at the objection urged by

---

[1] *Summa Theologica*, 1a–2ae: LI: 1, *ad* 2. Commentary, VI *Ethics, lect.* 1. Commentary, III *de Anima, lect.* 14, 16.

John Stuart Mill against the validity of deduction and in consequence against the good standing of the syllogism. He argued that
a begging of the question is involved, for though a psychologically
useful application of generalization, in strict logic the syllogistic
form supposes the truth of the conclusion before the premisses are
stated. Take the following first figure syllogism in *Darii*: man is
mortal—but John is a man—therefore John is mortal. Before you
can affirm the major premiss, namely that man is mortal, you must
know the conclusion, namely that John is mortal. For how can
you speak about all men until you know John? It is claimed that
this objection has force against every deductive argument; that all
labour under the false pretences of working from the general to the
particular, when a truly general idea can only be known after
acquaintance with the particulars comprising it.

It is here that the objection may not fail to avoid the fallacy of
ignorantia elenchi, or misstatement of the case. For in treating a
general idea as though it were a sum of singular ideas and the
major premiss, man is mortal, as though it were a contingent proposition, the product of a constant experience of incidents, the
argument runs like water off a duck's back to one who holds a
realist theory of universals. He bases his major premiss, not on his
historical sense or his experience of men dying, but on the analysis
of the idea: he does not need the spectacle or report of death to affirm
that mortality is a necessary attribute of every organic compound.
In other words he claims an insight into a nature that does not
require to be tested in every singular instance. Where contingent
experience enters, and where the argument becomes a miniature of
the problem of the junction of philosophy and history, is in the
minor premiss, which affirms that John is a man. That is a judgement of fact, John-that-thing-there is a man, and a contingent
judgement, since John is no more than an incidental embodiment
of human nature, and not a necessary emanation. The difficulties
are evident, also the contest between the philosophy of real form
and the philosophy of Mill; but the enquiry and contest lie outside
the bounds of logic.

The pure perfection of the deductive method is found when
the movement is entirely in the realm of necessary propositions
and when the mood of the argument follows Barbara Celarent; in
the loftiest demonstration all the terms are convertible; there is a

simple identity that approximates to understanding without discursus, the radial uniformity and repose of purely spiritual contemplation.[1] St Thomas does this, but without pretence of breeding facts without experience. When a pure philosophy claims to
provide a historical or political plan, it is not the mouse that is
ridiculous, but the mountain. That man is mortal, and John is a
man, and therefore he is mortal, is a true but not very inventive
argument, and if the method of deduction were no more aspiring
than that it would be rather like burning down the city in order to
obtain a piece of roast pig. So the purest and most profitable
function of deduction is to bring together necessary propositions
that they may be explained and expanded into fresh truths, as in
the treatises on the nature of the deity and on the analysis of mind
and will.

Yet such ideal analysis must be based on the affirmation that
real being is, and here we must at least note, if we cannot explore,
the traditional doctrine that such an affirmation of human metaphysics—in truth it may be doubted whether there is any other,
for a purely spiritual intelligence is past the need of such a science
—is elicited in a response of the rational animal to his material
environment. It is this biological imperative that differences
thomist philosophy from an ontology of essences and keeps the
thought in touch with things that are real in the humble, as well
as in the uplift, sense of the word. Even pure ideas must engage
on the interpretation of the historic world, even though the result
be that hybrid known as a working philosophy. Goodness itself,
says St Thomas, does not signify unless it refers to an existent.[2]
But the really exciting proofs are those that press forward in the
spirit of the empirical sciences,[3] and though they cannot be easily
accommodated to purely ideal forms, the characteristic deductions
of thomism are mixed demonstrations, or minglings of necessary
and contingent truths, such as the *quinque viae*, the proofs for the
psychophysical unity of man and, under conditions, his destiny
of eternal happiness.

Such problems loom round the logic of deduction, to which we
must now return. Having cleared deduction from purely logical
flaw, we must attend again to the distinction between *a priori* and

[1] *Summa Theologica*, 2a–2ae: CLXXX: 6.
[2] *Ibid.*, 1a: III: 4.   [3] *Ibid.*, 2ae–2a: CLXXX: 6.

a posteriori processes.   Take the remark that one would expect a
man who has joined a religion from adult conviction to be a better
practitioner than a man who has belonged to it from his cradle;
one would expect—that is a sign of an *a priori* proof, which works
from the top downwards.   The middle term of the argument is
drawn from one of the four groups of causes.   What is called a
demonstratio propter quid conforms to this type; this is a proof on
account of the 'reason,' which goes to the heart of the matter and
touches the proper and proximate cause of the conclusion, showing why a thing is, *propter quid ita est*, not merely that it is so, *quia
ita est*, as in the case of a *demonstratio quia*, presently to be described.[1]
An *a priori* demonstration so enters into the nature of its subject as
to live and move within it; the motion is from inside; the information is like that of a staff officer who works with his general
when the plan of campaign is drawn up and who does not have
to piece it together from hints and consequences.   The subject,
of course, may be somewhat thin, triangularity or such like, and
though the method has a certain cool perfection in itself, the conclusion does not always deserve the flourish which ushers it in, nor
have the results always equalled the richness of more tousled efforts
of empirical enquiry.

In *a priori* and *propter quid* demonstration the order of our
thoughts follows the order of things; what is prior in reality is
prior in the mind; we see first things first, and secondary things
as deriving from them.   Thus a philosophical theologian, having
ascended to the knowledge of a high truth, may from that
eminence see the reason for other and lesser truths.[2]   This, however, is not the case when the inference is from inferior to superior,
from effect to cause.   A true reason is given for the conclusion, but
this reason is not the real cause of the thing signified by the conclusion.   From effects the mind may reach a cause, but the effects
are not the cause or reason of the cause, merely the cause or reason
of our knowing the cause.[3]   The deduction is *a posteriori*; the argument is thought out backwards as in a detective story, effects put
us on the track of the cause.[4]   In this place we may take *a posteriori*

---

[1] Commentary, I *Posterior Analytics, lect*. 23. VI *de Trinitate*, 3.
[2] *Summa Theologica*, 1a: LXXIX: 8.
[3] *Ibid*., 1a–2ae: XIV: 5.
[4] *Ibid*., 1a: XLV: 7.

demonstration and *demonstratio quia* as equivalent.[1] This latter is a proof of the existence of a thing, but does not formulate an essential idea of its nature. The sequence of thought is the reverse to the sequence of things; the mind starts from the secondary and concludes to the primary, the movement is from the posterior to the prior.

An analogy to this twofold type of proof is presented when we consider how naval and military history can be written. Until 1890, when Mahan's classic appeared, naval warfare as a connected whole had never been studied. There were many naval narratives, but no philosophy of naval warfare; they described naval operations and how they happened, but they did not tell why they happened, and whether the policy that brought them about was well or ill conceived. In all human wisdom *demonstratio propter quid* is present. It may enter into rational theology once the existence of God has been established[2]; but the *a priori* approach must fail as an initial effort because we enjoy no insight into the nature of God, no immediate apprehension that real existence is implied in the idea we form about him: we cannot proceed as we do with geometrical figures, from which we can infer such truths as that the angles of a triangle together equal two right angles. For we have to start from the things about us, which are certainly not God; from observing how they are mutable, composite, contingent, various, and finalized, we are prompted to explain them, and this, by a process *a posteriori*, entails the conclusion that there must exist, other than this world, a being immovable in tranquillity, simple, necessary, sheer, the end and purpose of all things.[3] The demonstrations assign no inner reason for the existence of God; they show the reason why we must affirm that he exists.[4] If the natural theologian recognizes that he is like Mrs Piozzi describing Switzerland as 'the Derbyshire of Europe' he will avoid the danger of pertness.

---

[1] There is a type of *demonstratio quia,* known as the *demonstratio a simultaneo,* or *quasi a priori,* found in dealing with objects that are either correlatives or really identical, though a merely logical distinction interposes. Also a demonstration giving the common and remote cause of a subject, and which is therefore *a priori,* is also classed as a *demonstratio quia.* These departures from the simple classification may be neglected as scholastic luxuries.

[2] *Summa Theologica,* 1a: III: 1–8.

[3] *Ibid.,* 1a: II: 3.   [4] *Ibid.,* 1a: II: 2.

In learning a science, the elements and principles do not always come first[1]; the *Summa Theologica* begins by working back to the existence of God, and then afterwards, reflecting the evening and morning light of pure intelligence and meditating on the divine nature, is able to see the world again and re-interpret it according to eternal reasons.[2] The whole argument is one of ascent and descent, like the angels in the vision of Nathaniel.[3] In a similar manner the saints climb painfully to the heights, and thence are able to look down and see all things in their proper place and order. Wisdom is the judgement of things by their highest and ultimate causes[4]; its regard is contemplative though its preparations are alpine. That such high considerations, even in theological writing, need not blur our proper appreciations of the play of creatures is shown by the temper of all the writings of St Thomas, where other-worldliness is never intruded to decry the present, and the real is always now.[5] Prejudice in argument is the ape of the *a priori* method. It must be confessed that it can be adopted, not from insight, but from ignorance, and can look like an improvisation undisciplined by close attention to facts. Foreigners treat Winston Churchill as the cause of a dogged English spirit, his fellow-countrymen pay him the greater compliment of treating him as an effect.

---

[1] *Summa Theologica*, 1a: LXXXV: 8, *ad* 1.
[2] *Ibid.*, 1a: LXXVI: 6, 7.
[3] John i, 51.
[4] *Summa Theologica*, 1a: I: 6. Opusc. X, *de Causis, lect.* 1.
[5] *Summer Theologica*, 1a: LXXIX: 9.

Chapter XXVIII

INDUCTION

MOST of our working judgements are based, not on the inner evidence of the terms, but on their frequent association in experience. Every shark has a pilot fish; red sky at morning, shepherd's warning; history never quite repeats itself. Such cases reveal no interior connection between the subject and predicate when they are first looked at; though after studious inspection a reason for their agreement may sometimes be discerned. Philosophers of a mathematical temper have sometimes nourished the hope of extracting everything from a simple principle. Certain phenomena are frequently or invariably observed together, and the propositions expressing them are contingent.

Now the same proposition may be both necessary and contingent, though from different points of view. Mothers love their young; bus drivers suffer from gastritis; milk is good for them; exceptions make bad laws; crime never pays. They are enunciated in the first place from acquaintance with the run of things; and their force varies on whether they are nearly always or invariably true. Some may be old wives' tales. But however constant they may be, the mind can never proclaim necessity from an accumulation of instances or state an inevitable must, a bound to be, until some insight into the nature of the subject is enjoyed.

So we may be led to investigate the nature of motherhood, of bus driving, of law, of crime, in the hope of establishing a theory. If motherhood is seen to contain the notion of self-sacrificing affection, if petrol fumes are shown to have a certain effect on the belly, if the chemical action of milk is seen as a remedy, if the nature of law as a generalized directive for public actions with an eye to what happens in the majority of cases,[1] and if crime is seen to imply a refusal to abide by rules that alone can guarantee happiness,

---

[1] *Summa Theologica,* 1a–2ae: XCVIII: 4. 2a–2ae: CXX: 1, 2. Commentary, VI *Ethics, lect.* 9.

8

then our propositions are beginning to be invested with a necessity more lasting than the fashion of events.[1]

One note of the difference between necessary and contingent
judgements, and consequently between a deductive and an inductive conclusion, is sounded by the modern distinction between
judgments of value and judgements of fact. A value is taken as an
ideal, which may or may not be perfectly realized in this world,
usually not; it is not always an ethical exemplar, such as disinterested truthfulness, but may be an aesthetical form, such as
beauty, or a social pattern, such as utopia or the family of nations.
A judgement of fact, while lacking this sublimity and perhaps
unearthliness, is adapted to our workaday experience; it has a
shrewd and commonsense sobriety, it is the sound piece of work
and statesmanlike solution, the tolerance devoid of moral indignation and yet without cynicism—all our compromises with the
practicable. A thorough-paced thomist, to whom values are embodied in fact and facts sustained by values, is not happy with the
distinction, for a dualism is introduced he is compelled to reject.
He is suspicious of a comfort-loving philosophism which, unable
to adjust itself to the scandal of the real and present world, takes
refuge in another, escaping from untidiness and turbulence to a
privacy that is neat and safe for all its language to the contrary.
Metaphysics is not a loss of grip, but the ardent ability to cope.
Its silences are made from sound, not by stopping the ears; it does
not retreat before the world, but banishes this world at choice.
Moreover, the distinction between fact and value can become
dangerous, especially in social action, for the machiavellians are
quite content for the idealists to withdraw. Divorce between the
ideal and the real cannot be tolerated, in theory any less than in

---

[1] Jews are subversive, that again is a judgement, which may be repeated for
the relief of an obscure and irrational sense of grievance, or it may be expressed
soberly from what are considered to be a sufficient number of supporting facts.
It is then a contingent proposition. But if it is backed by an analysis into the
traditions and history of the Jewish people, how they are without roots, never
for two thousand years having a country to be loyal to, subjected to frequent per-
secutions by the communities in which they have dwelt, then the proposition in
some measure is setting up as a conclusion of a deduction, and is claiming a
certain inner necessity. That is a diffident theory, as every historical theory must
be; there are other theories which reach beyond to the more confident necessities
of the philosophy of nature, and beyond them to the philosophy of being.

practice. Plato had a noble vision, but since his time others have tried to use it to escape from a scandalous reality, which prevents us squaring the ought and the can. Yet a boa-constrictor cannot cope with its prey unless it first gets a firm purchase with its tail, and so dialectics must be bound up with things here and now, really here and really now.

The philosophy of St Thomas, despite, or rather because of, the range and power of his abstraction, never loses respect for the present world; a sense of fact is displayed for which there is no inclination to apologize.[1]   In this respect, the direction, though not the content, of his thought agrees more with Marx than with Plato. There is no accommodation—in the strict sense of the term —to facts, because the question of a compromise between the ideal and the factual never arises, no antagonism between them is allowed at this level. The conflict is conducted at a lower and practical level. There is a distinction, but not a division. History is not patronized from the lordly height of philosophical speculation, nor are philosophical theories made mere sweepers in a universe of what happens to happen. The offspring of heaven and earth, philosophy itself starts from a vigorous life of sensation and as a human science never loses its reverence for bodily things; bodily things as they are, without hocus pocus, sentimentality, or squeamishness; material substance, neither elevated into spirit, nor lit with glamour, nor left as vile. Throughout there is a sturdy, almost materialist, sense of the reality of the physical world; a high philosophy that is yet racy of the soil. The Order to which St Thomas belonged was born in protest against the doctrine of the Albigenses, the dualism of pure spirit and obscene matter, and his philosophical polemics were mainly against the averroism of those who would set up one world-mind and the platonism of their opponents who saw men as imprisoned spirits. His own metaphysics never washes out the distinctness of individuals in the expanse of being; his psychology never loses sight of the organic bases of consciousness; his moral science starts from the can and arrives at the ought.

From such a temper one would expect congenial support and encouragement for the inductive processes of the natural sciences.

---

[1] His inaugural professorial lecture (Opusc. XL) is arranged under the headings, the modesty of matter, the firmness of ground, the fruitfulness of earth.

Unfortunately the scholastics missed the tide and were left high
and dry. The course of events ran counter to the *a priori* promise;
the opportunity of making a partnership of philosophy and science
was missed three or four centuries ago. To the celibacy of the
medieval learned classes succeeded, as Whitehead says, a celibacy
of the intellect divorced from the concrete contemplation of the
complete facts. But the need is increasingly felt, and it is submitted that the thomist philosophy offers a suitable general
background and profitable principles of co-ordination to the work
of the particular sciences; they cannot do this for themselves, and
a strictly rational philosophy will serve the purpose more satis-
factorily than the vague humanism that is proposed instead. Just as
there is nothing in the philosophy of St Thomas to justify the
indiscriminate reduction of all problems to a logic polemical in
spirit and legal in form—look, warns Aristotle, see whether the
resemblance be that of a caricature, like the resemblance of a
monkey to a man, whereas a horse bears none; for the monkey is
not the more handsome creature, despite its nearer resemblance to
a man[1]—so there was nothing to justify the hostility of the
schoolmen at the period of the new learning to the great advance
of the physical sciences and to the new techniques of discovery.
This must be explained, not by the inherent tendencies of their
philosophy, but by the historical circumstances of persons and
events. And though some of the cloisters were not without a
Mendel, the tale of thought was of a widening gap between philosophy and science until the rise of the School of Louvain.

When we use induction we have at the back of our mind the
expectation that a characteristic or pattern of behaviour constantly
present in many individuals can be attributed to a group or class
as a whole. While supposing that a sufficient enumeration of
singulars is equivalent to a generalization, induction does not
claim any insight into a general nature, in the philosophical sense
of the term. From repeated observation and experiment it is prepared to make a general subject and attach thereto certain predicates. It differs from deductive reasoning inasmuch as it is based
on the principle that whatever can be affirmed of all, or approximately all, the parts and members of a group can be affirmed also

---

[1] *Topics*, III: 2: 117b.

of the group; while deductive reasoning is based on the principle that whatever is affirmed of a general nature can be affirmed of any particular contained within it.

Induction proceeds to establish a general law by the process of sampling many cases. If the enumeration is complete, that is if a complete division of the subject is made, then the argument will be a complete induction. Plants, animals, and men all exhibit self-initiated motion—but, plants, animals, and men, compose living things—therefore, living things exhibit self-initiated motion. The second premiss of the argument signifies that plants, animals, and men, amount to living things, or comprise the total; a semi-mathematical equivalence. This $a + b + c = d$ scheme should be noted, to point one difference between induction and deduction, the singular and collective ideas of the one and the distributive ideas of the other.

It may not be idle to note the social doctrines that have accompanied the development of the inductive method. To say that we have lost the idea of human nature is scarcely an exaggeration, nor have we gained instead a greater regard for the rights and dignities of the human person; for in place of the distributive idea, at once social and individual, we have a multitude of units, previously competitive, but now regimented into the collectivity. For units may be added up to make a total, but persons, never. Perhaps logic and a realist theory of universals are not so remote from human affairs after all. A purely experimental and mathematical method, unless corrected by humane philosophy of the Ideas, starts with the apparent freedom of facts, and nothing but facts, but will presently seek to make its method exclusive and will end with the total, the impersonal whole, the human mass without patience, pity, or consideration.

A sufficient induction is based on an adequate division, a virtually complete enumeration of the facts, and will produce a fair degree of certainty on the assumption that a characteristic that has hitherto been observed in all members of a class under diverse conditions will invariably be found in that class. The generalizations which are the conclusions of all the experimental sciences must inevitably be drawn from a limited number of particular instances assumed to be typical. Few would seriously doubt that all the penguins in the Antarctic look as portentous as those in the

Zoo, or that a wasp sting will produce a painful swelling. The enumeration of cases may be so partial that only an insufficient induction is possible, insufficient, that is, to produce certainty. Yet we may have a pretty shrewd opinion as to the truth of the conclusion; we may have sampled few medlars, but we know what to expect. Here is the opportunity for the inspired guess-work that jerks scientific discovery from one period into another, the field also for practical judgements of morality and the framing of human laws, where it is a mistake to seek the clear certitude proper to mathematics.[1]

It is doubtful whether there are many occasions when a complete induction—a complete enumeration in a deductive system is different[2]—can be used with much profit as a method of reasoning, nor would it be desirable, since no more than the articulation of premisses conterminous with the conclusion would be provided. When all the occupants of the field fall under one glance we are in the position to launch a deduction: the special value of induction lies in its power to work from limited knowledge and to add to it. Consequently, the scientific investigator customarily makes use of incomplete induction. He is called upon to be at once adventurous in searching and anticipating the lie of the land and cautious in not pushing too far ahead well beyond what the facts warrant; it is probable that he has to be more guarded with the philosophical statements he may be tempted to make rather than with his strictly inductive readings and forecasts, with his theories rather than with his hypotheses. The history of science abounds with warnings of how carefully data must be sifted and for how long. Time brings qualifications, the insect may act differently on the thousandth occasion: then, too, the presence of unrecognized factors must be allowed for. By and large, it appears that induction, though logically humbler than deduction, entails more drudgery and taxes more honesty.

A caveat should be entered against the habit of setting one method against the other. There should be no collision. While it may be true that some periods of thought have been marked by a deductive cast of mind and others by an inductive, phases that are repeated in the life of individuals and cultures, and while it is generally said that the English are more empirical than some other

---

[1] Commentary, I *Ethics*, lect. 3.   [2] *Summa Theologica*, 1a: III: 7.

peoples, less given to metaphysical speculations and unbending political doctrines, the facts of the matter need very delicate statement, more delicate, certainly, than is found in the *Westward Ho!* school of writers on the history of thought, to whom Francis Bacon and Roger Bacon his morning-star were robust and free-minded Englishmen, who with other hardy thinkers of the new learning swept away the *a priori* cobwebs of the schoolmen and gazed with a fresh and curious eye on the new world of nature. But despite the gusto for experimentation, the old tradition of abstract philosophy in the old tradition still ran strong; in the narrow sense of the word, Descartes and Leibniz are more rigid systematizers of thought than St Thomas; and the deductive method still flourished when Scotland began to export academicians as well as empire builders. Nevertheless a growing suspicion greeted such speculation, which the later cosmic pretensions of the new German idealism did nothing to diminish, and it was generally agreed to let the scholastic method fall into disrepute. Already in the seventeenth century Bishop Sprat could write of the Royal Society; 'While the old philosophers could only bestow on us some barren terms and notions, the new shall impart to us the uses of all the creatures and shall enrich us with the benefits of fruitfulness and plenty.' His confidence has not in the event turned out to be altogether well-placed, and in many fields we are discovering the need of concepts very similar to those old and barren conceits of the schoolmen; finality, faculty, usury, form, philosophy of law and the like; their disquisitions are now not so easily discredited as vain and unprofitable. In recent years, too, we have witnessed remarkable results from the entrance of deductive mathematics into physics. Even from the point of view of history, the movement of events cannot be simplified into a succession of tableaux, the centuries of abstract speculators and word spinners followed by the centuries of curious and ingenious researchers into the behaviour of things. Many of the representative medievals had the painter's eye, an intense concentration on what was before them, and were patient and empirical investigators, and not a few modern scientists, for all the display of apparatus and research, are not averse from making daring philosophical swoops; metaphysical and moral conclusions emerge from physics nowadays with no less exuberance than from the natural science of the middle ages.

The differences should not be heightened between two periods in the history of thought; if the methods of deduction and induction are pitted against one another, instead of being used for mutual support, we verge on the nonsense of the dispute in Surgeons' Hall when Roderick Random was examined: 'I affirm, that all wounds of the intestines, whether great or small, are mortal.'—'Pardon me, brother,' says the fat gentleman, 'there is good authority—' —Here he was interrupted by the other, with, 'Sir, excuse me, I despise all authority. *Nullius in verbis*. I stand upon my own bottom.'—'But, sir, sir,' replied his antagonist, 'the reason of the thing shows—' —'A fig for reason,' cried this sufficient member, 'I laugh at reason, give me ocular demonstration.' At the other extreme were the old physiologists claiming the name of aristotelean, who would not believe their eyes when, on the dissecting table, they saw nerves coming from the brain, because they had been brought up to hold that they issued from the heart.

A medieval practice that may prove misleading is the habit of adducing probable reasons, or *argumenta ex convenientia*, for things whose behaviour and characteristics could not otherwise be accounted for; sometimes they are supplementary arguments in favour of what had already been established and sometimes they are advanced in a spirit of hypothesis.[1] In some cases they may appear to be far-fetched to the modern mind and to match in the field of natural science some of the medieval efforts of biblical interpretation. But they are not always in deadly earnest. The scholastics had their own brand of academic drollery which may not be ours, and they were aware of the suggestiveness, little more, of such *rationes congruentiae*, hints of the reasons why a thing may be so, or at least of why we may be grateful that it is so. This habit of mind is active when all the details of the universe are expected to be interconnected, and accompanies a sympathetic assessment of facts that is not always solemn. To these reasonings may be joined the arguments *ad hominem*, of which the proper place in the *Summa Theologica* is the *sed contra* of an article, usually no more than a flourish and a preliminary statement of position.

---

[1] *Summa Theologica*, 1a: L: 3. A typical example, which deals with the multitude of spiritual beings incomparably exceeding the number of corporeal things. Such arguments abound in the field of natural science and philosophy, where, as St Thomas observes, we have to seek for clues all over the place. VI *de Trinitate*, 1.

What is certain is that the method of deduction is hedged with limitations in this world of stubborn, intractable, untidy, and surprising facts. One might suppose that the country which supports the largest urban population evinces a general taste for town life, yet the contrary is the case; or that heavier weights would fall more quickly than lighter weights, yet Galileo climbed the leaning tower of Pisa to disprove the conclusion. What literary science could anticipate the death scene in *Antony and Cleopatra*? Nature is not alone in baffling a purely deductive approach; the gentry build ruins in their grounds, architects embattle pediments, landscape gardeners plant dead trees; dialectic is full of ha-has and surprise symphonies. Millais falters to a decline, Wolfe climbs the Heights of Abraham, perhaps in some cases modern medicine causes the very ills it sets out to cure. Little wonder then, if logic should prefer the sententious and inevitable expositions of the deductive process.

The balance, however, must be adjusted, and it can be said that every adequate rational discipline will comprise both methods. The two are interdependent and complementary.[1]

> *Physics* of *Metaphysics* begs defence.
> And *Metaphysics* calles for aid on Sense.

The highest speculation cannot afford to disdain Locke's 'plain historical method'; real metaphysics originates and develops from crude experience and is not conjured out of thin air; there is a historicity in existence; while a practical and experimental science starts a process designed to yield a metaphysic. Deductive reasoning starts from the statement of a general principle, to which inductive activity is presupposed. This is clearly the case when the principle is arbitrary, as with the example of the ship in need of assistance and flying a red saltire, for by induction one accepts the trustworthiness of nautical instructors, of general agreement, and of exact and careful observation. But the relation of induction to necessary, not contingent, truths is not so easily determined. Let us take the judgement: composite beings demand a cause. Is that held to be true because effects and their causes have been seen as such; because smoke is observed from fire, coughing from smoke,

---

[1] Opusc. XI, *de Regno*, III: 9.

pain from coughing, and ill-temper from pain? To answer such a question would take us into critical philosophy: all that we need note at present is that necessary deductive principles are not wholly caused by experience nor by induction from experiences. They require experience as a necessary condition to be elicited, they are occasioned and prompted by scientific induction, yet their truth lies on another plane. Meanings are independent of their applications and embodiments; one may be certain that effects, that is objects that are not self-explanatory, demand a cause without knowing for certain whether one has experienced any effects, and certainly without knowing what the cause may be.

But this at least can be said, that inductive reasoning has preceded the statement of causality and that it is present in every deduction of a philosophy claiming to be in touch with the physical world. Though the mind can discuss the ideal implications of causes and effects without overt reference to the physical world, it can affirm that there are real causes and effects in the world only by drawing on experience and making use of induction. If metaphysical dialectic is to come down to earth, and some embarrassment may attend the transaction, as when the gods commit themselves to mortals, then its necessities and implications must be taken into human life, in its modest, tragic, comic, and companionable sense. It must not birk the statement of fact and must argue, not merely about effects as such, but about real effects in the world. Like St Thomas, in his proofs for the existence of God, it must start from the world presented to us through the senses and shaped according to the recurring patterns classified by induction. *Experientia constat*, that phrase echoes throughout his dialectic. His attitude is one of almost burly confidence in commonsense, coupled with a humility in respect of facts all the more impressive because of his extreme ardour for the highest speculation. Metaphysics should not be inhuman and remote, dwelling in a timeless world of essence in which facts are interlopers; action should derive from contemplation, and plain men should see that philosophy means a giving, not a withdrawing. Deduction is not interrupted by induction, but aided and comforted. We must think humanly, or not think at all.

Deduction, then, reposes on induction; but, not less certainly, induction implies deduction. For any sufficient induction sup-

poses this general truth; a wide enumeration of instances can safely
be taken to stand for a whole class. A law of constancy is assumed,
in the confidence of the deductive truth that part of our experience
at least can be made reasonable, and that the mind requires and
finds some necessity. Behind all our investigations rises the truth
of the first principles of metaphysics, for though the special
sciences are not departments of metaphysics, nevertheless their
guiding rules are contractions, as it were, of the general intelligibility of being.[1] Without this rational insight, we should be unable to consider the meaning of the simplest sentence or paragraph;
we should be content to take everything as it came, to live for the
moment, to register a succession of incidents, and not seek a continuity. Bath water, we notice, always swirls anti-clockwise out of
the plughole; already there is more there than an observation; and
then away we go instinctively seeking the reason, and wonder if
it be connected with the rotation of the earth.

All meaning without exception is of deductive force and
the meanings with which inductions are charged are no exception.
All attempt at explanation, as opposed to simple reporting, is a
motion of deduction. Mothers love their young: I may be ignorant
of the springs of maternity, unable to answer a physiologist who
says that it is just a question of physique and secretions, or a psychologist who says it is just a question of ego-aggrandisement: but
I have seen hens, mares, cows, bitches, and humans, and they have
all behaved in such a way that my statement remains secure, I am
conscious that I hold it as a general truth and that I have not just
acquired a set attitude on the subject. My readiness to entertain
exceptions is a sign of that. There is a meaning there, not just
a mechanical reflex. By its very generalization the statement is
lifted above the empirical plane; for while a practical habit of mind
may be content to leave it at that, and take for granted that a sufficient number of instances may represent the characteristics of an
entire class of objects, there remains a lurking desire to find more:
when we generalize by induction we are seeking an inner connection between the terms. To begin with, we may not be able to
explain why x belongs to y, but we load the statement with a
kind of necessity; this necessity is not just the sum of repeated

---

[1] V de Trinitate, 1, ad 6.

contingencies, but rather more; from what always has been we tend
to say, and always will be and should be, because—and then we are
beginning to form a deductive principle. Rain makes the grass
green; our experience of droughts and rainfall is behind us, but we
go a stage farther than marking the connection; if we are curious,
we seek an interpretation, and may find one. This temper of expectation has led not only to the discovery but also to the control
of such facts as that mosquitoes cause malaria, lice typhus, and
rat-fleas the bubonic plague.

From the very outset, before the generalized conclusion of an
induction is subjected to an interpretation or used to forecast and
control other events, when it merely states what always has been,
the process is already suffused with necessity, if only with the deductive necessity of the principle of contradiction: what always
has been is not what always has not been. It is impossible to
escape the grip of such judgements. They may be taken so much
for granted as to appear tautological when they are explicitly stated;
but their present interest is that they have a necessity transcending
incident, fact, happening, and inductive generalization. In other
words induction proceeds according to processes which are, to a
great extent, beyond its power to establish. Moreover, the dependence of induction on deduction is practical as well as theoretical. For we may talk about the practical value of the experimental and inductive sciences: but what is practical and why be
practical? The very itch to be experimental can be explained by
nothing less than a theoretical science, which on analysis will be
found to be largely deductive. All rational theory, as we shall be
in a better position to see after the next chapter, is an assumption
of the validity of deduction.

While induction cuts a different figure from deduction, and
often can be squeezed only with violence into syllogistic shape,
there is yet an underlying similarity of logical form, and its categorical expression will follow the same general rules; as we have
seen, it works with principles that are tantamount to the principles
of philosophy, which exceed experimental verification and can be
explained and defended by nothing less than the deductive science
of critical metaphysics.

It plays the principal part in the method of the experimental
sciences, whose first aim is to formulate general laws from singular

instances. Few or many of these will be required according to the nature of the field that is being worked: crystallography, for example, should be quick to class the regular geometrical structures enclosed by symmetrically arranged plane faces without calling for repeated and repeated observation; but other sciences, and especially those that deal with more complicated subjects, will demand a greater accumulation of statistics. Organic chemistry will call for a wider selection of facts than is required by inorganic chemistry. This observation, incidentally, is an example of an *a priori* deduction, for the greater complexity of a living organism compared with a non-living object is taken as the reason for the need of a wider and more detailed system of observations and checks, without entering on the inductive process of comparing two representative text-books on the two subjects and observing which has the greater complication of formulae. Most of all will the sciences that deal with human affairs require a prolonged and patient attention to facts,[1] otherwise they will be like those writers who would set out to explain foreign affairs from a smattering of their history.

---

[1] *Summa Theologica*, 2a–2ae: XLVIII.

CHAPTER XXIX

METHOD OF THE SCIENCES

IN the special scholastic sense of the term, science, *scientia*, meant the sure and certain knowledge of conclusions demonstrated from principles, the mental habit of knowing judgements arrived at by deduction, in contrast to understanding, *intellectus*, the habit of knowing principles.[1] But the term is applied in scholastic usage to all reasonable knowledge and indeed to all knowledge, thus *scientia Dei*, though there is no discursive or reasoning process in the divine mind.[2] In modern times the sense has been narrowed to mean tested knowledge obtained through trial and error, in contrast to intuition, or mystical ways of knowledge, also in contrast to automatic acceptance of current conventions. Tests, in this connection, are usually taken as practical and experimental trials, or mathematical measurements: that philosophy and theology can also be strictly scientific while dispensing with these aids may come with a faint sense of shock. While remarking that no thomist will restrict science to the material world or allow that the spiritual is beyond the reach of strictly rational investigation, and in submitting an outline of its grammar, we shall take the term to signify the systematic arrangement and development of phenomena which assumes the truth of Galileo's statement that the book of nature is written in the language of mathematics.[3]

It is commonly said that the sciences base themselves on facts; and more accurately, that they issue from sense perceptions. These are not facts pure and simple, in the sense of being things straight and natural as they are in reality—if indeed there are any such phenomena—but facts psychological, events as held in the medium of our consciousness. Without a critical science and philosophy to decide one way or the other it is open to doubt whether things are as we experience them. The reflection need not be disturbing.

---

[1] *Summa Theologica*, 1a–2ae: LVII: 2.
[2] *Ibid.*, 1a: XIV: 7.
[3] V *de Trinitate*, 3, ad 6. *Summa Theologica*, 2a–2ae: IX: 2, ad 3. Commentary, II *Physics, lect.* 3.

We begin to think from the phenomena presented to us in and through the senses; we must assume that our temperate sensations are fairly reliable guides, and there is a period when appearances must be allowed to speak for themselves.

The facts, then, are not the things in themselves, but their appearances: the black shine of this old typewriter, the boys skylarking outside the cabin, the whirr of the ammunition hoists, the tang of Bordeaux snuff in the nostrils still, the clammy discomfort of the Levanter blowing. Now there are two qualities to be noted here: first, that from the beginning these human sensations are penetrated by the mind, the *ratio particularis*,[1] and that one event is swiftly collated with others[2]; and secondly that they offer the sole opening to reasonable and sociable enquiry. A human perception is more than a response to a contingent and sensible situation, it is also a rapid and inchoate interpretation; and though our experience of a concrete event is not wholly reducible to a set of abstractions, what we call a plain fact is a common centre for many reasons[3]: the dart is seen to be sticking in the centre of the board and the implications are swiftly appreciated. Human perception does not stop at sensation: the consciousness is never stagnant, notions become judgements, and judgements become reasonings. Then secondly, however refined and complicated become our subsequent readings, and however detailed and elaborate the instruments that are used at a more advanced stage, their validity always depends on the initial and unsophisticated knowledge of the senses: the microscope reveals objects hidden to the naked eye, but would destroy itself were it used as a criticism of ordinary eye-sight: it would be like sawing off the bough on which you sit.

Science is built of facts as a house is built of stones, but, as Henri Poincaré warns us, 'an accumulation of facts is no more a science than a heap of stones is a house.' The exact sciences do not start from facts as they are registered by uninstructed common-sense; the scientists begins where the plain man leaves off. His method is technical experiment, not homely experience, and he goes beyond the organisation of the ordinary data. Yet he must never deny his origins nor forget that ordinary straightforward

---

[1] Disputations, *de Anima,* 13.
[2] Commentary, I *Metaphysics,* I: *lect.* 1.
[3] *Ibid.,* II *de Anima, lect.* 13.

sensation is presupposed and is present in all his experiments. Science is not a species of Indian rope trick, the production of an effect against the common rules of experience. All the same, a scientific fact differs from a plain fact: art has entered, in a sense the fact is now cooked, not raw; it is a specimen rather than an event; a select abstract, a point on a scientific map where scientific bearings intersect, and it is designated by the terms of scientific nomenclature not of ordinary current speech; a *troglodytes troglodytes troglodytes*, not a jenny wren.[1]

Where the ordinary man says cold, warm, hot, the scientist says 32° Fahrenheit, or 60°, or 104°, as the case may be; his fact is a rendered fact; thus the phenomena of temperature are stated according to a position established by a previous correlation of expansion and heat on a linear scale of a thermometer. Mercury serves in the first place, later on a more abstract thermometer may be used. Nevertheless scientific facts are elaborated and defined in terms of scientific instruments of measurement, compasses, clocks, rulers and so forth. There is an arbitrary quality in the representation: let such and such an expansion of mercury represent such and such an increase of heat. For the study of metabolism let the human body be considered as a machine in which the energy supplied is balanced by the energy liberated. An abstraction is made, which abstraction can be considered only as an approximation to the nature of the singular object. A scientific fact is therefore literally a fact, something constructed rather than sought, the *datum* has become a *factum*. It is important to note how the scientific instrument defines the object, for without detracting from the reality of the bases of the sciences it must be allowed that their immediate start is from data which are, in this sense, artificial.

Whereas mathematics can be separated from physics, since quantity underlies other phenomena and can be stripped of them by the mind, it is not possible for physics to work apart from mathematics, since quantity is the base of sensible qualities[2]; and consequently scientific facts will be defined and measured in mathematical terms. Every measuring instrument uses some sort of linear scale, either straight or curved, on which an indicator

[1] Commentary, I *Metaphysics, lect.* 1.
[2] V *de Trinitate*, V: 3.

moves. Scientific facts then become formulae rather than things; they are entities such as atomic weights, thermal capacities, melting points, coefficients, $C_4H_4N_2O_3$ as the notation for barbituric acid, solidifying points, enzymes, chromosomes, marginal economic utility, just price, third figure syllogism. Moreover it must be remembered that statistical methods, which are specially adapted to eludicate quantitative data affected by multiple factors, are indispensable in many sciences.

The quantitative formulation of phenomena, performed by habits of scientific knowledge midway between natural and mathematical science,[1] provides a useful system of reference and measurement. Furthermore, with the growth of knowledge mathematics may well absorb parts of what were previously thought to be physics. Provided that the artifice is recognized together with the consequent limits imposed, and the peculiar scientific status of the particular natural science is not impaired, then the results may be taken as approximately just. Because a performance of a sonata can be registered on graph paper we cannot conclude that the composer was a mathematician. Nor can we claim to have represented reality just as it is; it is a rendering—'a very fine poem, Mr Pope, but not Homer.' The scientist has no right to adopt a cocksure air, as though he were the man of sense and the philosopher the man of dreams or to forget that sophistication depends on naïveness; as if to say, I deal with facts, with no frills or fancies about them. In truth, if anyone is to be stigmatized for credulity it is the man of science who is unaware and uncritical of the assumptions he makes, and who does not allow for the tendency of abstract ideas to harden into concrete things. Scientific experiment itself, which plays such an important part in the method of the sciences, is the artificial production, or at least the artificial protraction of an event, under conditions that favour observation and control and that exclude, as far as may be, unknown factors that may cloud the issue. The scientist cannot claim to develop from such data a complete interpretation of the universe without falling into the fallacy we have referred to in dealing with the laws of the syllogism, of making the conclusion more sweeping than the premisses.

Scientific observation is based on the common or garden life of

---

[1] V *de Trinitate,* ad 5, 6, 7.

sensation and goes on to include experimentation and measurement[1]; and scientific induction starts from a collection of data that have been made scientifically presentable by being dressed up as mathematical pieces. The procedure is justified by success: facts are thereby more easily worked and the processes of technical exploitation made more convenient. Even this apologia cannot be submitted by the special and experimental science concerned but must come from a higher and directive science, philosophical in temper and method. For a particular science is neither self-defensive nor self-critical; in both respects it must rely on outside help.[2]

The next step is taken when the clusters of generalizations and abstractions called scientific facts are compared and their relations drafted, usually according to mathematical ratios, in suchwise that constant connections appear in the general untidiness of phenomena. Take, for example, Avogadro's Law: Equal volumes of gases contain an equal number of molecules provided that temperature and pressure remain the same. Notice the artificiality—not unreality—of the terms and the mathematical cast of the law. Take another example, from a field less amenable to mathematical treatment; Fechner's Law: Sensation increases in arithmetical progression when the strength of the stimulus is increased in geometrical progression. Again the medium in which the law is stated is mathematical, and justly so, for none other is so measurable, communicable, and technically tractable. A scientific law is the brief and economical statement of invariable connection and sequence under given conditions. No explanation is offered at the start; the law is merely a convenient way of expressing a statistical constancy.[3] The correlations of the happenings of nature according to the general forms of mathematics, and not seldom according to the models of mechanics, is largely the work of inductive reasoning; carefully guarded against undue philosophism, the classical masterpiece is Sir Isaac Newton's reduction of all known physical motions to three laws.

Now comes the third stage, when the scientist departs from his method of induction. He is in possession of a set of laws, sometimes in harmony sometimes apparently not, the codification by

---

[1] Commentary, I *Metaphysics, lect.* 1.
[2] *Summa Theologica,* 1a: I: 8.   [3] *Ibid.,* 1a: CV: 6, 7.

induction of an array of scientific data; his observations have been
checked, the facts have been grouped, and they are seen to behave
in accordance with the laws that have been framed; yet this mass
of material, though organized, is still without meaning, and the
scientific mind must remain unsatisfied until a reason is found.
And so the process arrives at the formulation of a scientific hypothesis[1] or theory, which gathers the empirical laws together, relates
and interprets them, and offers a reason for their existence.[2] This
is sometimes called a law, as in the case of the law dating the
periods of geological strata by the fossils found in them.

Though the terms are used interchangeably there is some
difference between a theory and a hypothesis. Theory has the
wider sense; it covers all knowledge that sees and contemplates,
from the understanding of principles to the scientific knowledge
of demonstrated conclusions; it is a knowledge of things as they
are, rather than a practical collocation thought out to save the
appearances and to provide one clue of why the facts should follow
certain lines; as the name suggests, a theory is an insight into
an explanation or reason, a seeing why the laws are necessary and
how they fit into one another. But a hypothesis has a more limited
sense; as the name suggests, it is a postulate, a working statement
that is imposed on the facts rather than drawn from them, a supposition to make their behaviour reasonable. We should require it
to be plausible rather than true. The psychological pressure
behind it is similar to that behind an act of faith, and the motion
is parallel,[3] though its object is a policy rather than a dogma, a
practical rather than a speculative truth; or if it be a theoretical
truth, it is that kind of theory which is read into things, or placed
upon them. To that extent, therefore, all hypotheses may
grudgingly be allowed the title of theories.

But not all theories are such hypotheses, for as we have said,
they may rest on an unalterable reason; in the highest sense of the

---

[1] The sense of the term is not restricted to that employed by Aristotle, an
assumption not requiring proof in the domain of the special science in which it
functions.

[2] Many examples will be found in the cautious cosmogony contained in St
Thomas' rationalization of the seven days of creation according to the science
of his day and patristic teaching. *Summa Theologica*, 1a: LXVII–LXXIV.

[3] *Summa Theologica*, 2a–2ae: II: 1. 2a–2ae: IV: 2. Disputations, XIV *de
Veritate*, 1, 2, 4.

word, the act of theorizing is the act of contemplation, the steady
sight of things as they really are,[1] and if a proof is engaged, then
it will be strict demonstration. A hypothesis, however, may do no
more than work with an argument *ex convenientia* to establish a
working arrangement of scientific facts and laws that may be
changed later for another, and perhaps contrary, working arrangement. St Thomas speaks of these two kinds of explanation[2]: the
first is joined with demonstration and goes to the root of the matter
the second postulates a reason which 'saves the appearances,' it is
consistent with what happens, and yet does not exclude another
explanation. There is nothing final about such a hypothesis offering one possible explanation of the way things work; there may be
others, but the one elected is recommended by its neatness and
utility. A theory, however, may signify a truth less provisional, it
may see what is and why it is, not what is as it were.[3] Then again,
a hypothesis may not so much proffer a reason as to suggest another
fact, one instance is related to an average struck from other instances: thus until recently there was a controversy about the
manner in which cuckoos placed their eggs in the nests of other
birds; nobody had witnessed what actually happened; the traditional hypothesis was that the hen lays her egg on the ground and
carries it in her beak to the nest; but some held that she lays her
egg directly in the nest: the dispute was bitter, but it was a clash
of hypotheses in the sense of 'previous facts,' which as such never
provide 'reasons' in the strict sense of the term. When used of
scientific enquiry the term theory should be restricted to the interpretation of laws by deductive reasons, and should not mean the
postulation of one fact to clarify another.

An hypothesis may be provisional, to be discarded when it has
served its purpose, or rather to go into solution, that is when
another supervening hypothesis appears to be simpler and more
successful. The history of science is like a caravan route in the
Gobi Desert, strewn with dead bones that once were living. Looking back on the past, there are not a few cases of memorable
observations and discoveries which now seem to controvert the
hypotheses of the men who made them. Scientific hypotheses may

---

[1] *Disputations*, XV *de Veritate*, 1.
[2] *Summa Theologica*, 1a: XXXII: 1, *ad* 2.
[3] *Commentary*, I *Posterior Analytics*, *lect.* 4.

sometimes scarcely amount to more than inspired guesses, yet, so long as they are not mistaken for assured deductions, they are none the worse for that. Science owes much to workers who have leaped to conclusions, who have ventured acts of faith, and jumped the bounds of their apparatus and laws, and returned with new knowledge to make fresh laws. It is a poor hypothesis, someone has said, that will not explain more facts that it was designed to meet. Furthermore, scientific speculation is tolerant of apparent contradictions, and perfectly good hypotheses may appear to be at loggerheads with one another when they are taken as separate and independent pieces, as when energy is pictured as acting sometimes like a bayonet and sometimes like a bullet. We do better to class them, not as true or false, but as good and bad, meaning useful or relatively useless. They are conveniences like gazebos and springboards. They should be preferred, as Einstein is to Newton, for their economy and elegance, according to the test of Ockham's razor, *entia non sunt multiplicanda, praeter necessitatem* or in Hamilton's adaptation, 'neither more nor more onerous causes are to be assumed than are necessary to account for the phenomenon,' and for their usefulness in opening up new routes of discovery.

That scientific hypotheses have been scrapped in the past is true, also that more has been claimed for them than was warranted, yet if they have thrown some light on the material world, and if this has served to show up the need for different and later installations, then they must be held to have been justified, and their incidental extravagances can be tolerated. The test of a hypothesis is pragmatic, namely that beneficial new developments should follow its adoption; though of course such benefit by no means need be the main intention of the exploratory scientist. Scientific curiosity has a bent for theory, and it is here when hypotheses are inflated into theories that we should grow cautious. A physical scientist should keep a stubborn modesty, if only to preserve his own independence; the classification and systematization of phenomena should not be committed to quasi-philosophical explanations. A useful hypothesis may be a false theory, in the sense of affirming a false philosophy. The scientific hypotheses of mechanism and atomism have carried us on the road of discovery, nor are they yet obsolete; this will be admitted by those who reject them as false philosophies. Similarly, the Freudian method and hypothesis is one thing, but its erection into a general philosophy and complete interpretation of human nature quite another.

As soon as he starts to theorize, which being a man he is bound to do, the experimental scientist is by way of becoming a philosopher. If he reckons with the element of cognition in his science he is raising the problem of knowledge. He then needs the backing that philosophy alone can provide. He may deny this. Then he is a bad philosopher, not a bad scientist. Some kind of philosophy is the inevitable consequence and the ultimate stage of experimental science. The worker whose first approach was empirical and practical eventually finds himself casting about for reasons, striving for a system of knowledge that is more than a chart of points representing scientific facts, joined by lines representing scientific laws, with diagrams superimposed representing scientific hypotheses. He seeks to understand more than that part of reality which is amenable to mathematical treatment. The teaching of the dynamic psychology displays this tendency of observation and controlled experiment to reach out for a philosophy, or for what lies on the threshold of philosophy.

At this place, let us allude to the difference between natural science and natural philosophy. It is difficult to draw the frontier between them, except as a kind of Curzon Line. There was a time when the natural philosophers optimistically believed that they could include all the natural sciences in their hegemony, then following the revolution inaugurated by Galileo and Descartes natural philosophy was largely displaced by natural science; even its name was usurped by physics. It should be mentioned that physics was a much wider concept for the medievals than for the moderns. By the time of Dugald Stewart there was nothing between metaphysical speculation on the one hand and experimental research on the other; the former studied the nature of the substance of the material world, its causal principles, and the reality of its existence apart from that of percipient beings; the latter observed phenomena and ascertained their general laws; and he warns us that it is of the utmost consequence that the principles of experimental science should not be blended with those of the former. Now once again the need for a theory in and about the material world is entertained and though there is a pause for the interpolations of mathematics, the place remains for a philosophy of nature on the aristotelean model. The difference between a general philosophy of nature and the particular natural sciences lies partly in the size of the picture but more profoundly in the character of the explanations that are offered.[1] Whereas a philosophy will attempt to give an all-over view, and will deal with such non-empirical inferences as primary matter, the experimental sciences are limited to their special fields of research and will turn to such elementary particles as electrons, protons, neutrons, and so on. Natural philosophy, of course, is less than metaphysics in not including *ens inquantum ens* in its scope and in being restricted to changing reality, *ens mobile,* nevertheless it can use the principles of metaphysics and at the very least serve as the general grammar of the sciences without being wholly absorbed in mathematics.[2] But the deep ground of difference lies in the quality of explanation; whereas a philosophical science will aspire to the wisdom of assigning the ultimate reasons for a thing, and a philosophy of nature will discuss the nature of change as such, the particular sciences will stop at the proximate conditions and factors for certain classes of changing being and sometimes perhaps do little more than resolve one set of facts into another set of facts which themselves are left unexplained. Nor can they negotiate with one another. Moreover they assume throughout a philosophy and a theory of knowledge. Their view is departmental, not synoptic. This is said without scorn, for so they consider particular and detailed problems, such as why some trout have pink-tinted flesh and others not, which philosophical science is quite incapable of entertaining, and still less of solving. We face again the familiar gap between the general and the particular, between horse and the white horse of Kung-sun Lung Tzu.[3]

Let us recapitulate the passages of scientific enquiry. First there is ordinary human experience; the level is higher than that of mere sensation, for the experience is quickened, ordered and enlightened by intelligence, and the data are those of sober and instructed commonsense, neither elaborated nor scientifically processed. For example, the concept of *sweet.* There follows the

---

[1] *Summa Theologica,* 1a: 1: 6, *ad* 3. Prologue to the Commentary on the *Metaphysics.*

[2] Commentary, III *de Anima, lect.* 8.

[3] *Ibid.,* I *de Anima, lect.* 1.

period of observation and classification, which is yet too rough-
and-ready to pass the standards of a polished and technical scientific method; the result may be crude and provisional as with the
division of the four elements, earth, water, fire and air, or bluff
and final, as with the difference between male and female. Let us
take as our example the concept of *sugar*. Then comes the attempt
at exact measurement and translation into a scientific formula.
The data are defined by scientific instruments and are transmuted
into scientific facts. Instead of sugar we have the concept of *CHO*.

Then we leave facts, and seek to enunciate a general law that
will govern the connections of different sets of scientific facts.
For instance, if I am a physiologist working on the human body,
I may seek to determine the relation between the amounts of
nitrogen and glucose excreted, and I will talk about the *DN ratio*.
Then I may try to explain how this comes about and may submit
a hypothesis concerning the power of the pancreas to utilize glucose; I may even make a model to show how it works. The hypothesis will preferably also make reasonable other and related functions of the body. With an increase of technical skill new facts
may issue from this interpretation, new laws may be formulated,
new hypotheses suggested, and new methods employed of con-
trolling phenomena; for example, a new method of treating
diabetes.

Finally, the enquiry may enter into the higher and quasi-
philosophical field of discovering general reasons and relations
with other phenomena outside the field of bio-chemistry, and perhaps of setting the question in its place against the wide background of natural philosophy. Questions of psychology and
morality may also be involved; indeed, as Cardinal Manning says,
all problems of human interest are theological, at least by implication. What is certain is that the reason cannot touch anything
without waking a philosophy.

Now these different stages of enquiry must not be taken in too
mechanical a sense; the mind is not composed of different com-
partments which fill up one at a time, as when liquid is poured
into a motor-car battery. Science is a criss-cross of fact, law,
hypothesis and theory; scientific material shimmers and the mind
is no less glancing and allusive in its response. Nevertheless the
periods we have marked do represent different moments of accent

in the method of the sciences. They cannot themselves successfully define the grammar of their method; this must be expected
from that part of logic which deals with the critique of the
sciences.[1] The order of their development is fact-law-hypothesis:
facts, at first wild and then later groomed; laws, the mathematical
expression of constant ratios that are observed; hypotheses, the
working principles that are imposed to interpret the behaviour of
the facts and the ruling of the laws; which hypotheses may
amount to true theories, reflecting what really is in the nature of
things. A more refined technique may be then introduced, which
in its turn uncovers new facts, to be related by new laws, to be
interpreted in the light of new hypotheses. And so it goes on:
science advances, not steadily and in a straight line, but with a hop
skip and jump, and in a roundabout way. Notwithstanding the
direct trajectories of particular processes, the total effect is one of
convolution. The movement is not that of a vicious circle coming
back to the same point again, but rather that of a growing and
ascending spiral.[2] For the hypothesis returns to a new fact, or to
the old fact in a new light, and brings new methods of treating
facts. There is a sense in which the experimental sciences are
always in process of becoming obsolete; that is the gauge of their
success. Even natural philosophy, observes St Thomas,[3] is always
revising and is rational in the special meaning of not being at rest,
nor has its development the formal perfection of the mathematical
method. Too final a theory can hold up advance: English natural
science after Newton was not unlike English music after Handel;
and for centuries natural philosophy suffered from the very greatness of Aristotle.

Furnished with improvements in equipment and techniques
the experimental sciences can march from success to success, at
least as regards the development of the inanimate world. The

---

[1] Experimental scientists are not always happy in their definitions of the
logical meanings of the terms they use, as, for instance, in the following quotation from a dictionary of scientific terms: 'Hypothesis, a natural explanation of
a phenomenon warranted by consideration of the facts observed: a provisional
explanation, which, if partly confirmed, becomes theory, and, if fully confirmed,
becomes law or fact.' The terminology adopted in this chapter seems better
fitted to match the method of the sciences.

[2] Commentary, I *Posterior Analytics, lect.* 8.

[3] VI *de Trinitate*, VI: 1.

control of purely human factors tends to lag behind. Perhaps as the attention to detail becomes closer, and that detail itself becomes more intricate and specialized, the universal balance of wisdom is upset. The need of a higher directing knowledge was never more urgently practical: the particular sciences offer no deep explanation of our world unless they are taken into a general philosophy; our emptiness, as well as our precariousness, is displayed unless we match our cleverness with a wisdom that will demand contemplation; the mastery of technique leads to a new and frightful barbarism unless controlled by a humane philosophy, and this can be completed only by a theology: you are not my brother or sister, nor even my neighbour, unless God is our father and lord.

The inductive method is predominant throughout the experimental sciences, but there are always the undertones of philosophical intelligibility. Some exponents of physical science do not hesitate to proclaim contrary principles within the same system; but they do not necessarily offend against the principle of contradiction. As we have seen, a paradox is one thing and a self-destructive position another: Christianity simultaneously declares rational and supernatural truths of religion, a synthesis is found in a contrast, there is a hush and a great cry at the peak of joy. All experimental science works within a philosophy, whether or not this be recognized. Though the pattern of history does not conform exactly to the process of logic and the course of events cannot be deduced by a dialectic of necessary propositions, yet an assertion of some necessity is present in the most drifting and fugitive human statements. All necessity is ultimately a category for philosophy to investigate, and this demands the use of the deductive method, the evaluation of the particular within the general, impossible without recourse to the theory and art of logic, uninteresting without the play of dialectic.

THOUGH our subject is not, to apply Dr Johnson's phrase, a dull collection of theorems nor a rude detection of fallacies, we must devote some attention to recurring patterns of mistaken thinking. The misapprehension of notions, the misstatement of propositions, and the incorrect development of argument are the fallacies properly subject to the censure of logic. They may not lead to error, but any conclusion derived from them must be rationally hollow however consolidated on other counts.[1]

Logic, says John Stuart Mill, is not concerned with the false opinions which people happen to entertain, but with the manner in which they come to entertain them. The fallacies exposed fall into two classes, the purely logical and the semi-logical fallacies. Typical examples of the former have already been mentioned in speaking of the eight rules of the syllogism; for instance, the fallacy of the undistributed middle, of the four term argument, of illicit inference from negatives to affirmatives, and from particular principles to sweeping conclusions. Most of the current and interesting fallacies, however, are semi-logical, there is a breach of mental behaviour, and also a spill over into statements about the nature of our environment. Yet certain well-worn types are close enough to logic to be treated here.

Often they can be spotted without expert information, as in the remark of the man who said, 'When I look at the various religions, thank God I'm an atheist.' In logic, as in gardening, it is difficult and sometimes unprofitable to draw the line between bad cultivation, diseased plants and weeds; and for a full and

---

[1] In addition, mistakes may be made from the imperfect appreciation of reality without any fault in the mode of thought. Ignorance breeds error, and there are psychological and moral hindrances that cannot be examined here—prejudice, impatience, custom, lack of instruction, laziness, illness, foolishness, fear. Our thoughts are vitiated before they come to be arranged in orderly form. Nor need we reflect on our solecisms, flaws of grammar, mistakes of rhetoric, *nugationes,* babbling and futilities, baldness, sham ornament, and other offences against good taste.

systematic catalogue of fallacies the reader may be referred to the text-books: the treatment is copious, but not always unanimous. But indeed they are untidy and overlapping like sins and also, in their way, subtle; a logical dissertation can hinge on them no more successfully than a moral theology can take the various sins as its cardinal points, though at one time this was the procedure of the manuals. The stock examples can be knocked down as easily as ninepins; the underlying exemplars are not so easily dealt with. St Thomas wrote a short treatise on fallacies for the benefit of gentlemen students for an arts degree.[1] In this section we shall follow the order of its headings, and take, first, the logical, and then the dialectical fallacies, the misreadings of reality.[2]

---

[1] Opusc. XLIII, *de Fallaciis ad quosdam nobiles artistas*. Genuine according to Grabmann, scarcely doubtful according to Mandonnet, who dates it 1244–45, which will make it the first of the works of St Thomas. The treatment closely follows Aristotle's *Sophistici Elenchi*.

[2] St Thomas adopts the traditional division of fallacies *in dictione*, in the language used, and fallacies *extra dictionem*, independent of language: the former lie in the very form of expression, *ex parte vocis*, the latter come from a misjudgement of reality, *ex parte rei*, and can be treated as sophisms.

CHAPTER XXX

MISUSE OF TERMS

GOD bless you until we meet again, somebody said at parting; the phrase contains the two principal fallacies that come under this heading, for the six types enumerated by the scholastics, namely, equivocation, amphibology, figure of speech, wrong accent, composition and division, can be reduced to the two main classes of double meaning and bad mixture, which again can be contained by the general fallacy of confusion.

Let us first take double meaning. Equivocation, or ambiguity, the deceptive use of one and the same term to signify different meanings, is not confined to popular language, but may enter scientific terminology. Any statement, of course, can be called ambiguous because it can be split up into different series of echoes according to the private sensibility of the reader. But there are limits to useful analysis. The duplicity is blatant in such cases of *gallus* for Frenchman and for cock, or rank for stinking and for an ordered stage, but there are other nuances of meaning sufficient to split an argument. Religion may be used for religiosity, or theology, or the bounden duty of worshipping God; cause may be used in the same argument for a statistically constant antecedent or a metaphysical principle; crime for an offence against the police or against God. Piety, charity, immoral, creative, matter, theoretical and so forth call for definition when they are used; terms with an ethico-political meaning are especially liable to be bandied about in different senses, freedom, dogma, privilege, private property, violence, fascist, imperialism.

It is curious that words of a language become vaguer though the vocabulary increases. Words change with the years, sometimes growing stronger, as with belly, cancer, and cad, and sometimes weaker, as with charity, respectable, nice, myth, and mistress. Exegesis requires a sense of period: how strangely read the epitaphs of a past century, on a Vicar Apostolic in a Staffordshire churchyard that he adorn'd a respectable mitre, on a young wife in an Oxfordshire church that she expired a martyr to excessive sensibility, on a sound churchwoman that she was devoid of enthusiasm. Passage across the Atlantic, either way, can make some terms equivocal; also translation from one to another literary medium, or culture, or philosophical system: English and Russian delegates may use the same words, and still be at cross-purposes.

Most controversies start with an ambiguity, hence the rule in formal debate of seizing on the operative term that conveys different meanings to either side and fixing its sense. Double-meaning that extends to the length of a sentence is sometimes called amphibology, an aiming both ways, a quibbling or ambiguous statement that will bear two or more interpretations, as in the following statements; English humour is not to be laughed at, discretion is the better half of valour, or that teasing phrase in the Rule of St Augustine, it is better to have little than to need much, or the doorplate in Albemarle Street, *The Society for Visiting Scientists*. Double-meaning is much employed in entertainment; the pun, beloved of our great-grandparents, is a subsidiary form. The force of the humour lies in the recognition of the ambiguity; this is the world of coarse fishermen and the like.

A refined form of equivocation is known as the fallacy of figure of speech, *figura dictionis*, where, without the clumsiness of using the same term to signify two entirely different things, different aspects and shades of meaning are confused. Here comes the fallacy of switching the categories in the course of an argument. Only men can argue—therefore women can't: the concept of man is philosophical in the antecedent, but biological in the consequent. Or the change may be from quantity to quality, or vice versa: three is greater than one, therefore three prayers are better than one. Dancing, joyousity to Mary Queen of Scots, was skipping, not very comely for honest women, to John Knox. In such cases the middle term exhibits some identity of meaning, but the bearing has been altered, even beyond the bounds of analogy. Most arguments of which the conclusions are rejected after their premisses have been distinguished are examples of this fallacy of figure of speech: found in writers who put most of the revolutions of western man into the same category, for instance, the Reformation, the Civil War, the Glorious Revolution, the North American Revolution, the French Revolution, the revolt of the Latin American Colonies, the Bolshevik Revolution, whereas one was a

movement of the owners for more privilege, another a movement
of the poor for property, another an anti-Liberal reaction, and so
forth.

Another fallacy that falls into this group is false emphasis, or
the fallacy of accent, *fallacia accentus*, which occurs in spoken language, as with the notice on the escalators, 'Dogs Must be Carried.'
The beat of syllables may also vary the sense. We touch here the
persuasions of rhetoric, for there are accents other than those of
sound: subtler psychological stresses can be set up by the position,
or repetition, or emotional tone of words, by the archness in the
pauses of a radio news announcer and the overcharging of a thesis
by a research scholar. The mind is an opal, rather than a clear
crystal; its words are echoing chords, not single pings. Argument is best conducted in level tones, and the shout and the
whisper avoided, and terms avoided that excite a strong reaction
but carry little evidence; subversive, blasphemous, boss, No
Popery, Cheaper Food.

It is not unknown for arguments to be launched merely from
the verbal likenesses and associations of terms; a weakness of some
medieval arguments came from overloading the etymologies of
Isidore. The habit is usually too petty to be dangerous, and
belongs to the same class as misprints, such as *casual* for *causal*. The
fallacy becomes dangerous when phrases are substituted for ideas
on matters of great moment, and when a blurred emotional reaction does duty for an apprehension of meaning. We come back to
the logical need of definition, nominal and real. Argument depends on an exact appreciation of the meaning of words, and of
their analogical usage. Fluent intercourse is impossible when stiff
pedantry insists on one wooden meaning, and blocks any trans-
ference of ideas. As we have seen, dialectic is not restrained to the
arrangement of quasi-quantitative symbols, but can stretch itself
with the sinuousness of metaphysics and match the movement of
reasonable rhetoric.

Consider now the second type of fallacy, the bad mixtures that
are found in the fallacies of combination, *fallacia compositionis*, and
of separation, *fallacia divisionis*, where, respectively, meanings are
slurred when they should be considered apart, as when you are
asked three different questions in one breath, or cut up when they
should be run together, as when a text is entirely divorced from

its context. Meanings are built up into compound notions and expanded into judgements, then analyzed into their parts: the fallacies we are about to consider attend this composition and division. They may be called the incorrect punctuation of thought, over-punctuation being the fallacy of division, under-punctuation the fallacy of composition.

Now it is not difficult to smudge meanings by mixing them up. False antithesis is a case in point, as in the question: Which would you choose to be, a good pagan or a bad Christian? Well, we hedge, it all depends; and the mind vainly seeks for the composition of a rational ethical code on the one hand and intellectual belief in a revealed mystery on the other. The meaning of the question is blurred by a false composition. The fallacy attends every case of what may be called potted thinking. Take as an example a popular form of fatalism, which holds that since it is already settled what I shall be doing this time next year then I cannot help doing it. But in truth the springs of freewill are independent of the time-factor, and the inescapable future fact that quite certainly I shall be performing such and such an action this time next year no more affects the freedom of the action than the fact that something I did freely a year ago is now irrevocable.[1] The fallacy lies in treating a coupled notion, my-action-on-1st-June-next-year, as though it were a specific notion, my-free-action. Or put the fallacy in this way: everything foreknown by God is bound to be. Now the statement is true when the event and the foreknowledge are taken in composition and the sense is, when God foreknows an event it is bound to come to pass. But it is not true when they are taken in division and the sense is, whatever God foreknows is a necessary kind of event.[2]

Just as we can fallaciously coalesce our thoughts so also we can fallaciously split an idea and treat the parts as though they were equivalent to the whole. Thus we can take a collective notion, such as a heap of stones, and ask: when is a heap of stones a heap of stones?—eight are a heap, so are seven, yes, and six, but are five? —four?—three?—two? Whence this fallacy is sometimes called a *sorites*, or heap.[3] Perhaps you have heard a remorseless and over-

---

[1] *Summa Theologica*, 1a: XIV: 13.   [2] *Ibid.*, 1a: XIV: 13, *ad* 3.

[3] To be distinguished from the aristotelean *sorites*, meaning a group of syllogisms.

bearing logician pressing an opponent, who can but reply; well, I suppose one must draw the line somewhere; and yet not rarely it is the aggressor who is breaking the canons of logic and performing an illegitimate dissection; with every appearance of forensic skill he is dividing what cannot be divided and demanding measurements that cannot be taken. That a sense of proportion is wanting may be evident, but timidity may prevent us urging the laws of logic—Taylor said, a small bull-dog was as good as a large one. Johnson, 'No, Sir, your argument would prove that a good bulldog may be as small as a mouse!'

A specious logic may pose unanswerable questions, force issues that should not arise, produce difficulties that do not occur, and dig divisions that cannot be closed. Against all this we must learn to respect some concepts as indivisible and merely approximate: what is a mid-Victorian and when does an offence become grave? At one time casuists were fond of applying weights and measures to determine the seriousness of sin: if five scudi constituted grave matter in theft, did four? three-and-a-half? three-and-a-quarter? and so on. The process may serve well enough in the treatment of crime, but sin is another matter: the concepts of canon law can be transferred only by analogy into the science of moral theology.

Avoiding the fallacies of composition and division is a trait of an informed and balanced mind, knowing when to join and when to separate, respecting the natures of things and judging when to resist the aggressions of a barbarous logic, appreciative of the idioms that express a truth in non-formal language; you cannot make a silk purse out of a sow's ear, a miss is as good as a mile, a rolling stone gathers no moss.

Before the days of Pearl Harbour, when Europe was ravaged by war, an American prelate was reported as saying that all the belligerents were equally to blame, and the whole tragedy was the result of sin: this was a compound judgement on a divided situation involving the fallacy of composition. Then in his advice he fell into the opposite fallacy of division, for the remedy he prescribed was penance and going to church. But the enemy was round our shores: was penance enough to keep him out and were religious observances a substitute for warlike preparations?

There is a tendency for the pronouncements of ecclesiastics to fall into such fallacies when the sacred and the profane are not

9

co-ordinated and when the problems of life, for the individual and the community, in peace and war, are treated as though they could be solved by slick formulae. But they are by no means limited to the pulpit, but are present in most sectional thinking on large and complex subjects, as when the nation is treated as the man in the street, or the economic man multiplied a millionfold; all the many races, religions, and civilization, between the Himalayas and Ceylon are judged to be one people. Nor is philosophical thinking immune. A mistake in dealing with coupled notions and collective terms, and the reverberations are felt in the practical conduct of affairs. We may take the case noted by Coleridge, when 're-ligion becomes a noun of multitude, or *nomen collectivum*, expressing the aggregate of all the different groups of notions and ceremonies connected with the invisible and supernatural,'[1] there follows, as he foretold, on the plausible pretext of the multitude and variety of religions, and for the suppression of bigotry, a final sundering of national education from the social action of the Christian religion.

---

[1] *Church and State.*

CHAPTER XXXI

SOPHISMS AND DIALECTIC

THE fallacies hitherto selected are wrong in advance, like the judgements a man may make on the books he has not read. Those we are now going to consider are more deeply involved in the science of reality. As we have remarked, one fallacy does not exclude another and the misuse of terms can enter into sophisms, for just as one human act may be spoilt by intemperance, cowardice and injustice, so one process of reasoning may quibble and miss the point and argue in a circle all at once. The dialectical fallacies misinterpret the conditions of being, and usually they extend to the length of an argument. A sophism is a deceptive argument. An unconscious sophism is called a paralogism. A sham argument, *argumentum apparens*, is found not only when the flaw is purely logical but also when the premisses are unduly assumed, as in begging the question, or when the conclusion is irrelevant, as in *ignorantia elenchi*. There are many ways of misreading a situation near enough to logic, which acts like a cowcatcher for the sciences, to merit inclusion here.

Seven types are enumerated by the scholastics: the red herring, *fallacia accidentis*; thinking in blinkers, *fallacia secundum quid et simpliciter*; Aunt Sally argument, *fallacia secundum ignorantiam elenchi*; begging the question, *fallacia petitionis principii*; cart before the horse, *fallacia consequentis*; wrong scent, *fallacia secundum non causam ut causam*; omnium gatherum, *fallacia secundum plures interrogationes ut unam*. We shall take them in turn according to the order St Thomas adopts from Aristotle. As he bases his treatment of the various sins according to the hierarchic order of the virtues, so also he relates these seven rather sprawling fallacies to seven pondered meditations on the nature of the universe.[1] Perhaps the chief value of this chapter will be to throw these into relief, and so exhibit the fashion and spirit of his dialectic.

---

[1] Opusc. XLIII, *de Fallaciis*, Ch. 9–16.

(i)

The view of the world as composed of types and events is not
peculiar to any one school of thought nor to philosophy itself, for
the tension of general issues and individual sensibility composes
the dramatic significance of every person's life; there is a wide-
spread sense of the difference between the necessary and the incidental; and the distinction between the *per se* and the *per accidens* is
indispensable for all orderly enquiry. The special strength of St
Thomas consists, not in insisting on the world of necessary ideas,
but in pressing with great hardihood and equanimity for a religious philosopher the doctrine of Aristotle that physical facts are
very real. Reality rounded off in this world is not found as a pure
kind of meaning; everything is embodied and individualized by
matter, sprigged out and enlivened by all manner of considerations.
Pure humanity does not exist, nor the man *per se*, the rational
animal is but real because its examples are real; what do exist are
human individuals, all with different details, and all flawed—this
conception is always present in the *Summa Theologica*, not merely
because of the underlying theological doctrine of original sin, but
also because its psychological and ethical judgements are modulated
by the observation of fact. Consequently half of the movement of
St Thomas's thought is left out when his dialectic is represented
as the march of pure ideas; always there is a tug from the movement of physics and the tide of history. Pure rationalism is but a
temporary period; meaning does not hold aloof from matter; real
forms as existing are variable[1]; spirit is not contaminated by the
body; philosophy is not separate from events. It is because of
these sympathies that we must preserve the distinction between
necessary meaning and contingent incident, signification and application, remembering always that the paramount purpose of
distinction is not exclusion and rejection, but the retention and
enhancement of identity.

The non-observance of this distinction leads to the fallacy of
the incidental, *fallacia accidentis*,[2] recognized under many names
and forbidden by many precepts. We speak of wandering away
from the question, of speaking beside the point, of seizing on the

---

[1] *Summa Theologica*, 1a: IX: 2, *ad* 3.
[2] Disputations, I *de Veritate*, 8, *ad* 1.

irrelevant and the trivial; we are warned to cut out the frills, to cut the cackle and come to the 'osses; we are accused of trailing a red herring. The fallacy is present in theory and in practice: in theory, as when an argument is to the effect that substance is a solid body, and therefore were the soul a substance it would be a solid body; in practice, as in the action of the Roman Senate in sending troops to Spain when Hannibal was at the gates of the city. Yet let us make no mistake, what appears to be a side-show is sometimes primary in the long run; there was a sound strategical insight in sending troops to Egypt when England was threatened with invasion after Dunkirk, and in the realm of ideas St Thomas not seldom stresses questions, such as the rationality of law and freedom, that have grown in importance since his day.

If we are distracted by side issues, for instance, if we defend British rule in India 'because if we didn't Russia would'; or if we fix on the picturesque rather than the significant, as when it is said that Labour represents the people who watch soccer and the Tories the people who play rugger; or if we fasten on the non-essential, as when the Germans are blamed for using V.1 bombs 'because they daren't send pilots' or severe reprisals on Italy are advocated for any damage done in Greece—'why if Athens is bombed should Rome be spared, does Rome sound more greatly in the ear of civilized man than Athens?'—or if we argue that religious men usually find reasons for what they hold on non-rational grounds and therefore the philosophy of Aquinas is special pleading, then we fall into the fallacy of the accidental.

Much of our reasoning is conducted with contingent propositions. The fallacy easily crops up when three terms are engaged, of which two are connected *per accidens*.[1] Then we have to be on our guard against jumbling the accidental with the essential, the *de facto* with the *de jure*; for instance, concluding that holiness must be queer because it is rare. One of the first distinctions a student of scholasticism must draw is between an essential requirement and an adventitious condition, however frequent and almost inevitable the latter may be. Thus a knower and a known is essential to knowledge, but that there should be a causal relationship between them, or that they should be numerically diverse is incidental.[2]

---

[1] Opusc. XLIII, *de Fallaciis*, Ch. 10.
[2] *Summa Theologica*, 1a: XIV: 4.

Similarly whether or not the links of the chain of secondary causes are limited is irrelevant to the conclusion demanding a first cause.

The fallacy works both ways; to argue from the essential to the incidental is perhaps less frequent to the national frame of mind than to argue from the incidental to the essential, but it is as wrongheaded. To spin facts out of theories is the temptation of the *a priori* philosopher and, at a lower level, of those who seem never to be at a loss for an answer.

(ii)

Next comes the distinction between the entire and the partial, *secundum perfectum et imperfectum*,[1] with the related fallacy of mistaking part for whole and of shuttling between absolute and qualified terms. Often the mark of cheap thinking, yet what pain is here and what frustration: this is no place for ridiculing a fallacy that is the peculiar danger of a mind that must think abstractly or not at all. Each complete substance in this world is unique, rounded off and concrete, so entirely itself as not to be intimately reducible to general categories. Contingent events are not to be resolved into necessary essences.[2] Every person, indeed every individual object, is fundamentally a mystery to the reasoning reason, which may indeed touch but cannot expose. Generalizations however particularized cannot hold the heart of anything. Direct and immediate possession belongs to a higher flight of knowledge, a supra-rational mode to which the reason itself aspires and of which poetical and mystical experience is an earnest. No natural desire is pointless, and the natural desire of the human mind least of all. The present condition of the human reason is not self-explanatory. The more reasonable we are the more restless we become for a way of life beyond exposition and the showing forth of reasons. Nevertheless the rationalization of the things about us, if inadequate to the comprehension of ultimate reality, is not untrue so long as the limitations are recognized: moreover the construction of such a rational scheme of things is inescapable if we are to be reasonable and human. The work of the reasoning reason is a necessary prelude to a higher vision. The fruit of know-

---

[1] Opusc. XLIII, *de Fallaciis*, Ch. 11.
[2] Disputations, XV *de Veritate*, 2, *ad* 3.

ledge will not fall into our lap; we must plant and prune and set up ladders.

Now in this medium of the reason, where unique figures are translated into common dimensions and singular objects are expressed in communicable forms, there are still standards of completeness; and the mind is required to see things steadily and see them whole,[1] and to judge a situation, as we say, by and large, *simpliciter*, avoiding such phrases as that of Hobbes, 'for what is the *Heart* but a *Spring*; and the *Nerves* but so many *Strings*; and the *Joynts* but so many *Wheeles*?' For a balanced judgement many factors must be taken into account, and we must be alive to the dangers of purely sectional thinking. Even within the general limits of conceptual knowledge there is always the possibility of excessive formalization, of obsessional writing to a formula, of discussing philosophy in the spirit of party politics, of running in blinkers, of imitating Thackeray's treatment of the Hanoverian Kings. Thus Hitler's charge against the British Empire; forty-four million Englishmen own more than a quarter of the world's territory: or again, when the drinking of malt liquor or ardent spirits is treated as the consumption of alcohol, and alcohol itself is narrowly regarded as a narcotic, a depressant, a lowerer of temperature—the conclusion obviously has to be corrected by some such picture as St Bernards with kegs slung round their necks succouring frozen wayfarers in snowdrifts. This attitude releases the fallacy of mistaking the partial for the entire, *fallacia secundum quid et simpliciter*, of identifying the narrow aspect we see with the complete nature and setting of a thing, as complete, that is, as the reason can make it.

I may go to a dentist very much against my will, and in a way my action is involuntary, that is *secundum quid*, or considered under one respect, *in aliquo genere tantum*; yet by and large, and taking into account the whole circumstances, the pain and the poisoning, I go willingly, though not gladly. My decision is voluntary simply speaking, *voluntarium simpliciter*; other factors that would withhold me were they taken by themselves become subsidiary and partial aspects. St Thomas takes the example of a merchant who willingly jettisons the cargo to save himself and his ship, willingly *simpliciter*,

---

[1] *Summa Theologica*, 3a: L: 5.

that is with respect to the whole situation, but not willingly *secundum quid*, that is with respect to the damage he suffers.[1] The distinction is important in moral matters where we are judged by what in fact we do, not by our incidental regrets or ulterior motives; and it applies as well to all matters of reasonable judgement, not least in the writing of total history, where objects should be seen all round, and not merely from one angle.

Shibboleths, special pleading, grinding an axe, oratorical simplification, gazing at things through tinted spectacles, persecution mania, obsessional thinking, treating every question as political, polemical, or as personal, cynicism, sectarianism, all these in their various ways are cognate to the fallacy we are considering. The mind is not seldom colour-blind: in politics some see red everywhere, others do not see it at all. Most of us are reluctant to face facts, and are inclined to take those features alone that suit our tastes and ignore or explain away the rest. A respectable journal cannot be accused of *suppressio veri*, but yet may turn a blind eye where it does not suffer from mere inability to see. In philosophy, too, as in all science, there is the danger of selecting the evidence to support a doctrine and dismissing the rest. St Thomas is conspicuously not a sectary, for it is his rare achievement not to ride one particular theory to death, but to hold together a team of truths, combining the stoical with the the epicurean, the philosophy of ideas with the science of material facts, a spiritual psychology and a bodily biology, the single integrity of a human act with the analysis of its parts, intellectualism and an urgency of love, to name a few headings of his synthesis.

A little learning is a dangerous thing; but if lack of information is one of the causes of the fallacy so also is excess of ingenuity, which, whatever the situation, will find what it is looking for, and turn all the evidence to suit its purpose. Refined idealism is no more exempt than blunt materialism. Reality must not be whittled down until only a wisp is left. In working with a special aspect of things, the limitations of the appropriate method must be recognized; the result must be combined with other special

---

[1] *Summa Theologica*, 1a–2ae: VI: 6. Here, incidentally, some later scholastic moralists reverse the terminology, describing the ditching of the goods as *voluntary secundum quid* but not *voluntary simpliciter*, and so miss the point of the doctrine.

findings so that eventually some sense of the whole question may be obtained. Every abstraction, in brief, should carry a criticism of itself.

(iii)

The third general condition is that the universe abounds in contrasts, signs and counter-signs; being is divided into opposed and non-opposed being, *secundum oppositum et non oppositum*.[1] There is no level and general pervading reality, a settled mist and always 'the holy time is quiet as a Nun'; but storms and peaks, mammoths and grains of sand, conflicts and extrusions, as well as agreements and communities of being. The free play of Hellenic pluralism against the vast despotism of Persia is redoubled in the thought of St Thomas; he is no monist, not even in the religious and practical sense of regarding God as the exclusive object of sacred love; his theology comprehends Juliet's cry, 'O God! O nurse!' and has a feeling for the multitude, for the world of many things, for dapple and pied markings; in his metaphysics there is a responsive delicacy and he knows how there are other beings and goods besides the all and complete being and good of God.[2]

There is an ironical quality here, a reflex sense of things and their drawbacks, an edge in the taste which prevents them from cloying. The mind that would know these things must be firm, yet gentle, even tender and warmed with respect.

Sometimes we must twitch off the bandages. But rudeness and coarseness have no logical excuse, when, instead of developing a dialectic of contest and contrast, they lapse into the fallacy of the false antithesis, the slapdash either-or, the take-it-or-leave-it mentality. We then verge on the fallacy of sectarian thinking; an undue simplification is made, one side is isolated and made the exclusive object of assent. The tension within being is lost and the living idea stiffens into a set formula, regardless of the aphorism, better for all to be different and friendly than to be all alike and at enmity. Such is the philosophy of moral indignation and means-tests and party lines and special oaths, all very well, no doubt, for *ad hoc* measures, but a paralysis of the spirit. Rigid pacificism would deny to constitutions founded on evidence and

---

[1] Opusc. XLIII, *de Fallaciis*, Ch. 11.
[2] *Summa Theologica*, 1a: XLVII. IV *de Trinitate*, 1.

agreement the protection of force to defend themselves against the dark and violent appetites at loose; jansenism would deny the goodness of human nature in the name of a higher good; because virtue is often difficult in fact rigorism would treat the pleasant as vicious, or at least in need of apology; because religion is expressed in the act of public worship, all other actions are considered to be religiously irrelevant unless they be justified with an explicitly church-going reference: all these are examples of toppling the balance established in the universe.

The mating of opposites has continued in European thought since the days of Pythagoras[1]: even-odd, light-darkness, warmth-cold, male-female, action-passion, dominant-recessive, nature-law. From the struggle between the later Ionians and the Eleatics issued the dialectic of Socrates, Plato, and Aristotle. From the tension between the Hellenic philosophy and the Judaic religion issued the theological synthesis of St Thomas. Much beauty depends on contrast, and truth as well: opposites must not be made the same nor heights levelled down to flatness and consequent neglect. But we must be sure that the contrasts are just. Every contrast implies a match. Objects can only be opposed when they are relevant to one another; sweet to bitter, day to night, Pascal to Montaigne. There is no contrast between sweet and angular, duty and pleasure, character and intelligence.

As we have seen, there are various kinds of opposition; notes may be contrary or they may be contradictory. They are contrary when they exist in the same kind of subject, as love and hate are both in the will; one excludes the other, but there are intermediate stages between them and one supposes the other; idiom recognizes the obverse and reverse when it speaks of love turning into hate. But contradictories are in complete opposition, thus love and not-love; no common subject is supposed, no intermediary is possible, the exclusion is final. As Charles Lamb wrote of a Temple worthy, 'He had that in his face which you could not call unhappiness; it rather implied an incapacity of being happy.' Then also, there are two kinds of negation, pure negation and privation. Because I remark that I do not abstain from reading the *Manchester Guardian*, you must not therefore infer that I peruse that journal,

<hr/>

[1] Disputations, III *de Potentia*, 6.

for there are shades of negation: I do not read the *Manchester Guardian*, I abstain from reading it, I read only the *Daily Telegraph*.

The swing of alternatives plays a great part in the movement of dialectic. For instance, you may not be able to argue directly in favour of a position that has been adopted, but you may be able to take an opposed position and show its impossibility. If God did not exist, it would be necessary to invent him, if first principles were not true, it would still be necessary to adopt them in order to attack them; or again, I do not know much about the Jews but I can tell you more against the anti-Semites I have met. Light is known from shade, music from pauses and silences, and reasoning may advance by the opposition of notions. Analogy is the underlying principle, the glimpse of kinship in strangeness: 'Govern a large country,' said Lao Tzu, 'as you would cook a small fish.'

Yet if we avoid the abrupt forcing of issues, we may find ourselves at the other extreme of oscillating without making any advance. We know the long sentences that swing from side to side and never move forward, nor are they meant to; the pendulum movement in press and parliament; 'While on the one hand few cannot but bring themselves to admit that such a proposal provides not inconsiderable nor remote grounds for concern, yet on the other hand not many would venture to deny that it is premature to assume that the situation warrants the attention customarily accorded to a question that will not allow of delayed decision.' The fallacy of bad opposition, however, is more evident when argument presses for a premature decision; it attends statements that present a pistol at your head, with a swagger and a stand and deliver manner long before the time for decision has come. Faced with such a fallacy of the *either-or*, we are inclined to reply, in some cases *neither*, in other cases *both*. When the slogan, quality not quantity, is used by those who favour the limitation of families, there is the unproved assumption that there is a connection between having few children and bringing them up well.

Deep mental splits are not wise nor are they healthy; but we are in a hurry and divorce is all too easy between value and fact, idealism and realism, theory and practice, the rules of logic and the conduct of life, God and mammon, the Here and Hereafter; some are justified, but in many cases it is better for our peace of

mind, unless we run away from the problem either by ceasing to
worry or by embracing a simple cause, to resolve the opposition, to
take the contrasting notions in the spirit of wisdom[1] to their
highest cause, where neither is suppressed nor suffered to clash, 'to
find in contraries above their contrary causes their common universal cause,'[2] for the One produces multiplicity and the Invariable is the source of change.[3] Such is the method of St Thomas
with the so-called antinomies, or philosophical mysteries that can
be reached, but not positively resolved, by the reason; the enigmas
of the One and the Many,[4] the determinism of mind and the
freedom of will,[5] the immobility of perfection and the leap of
life,[6] the justice and the mercy of God.[7] As a novelist reveals
human character in the union of contraries, so the philosopher respects the oppositions within being. Flashes of temper may light
a subject, but philosophy calls for composure. The tests for philosophical truth and error are not like litmus paper for acid and
alkaloid: the temper is not that of the heresy hunt or the party-
line.

The great virtue here is the power of synthesis where, after the
period of temporary and methodic exclusion, differences are
brought together in society, not merged in community; as when
creatures are known in God and yet remain creatures and themselves,[8] when bodies are infused with spirit and become better
bodies,[9] time is taken to eternity without ceasing to move,[10]
pleasure is none the less because integrated with duty,[11] and
secondary causes lose none of their force because they are energized
by the first cause.[12] A synthesis is neither a mixture nor an eclectic
collection; the Summa Theologica itself is not a mosaic of philosophical truths from Aristotle and Plotinus set in the cement of

[1] Summa Theologica, 2a–2ae: XLV: 1.
[2] Ibid., 1a: XLIX: 3.
[3] Ibid., 1a: XLI: 1, ad 2. 1a: LIII: 1, ad 2. Commentary, III Physics, lect. 4.
VIII: lect. 9.
[4] Summa Theologica, 1a: III: 1, 2, 3, 4, 6, 7, 8. 1a: VII: 2. 1a: XI: 2.
[5] Ibid., 1a: XXIII: 6. Disputations, XXIV de Veritate, 2. VI de Malo.
[6] Summa Theologica, 1a: XVIII: 2, 3. 1a–2ae: XXXI: 1, 2.
[7] Ibid., 1a: XXI: 4.   [8] Ibid., 1a: XIV: 6.
[9] Ibid., 1a: XLIV: 2. 1a: LXV: 1, 2. 1a: LXXVI: 1.
[10] Ibid., 1a: X: 1.   [11] Ibid., 1a: XCVIII: 2. 1a–2ae: IV: 1, 2.
[12] Ibid., 1a: CV: 5.

the Christian revelation; it results from the collaboration of contrasting truths at their highest peak of development; and its conclusion is not a composite image wherein different objects are blurred or the sort of conclusion that makes do with ambiguity and compromise, and finds itself faced in the end with the humiliating consequences of appeasement.

A truly synthetical philosophy practises what may be called a free trade of ideas. An open mind will meet an open world; a closed mind will create barriers and blockades; differences will be drummed into hostility, and philosophy, instead of being lively and calm, will find itself cramped with a set of artificial restrictions and excited with clumsy anathemas. Yet in truth a tankard may be either half-full or half-empty according as you are of a sanguine or melancholic temperament. An exact sense of opposition is a precious quality, if it goes with the ability to hold a balanced conviction which can appreciate the true strength of objections and discern the temptation behind the attractive forthrightness of black-or-white thinking, the dangers of acting on a simple and exclusive test, the weakness of false contrasts and bogus dilemmas. All ills, said John Brown of Edinburgh, are either depressions or excitements; to be treated respectively with alcohol or opium. His own ills were depressions, and he died of the cure.

An opposition should be stated only where a real division exists, and at no greater strength; a difference of emphasis should not become a contrariety, nor a contrariety a contradiction. Moreover the contrasts should be accurately paired; obedience should not be pitted against freedom, nor supernatural against material, nor piety against scandal, nor ecclesiastical against worldly, nor eternal against natural, nor duty against pleasure, nor right against self-interest. The statement, for instance, that the moral sense of duty is lifted above all rational considerations and may even be opposed to them leaves to the utilitarian and pragmatist the scientific control of material forces. In a sense the fallacy of false exclusiveness is present in all sophistical argument; yet there is a special name for setting up a pseudo-opposition, then proving or disproving one side under the mistaken impression that it bears on the other. Night and day are contraries—but the house is not locked up during the day—therefore it is locked at night.

This is the fallacy of false issue, to which belongs, as a parasite on refutation,[1] the fallacy of *ignorantia elenchi*, which sets out to prove what is not denied or to disprove what is not affirmed. If the question is whether poaching a rabbit from a rich man's preserves is wrong or not, and it is argued that the rich man will not miss it, then there is *ignorantia elenchi*. A similar fallacy in the law courts shifts the grounds of dispute or abuses the plaintiff's attorney. To this class also belong the trick of setting up Aunt Sallies and knocking them down, or arguing against men of straw.

Fallacies, as we have noted, are not mutually exclusive, and to isolate one for examination without including another is not always easy. The fallacy of forced issue and false contrast is the one that lies in wait alike for the gentle rocking motions of an antithetical argument and for the urgent ultimatum, and the result is not always so agreeable as the temperance sermon from the Irish parish priest in the days of Captain Boycott: 'Drink,' he cried, 'is the greatest curse and the cause of every sin. What makes you shoot at your landlord? Drink! And what makes you miss him? Drink!'

(iv)

The fourth condition of being and occasion of fallacy is a corollary of the third. In a heterogeneous universe the mind must appreciate identities and diversities and judge *secundum idem et diversum*,[2] separating principles and derivatives, and scrupulously observing the difference between them in its discourse. For instance a conclusion is proved by principles that are distinct from it, and consequently the attempt to demonstrate the conclusion by itself falls into fallacy. The substitution of the conclusion for the premisses has already been remarked in treating of the third rule of the syllogism; it is called the fallacy of begging the question, *petitio principii*, of which the typical case assumes precisely what is to be proved. Foxhunting is not cruel because the fox enjoys the sport; there are no miracles at Lourdes because miracles do not happen; atrocity propaganda is true because the enemy will stop at nothing, which we know from atrocity propaganda.

A common and stronger variety of begging the question is called the vicious circle, *circulus vitiosus*, or proving the same by the

---

[1] Opusc. XLIII, *de Fallaciis*, Ch. 12.   [2] *Ibid.*, Ch. 13.

same, *idem per idem*, as when two conclusions are based on each other. I know the Bible is true because Christianity guarantees it, I know Christianity is true because I can prove it from the Bible. We frequently argue in a circle, not all circular arguments however are vicious, far from it. Scientists must often go beating round the Horn; the educator, as Marx says, must himself be educated. The example we have given can be taken in a perfectly valid sense. The movement of philosophy does not proceed from point to point in a straight line, though Descartes tried to make it so, but is, as it were, four-dimensional[1]: if we must represent the movement by a line we must make it double back on itself and coil and expand. Though he agreed with Aristotle that merely rational processes tend to go in a straight line,[2] St Thomas was influenced by the mystical teaching of the *de Divinis Nominibus* and the great twelfth century school of the Victorines in representing the ebb and flow and circlings of enlightened contemplation; he cites the Scotsman, Richard of St Victor, on the flight of birds.[3] One truth illumines another and is itself illuminated. The parts of the universe all go together. Beauty is strange and familiar; wisdom is knowledge returning home.

As in the highest form of love, which is friendship,[4] there is a giving and a taking, more perfect than the outgoing of unselfish and disinterested affection, so the highest form of knowledge, if motions be ascribed to it, is not in one direction only, but is a circling and interpenetration; at once a memory and a recall, a discovery and an invitation.[5] This is found at levels lower than the heights of mystical contemplation. What has been a conclusion becomes a principle, and the old principle becomes a new conclusion. The movement is spiral and ascending, not that of a flat circle, as we have seen in discussing the scientific method of fact, law, hypothesis, new fact, new law, new hypothesis; the mind does not arrive at where it started from, or if it does, there has been a strengthening, and the repetition is not meaningless.

---

[1] Disputations, I *de Veritate*, 2.

[2] Commentary, I *de Anima*, lect. 8.

[3] *Summa Theologica*, 2a–2ae: CLXXX: 6.

[4] *Ibid.*, 2a–2ae: XXIII: 1.

[5] *Ibid.*, 1a: LXXIX: 6, ad 2. 1a: LXXXVII: 1, 2, 3. Disputations, X *de Veritate*, 1–9. Opusc. X, *de Causis*, lect. 3, 15.

Sensitive to bumbledom the logical censor should not hurry to pounce on arguments that seem to go round and round in a circle. The same holds good about arguments that seem to land themselves in verbal contradictions, for sometimes scientific investigation finds it convenient to assume in the first instance what it hopes eventually to be able to prove. In such cases the background and context must be sympathetically taken into account, as in the following dialogue from Stephen Leacock: 'If you had asked a Canadian just before the outbreak of the present war, "Does Canada have to go to war if England does?" he would have answered, "Of course not." Then if you had asked him, "And will Canada go to war if England does?" he would say, without hesitation, "Oh, yes." Then if you had gone on to ask, "Why?" he would have reflected a little and said, "Oh, because we'd *have* to." ' Circular arguments are only vicious when they are as destructive to the process of reasoning as the action of a worker wasp to the life of its larva, which, lacking other food to present, was observed to bite a portion from one end of the larva's body and offer it to the other end to be eaten. In the same way a universal empiricism that rests entirely on experience and experiment falls into the fallacy, and is consequently self-refuting; for it must involve some general propositions about the dependence of rational knowledge on experience which in themselves are not the object of experience. Arguments are fallacious and endlessly repeating when they turn full circle and curve back to exactly the same point and nothing is gained.[1]

Yet the mind is so lively as to profit from apparent tautology; circular thinking can be informative and add a necessity even when the advance is very slight, for instance in the book review which began, for those that like this sort of thing, well this is the sort of thing they like. But it must be confessed that whatever may be the motion of the mind in the higher reaches of contemplation, the logical reason prefers the straight advance and the succession of theorems, at any rate in a set treatise, and tends to greet circular processes with the reserve it shows to the observation in *Sylvie and Bruno*, that if a crocodile should turn round and start walking up its own tail it would eventually stand on its forehead.

---

[1] Commentary on the *Posterior Analytics*, I: *lect*. 8.

There are vicious circles in practice as well as in theory: people are too tired to be patriotic, but because they are not patriotic enough they are too tired. Or again, there is unemployment because there is no market, and no market because there is unemployment. In these, as in the psychological problems of personal relationships where a similar endless circularity may come about, the remedy is the same as in logic; the ring must be broken, one of the terms must be distinguished or fractured, possibly painfully, and the circle converted to a spiral.

(v)

To the scholastics the world was a hierarchy of things, arranged in differences of importance, *prius et posterius secundum dignitatem*. Some objects are primary, others secondary; though often forced to begin from secondary considerations, for they may be more evident to start with, the reason should arrive at a judgement of things according to their proper order and sequence and see first things first. Apart from our tendency to start with conclusions and then make up premises to fit them, there is here what may be called the general danger of the preposterous, the fallacy of putting the cart before the horse, of getting hold of the wrong end of the stick. 'You don't know how to manage Looking-glass cakes,' the Unicorn remarked, 'hand it round first, and cut it up afterwards.'

Under this heading falls the special fallacy of the consequent, *fallacia consequentis*, which consists in misjudging the connection in an argument, and which affects conditional rather than categorical arguments,[1] where it is included in the fallacy of the incidental. The fallacy of the incidental works both ways, from antecedent to consequent and in the reverse direction.[2] Thus to conclude that if a consequent in a conditional proposition is verified then the antecedent is true: if Peter is running he is moving—but he is moving —therefore he is running. Such a mistake can enter into the sciences that rightly make use of conditional hypotheses to rationalize a collection of laws. Yet because the laws are true, at least in this sense that the scientific facts are observed to behave in accordance with them, it is erroneous to infer that the hypothesis is

---

[1] *de Fallaciis*, Ch. 14.
[2] *Summa Theologica*, 1a: XIV: 13, obj. 2. I *Contra Gentes*, 20.

true in the same way. That Peter is running is like a hypothesis to
explain that he is in motion, but there are also other hypotheses,
he might be crawling on all fours, or marching in slow time. The
fallacy works in the reverse direction when it is assumed that a
consequent is not true because the antecedent is not verified: if
Peter is running he is moving—but he is not running—therefore
he is not moving. Such a mistake, too, is not unknown among
scientific men, who, finding facts not behaving in accordance with
the laws of their hypothesis, choose to modify the facts rather than
the hypothesis.

Were the universe the work of God, then it would be more
perfect than it is: the *fallacia consequentis* enters when the conclusion
is slipped in, therefore the universe is not the work of God. For
the argument forgets that limitation is inherent in finite being.
and reflects no imperfection in the power of the creator.[1]

(vi)

In many cases the principles and derivations in the universe are to
be seen as real causes and causal dependencies, indeed a universal
division of being is into cause and effect, for every substance is
either cause or caused, every finite substance is both cause and
caused. Hence the general judgement on things *secundum causam et
causatum* and the lurking fallacy of getting our causes wrong, the
fallacy of false genealogy, *fallacia secundum non causam ut causam*, as
when the increase of a population is treated as the cause of unemployment, or when Christianity is condemned because Christians
have failed, or when democracy is rejected because of the democrats one meets. This is less the mistake of jumping to conclusions than of jumping from conclusions to the wrong premiss.

The workings of causality need to be tracked very carefully and
patiently, bearing in mind the difference between the judgements
of experimental science and the judgements of philosophy, that is
the difference between the mere sequences of phenomena and the
real dependences of causality. The relationship of a constantly
antecedent fact with a subsequent event is an adumbration, but not
a clear statement, of the relationship of a positive principle with
another being which it produces and sustains. Moreover, in a

---

[1] *Summa Theologica,* 1a: XXV: 6.

system of multiple factors, the relevant ones have to be isolated deftly and in an impersonally surgical manner; preconceptions and party passion will make us clumsy; for instance, the fact that the proportion of Conservative members of parliament killed in action for their country was very much higher than their parliamentary majority does not by itself prove the greater patriotism of their party by comparison with the Labour Party, for there are other causes to explain the effect. It is no use tugging or slashing at the cordage of causality, the hitches and bends have their proper functions and we must handle them according to the manner they have been laid.

One of the clumsiest mistakes is labelled *post hoc ergo propter hoc*, afterwards therefore because of; thus, to attribute an earthquake to a notably licentious carnival; to adduce the sterling fighting qualities of the Russian soldier as an argument for communism; to explain Christianity as a product of conditions under the Roman Empire; to cite cancer as a disproof of the goodness of God, or its higher incidence with the increased consumption of tinned goods. The fallacy takes a subtler form when it enters that special type of argument known as a *reductio ad absurdum*, a pushing to absurdity which consists in disproving a conclusion by showing that it involves denying an admitted truth, or in proving a conclusion by showing that its denial entails an equally embarrassing consequence. To quote from Thoreau's *Walden*; 'One farmer says to me, "You cannot live on vegetable food solely, for it furnishes nothing to make bones with"; . . . walking all the while he talks behind his oxen which, with vegetable-made bones, jerk him, and his lumbering plough along in spite of every obstacle.'

What deeper principle is there to back the statement that for a thing to be and not to be at the same time in the same way is impossible? To attempt such a proof would be to fall into the fallacy of the vicious circle; that very truth would be taken for granted of which the demonstration is essayed. Consequently the principle has to be approached indirectly and negatively by a *ducens ad impossibile*[1]: if you deny the principle of contradiction, *ipso facto* you affirm it, which is illogical, and a different kettle of fish altogether from assuming it when you affirm it.

---

[1] Disputations, III *de Potentia*, 4.

Reductions to absurdity are legitimate types of argument, and sometimes the only ones available, but they call for discretion. They fall into fallacy when the cause advanced for a conclusion is not really the cause. Say that one wishes to disprove the statement, the more the merrier, and one argues, what? do you seriously maintain that a crowd of ten thousand makes for a more frolicsome party than ten? A false reason or cause of the thesis has been assumed for disproof, namely the greater the numerical size of a gathering the greater the fun. Or say that I am trying to prove that life is worth living against a pessimist, and I argue; well, if it is not worth living, the only alternative is to commit suicide as quickly and quietly as possible; but he has merely said that life is not worth living, not that dying is any better.

We need not unravel here the details of the fallacy *secundum non causam ut causam*; enough to observe what care is called for in the complications of causality for there are, to speak of efficient causes alone, primary causes and secondary causes, and secondary causes may be either total causes and partial causes, principal causes and instrumental causes, essential causes and accidental causes, causes of being and causes of becoming, applications, conditions, and occasions. What patient analysis is necessary in enquiring why the proportion of R.C's. is so much higher in the criminal than in the non-criminal population. How easy it is to get the causes wrong by making the position too simple: to assume that a theory is true because it appears to be verified by facts, as when a psychological theory leads to a procedure that happens to cure people. In a deductive system the truth of a conclusion may recommend, but does not finally confirm the truth of the premisses alleged.

(vii)

From consequence and causality we return again to an earlier consideration of the universe, namely that it is composed of many diverse things. To be one and to be many is a general condition of being. Behind this consideration, *secundum unum et multa*,[1] lies one of the original, and still most profound, problems in philosophy. Unity or multiplicity, unity and multiplicity? If monism be true,

---

[1] *de Fallaciis*, Ch. 16.

if at last analysis everything be one, a doctrine as old as Parmenides, then the variety and change and distinction we observe in the world are but illusions, or at least trivialities and surface excitements that will pass, leaving behind being alone, unwinking, motionless, and dead. If, at the other extreme, the world is but a tumult of events, a restless throng of incommunicable and fugitive points, then there is no ground, no source, no centre of reference, no end; peace and tranquillity are but a dream, for everything is thrust and change.

We may note one reflection in logic of this cosmic problem. The fallacy of composition may take in argument the special form of running many questions together, *fallacia secundum plures interrogationes ut unam*.[1] We have already referred to the difficult art of asking proper questions, here we have confused and improper questions, mix-ups, mental scrimmages, and *omnium gatherums*. A few days ago a naval officer remarked, 'I feel there is something in this philosophy business; would you in a few words let me have the dope?' It is met when we are asked to bite off more than we can chew: what do you think of things in general? When a diatribe ends with a series of rambling and rhetorical questions. When two or more questions are merged and a single answer demanded: Will you stop beating your wife? Answer me yes or no!

One of the purposes of logical discipline is to train us in the appreciation of the formal object, and to prevent us from being intimidated by the gigantic size to which a muddled question can tower and from allowing personal morals to cower before totalitarianism so that war ceases to be either seamanlike or soldierly. Confronted with a hash or hodge-podge, logic will demand a pause, a restatement, and will insist on dealing with one thing at a time. This indeed is one condition for profitable argument; otherwise fallacies seem to get away with a flying start before the answer is attempted; unless you are prompt to cry stop, they will romp away and leave you puffing and angry behind. On this account the scholastic method of debate provides for pauses and repetitions. All fallacies tend to spread; they are like a spot of sulphuric acid splashed on a coat, to be got out at once.

---

[1] *de Fallaciis,* Ch. 16.

In the use of terms the most frequent fallacy is double-meaning, in the use of argument the undistributed middle, together with the fallacies of the irrevelant and the partial which are its reflections in the interpretation of evidence. Perhaps the majority of faulty arguments conform to the following type: the myths of other religions taught miraculous births and sacrificial deaths of saviours, and therefore the Christian mysteries must be equally mythical.

DISCIPLINE, said Mr. Midshipman Easy, is a matter between officer and officer, but manners is a matter between gentleman and gentleman. By illustrating the method of scholastic debate we hope to show how the amenities of rational intercourse were preserved despite the keen exchanges expected, and indeed demanded. Even cats lose their dignity when they debate, but here there is no occasion for Cowper's fear:

> Preserve me from the thing I dread and hate,
> A duel in the form of a debate.
> Vociferous logic kills me quite,
> A noisy man is always in the right.

A disputation is a social argument, a dialogue not a monologue, a talking with another, extroversive like justice, *ratiocinatio ad alterum*, a reasoning conducted between two persons, *opponens et respondens*, to expose the truth, *actus syllogisticus unius ad alterum ad aliquod propositum ostendendum*,[1] a conversation rather than a cross-examination. The scholastics refer to various kinds of disputation: a sophistical disputation, also called quarrelsome, *litigiosa*, competitive and contentious, which seeks victory and fame and will stoop to the unscrupulous means of hucstering and electioneering and sectarian polemics; a didactic disputation, *doctrinalis*, between teacher and pupil, working from the principles to the proper conclusions of a science, a piece of instruction whose course is set beforehand; and an exploratory and dialectical disputation, *tentativa et dialectica*, seeking the tranquillity of truth from the contrast of meanings.[2] We are concerned with the second and third.

Thomas More writes of Pico della Mirandola, perhaps the most celebrated disputant in history and who ends the ornate period of scholasticism, when debates were held with all the display of a tournament, and terms used were armoured, not with the

---

[1] Opusc. XLIII, *de Fallaciis*, Ch. 1.
[2] *Ibid.*, Ch. 2.

chain mail of the thirteenth century but with cumbersome plate, more suitable for jousting than for war; 'It was a common saying with him that such altercations were for a logician and not meetly for a philosopher. He said also that such disputations greatly profited as were exercised with a peaceable mind to the ensearching of the truth in secret company without great audience. But he said that those disputations did great hurt that were held openly to the ostentation of learning and to win the favour of the common people and the commendation of fools.'[1] A peaceable mind to the ensearching of truth; we must go back to the high middle ages for disputation at its best, such as will be found in the series of disputed questions, the *Quaestiones Disputatae* of St Thomas, which represent the systematic series of debates, *disputationes ordinariae*, held twice a week during the academic term as part of the curriculum. They often include two sets of objections arguing for opposite extremes. More solemn functions were held during Lent and Advent, and such debates on isolated subjects will be found in his *Quaestiones Quodlibetales*.[2] Ordinary disputations, or circles as they are called, still enter into the weekly programme of Dominican schools.

A rumbustious display of logic, a hard-hitting rough and tumble is all very well on occasions. Of course it is possible to go to St Thomas in the spirit of an excursion to Skegness, and return with a similar feeling of invigoration and rude mental health. Nevertheless the logic in the authentic tradition of the schools is a quieter affair altogether. It aimed at the discipline that produced the calm of the English line, so impressive to the advancing enemy. The enthusiasm is more restrained, the purpose of controversy is agreement and peace. Allowing for the vanity of the participants there is a deep seriousness at work, neither content to live and let live nor out to down every opponent. No doubt the sporting element of combating an opponent is often present, and doctrinal disputations are sometimes held as exercises for sharpening the wits, teaching the power of exposition, meeting objections, and rehearsing what is already known. To this extent they are so much window-dressing. But the dialectical disputation

---

[1] *The Life of John Picus Earl of Mirandula.*

[2] Thomas Gilby. *Introduction to On the Power of God*, the translation of the Disputations *de Potentia.* London 1932.

should seek agreement in contrasts, not by compromise, each side ceding a point, but by the active and co-operating opposition of truths, the pitting of contraries against one another, the clash of two to produce a *tertium quid* or a *tertium gaudens*. This is to take the highest view and to judge the entire sweep of the thomist philosophy as one great debate and one piece of team-work; the same grandeur and growth will not mark one given academic occasion. Yet a typical outline will show the practice of dialectic in the days when men were very confident in the power of the reason. Their temptation was not to be mousy, mawkish, or mystified, but on the contrary, to be bold, brisk and perhaps irreverent. The ghost of Abelard was never laid.

CHAPTER XXXII

FORMAL DEBATE

LET our subject be human freewill, here put forward in a series of exemplar syllogisms for its logical interest; the various arguments will be purposely kept as short as possible and this compression, together with the use of curt technical terms, will inevitably detract from its value as a piece of psychological interpretation. Yet the pattern of the dialectic will be made clear, a dialogue of contrasts developing like a classical concerto. It will be observed how the question is refined and refined again, subjected to a constant process of distinction. The method is economical despite the courtliness and repetition. There is freedom under the law. The movement is divided into periods, each syllogism marking a pause; the argument is not allowed to rush on out of hand; point by point is settled without vehemence; the effort is to trace the disagreement to its source. The different arguments are really all variations and developments of the same theme; the objector is not hunted from pillar to post. There is the same finish and skill as in the naval tactics of the eighteenth century, with both sides manoeuvring to obtain the weather gauge. Both sides, in other words, have their eye on the same object, keep to the same point, and talk the same language.

Two people are engaged at the start, the defender, *defendens*, of the thesis and his antagonist, the objector, *objiciens* or *arguens*. There are local variations in the accepted styles and figures, but in the main the debate proceeds along the following lines.

The defender begins:—

> The thesis to be defended to-day is this: that human acts are free.

He explains the terms of his thesis, defining what is meant by a human act and what by freedom, and then, after expounding at some length his main proof,[1] concludes:—

---

[1] He investigates the nature of the human will according to philosophical psychology and the mode of its response to certain objects: 'the heart is not suffi-

And this is enough at present to prove my thesis: however, should any difficulties remain perhaps they may be cleared up in the reply to the objections.

The objector replies courteously:—

Well said, sir—or if they are Dominicans, *optime frater*—all the same, the opposite is the case, *sed contra est*; human acts are not free, and therefore your thesis is false.

And the defender responds:—

Human acts are not free? In these terms my colleague has thought fit to gainsay my thesis. Will he kindly prove his statement?

The stage is now set, and the objector opens:—

I prove my statement: predetermined acts are not free—but, human acts are predetermined acts—therefore, human acts are not free.

The defender repeats the syllogism entire, to make sure that he has caught it correctly, and then takes it proposition by proposition:—

As for the major premiss—predetermined acts are not free—I distinguish, *distinguo*: predetermined by a secondary cause, I grant, *concedo*; by the first cause, I deny, *nego*:

As for the minor premiss—human acts are predetermined acts—I counterdistinguish, *contradistinguo*: by the first cause, I grant; by a secondary cause, I deny.

As for the conclusion—human acts are not free—I therefore deny it and that it follows, *nego consequens et consequentiam*, and will explain my distinction.

---

cient for a kite's dinner, yet the whole world is not sufficient for it': an irresistible attraction is exercised only when it is confronted immediately with complete and infinite goodness; in its present situation, in the face of incomplete and finite goods which it does not find compelling, there is within the will a certain suspense and indetermination, an inner poise and reluctance: he may here touch on the evidence of empirical psychology. Now if one of these goods is accepted, then we must look for a factor of self-determination within the human organism; physical determinants will be examined, and, after drawing a distinction between involuntary and non-deliberate acts on the one hand and voluntary and deliberate acts on the other, he analyses a typical example of the latter, and shows that liberty has its springs in the nature of intelligence, from which the will is a derivative faculty.

Let us pause here to observe what has happened. First of all, the objection has not been rejected out of hand; the defender has recognized its considerable force, and the elucidation of the distinction he has made will show that he is not shying away from the problem. Nevertheless he has driven a wedge into the argument that splits it apart by dividing the middle term, namely *predetermined acts*. The two premisses do not match one another in the sense in which they are true; the distinction, which is applied twice, a left and a right, convicts the argument of the fallacy of equivocation, for two meanings are discovered in one and the same term.[1]

In the second place, the distinction, which has been couched in general terms, has the merit of leaving the matter still open. The objector is free to press for a closer conclusion. The terms are brief but their explanation is not skimped. Much greater qualification would be required for a more complete statement of the position. Were the defender in a hurry to bring the debate to a close he would reply with what is known as a sub-distinction and he might, for instance, reply to the minor premiss:—

Human acts are predetermined—I distinguish: predetermined by the first cause, I grant; by secondary causes, I sub-distinguish; partially, I grant, totally, I deny.

---

[1] Counterdistinction, or contradistinction, signifies that the qualification accepted in the major premiss is denied in the minor premiss, and the qualification rejected in the major premiss is admitted in the minor premiss. The position may be made clearer by the following formulae: let M stand for middle term, P for major term, S for minor term. As in the first objection of the disputation, we have a first figure syllogism, which reads:—

M is P
S is M
therefore, S is P

It is counterdistinguished:—

$M(x)$ is P, yes: $M(y)$ is P, no:
S is $M(y)$ yes: S is $M(x)$, no:

and the argument is rejected on reduction to the form:—

$M(x)$ is P
S is $M(y)$

which is a four-term argument in which the conclusion is caught on the wrong foot.

Our defender, however, does not take this course; confident that necessary qualifications will emerge in the swirl of the subsequent discussion, he is content at this stage to show the difference between the action of the first cause and of secondary causes on the human will and to remove any impression that the former is compulsive.[1] It need hardly be said that metaphysical theology here has considerable difficulties; behind the bald distinction there is a fruitful field for discussion, *doctrina copiosa*, on the inalienable rights of the creature. But for the present discussion, the clearing away of difficulties arising from divine predestination is a great advantage. The defender, having explained his distinction and narrowed the question, concludes:—

Therefore, the objection fails, *ergo nulla difficultas.*

The objector has no intention of leaving the matter there, for he has scarcely begun. Two courses are open to him: either he can contest the distinction and keep the debate to more general issues, arguing that any predetermination is the death of freedom, in which case his objection will revolve round the treatment his major premiss has received; or he will keep the question to the psycho-

---

[1] The first cause is the author of all nature, all being, all activity, and moves all things from above the particular and creaturely categories. Consequently this premotion is congenial to the nature of the thing moved and offers it no violence. The first cause is not one kind of thing to make another kind of thing act according to an alien inclination: there is no compulsive force, as we understand the word, no imposition of one particular form of action on another form of action, the causality is as universal as the being and activity are pure, *actus purus.* (*Summa Theologica*, 1a: CV: 5.) Thus predetermination by the first cause is unlike predetermination by a secondary cause, which sets up a necessity. This may amount to a forced action, as when one kind of thing invades another and compels its action. (*Ibid.*, 1a: LXXXII: 1.) The resulting action may be against the proper inclination of the thing acted upon, as when animals are driven into the slaughter yard, or it may surpass the natural aptitude of the patient, as when marble is shaped into the figure of a goddess, or when mysterious forces make a servant girl in North London speak what is thought to be fluent Aramaic. The first cause as such, however, cannot be such an imposition, since it is already working at the springs of being; it cannot invade when already in possession, it cannot force where it preserves and fosters. (*Ibid.*, 1a: XIX: 8.) God has no victims. In brief, the distinction has drawn the line between the spontaneous or natural and the forced or violent. (*Ibid.*, 1a-2ae: VI: 4, 5. I *Contra Gentes*, 85.) Human acts belong to the former category, and their predetermination by the first cause does not destroy this character.

logy of human acts, in which case he will pick up the challenge to his minor premiss. Let us suppose that he takes this course; he therefore asserts what the defender has denied in his distinction:—

> But human acts are predetermined by secondary causes, and therefore, the difficulty remains.

To which the defender replies:—

> Human acts are predetermined by secondary causes? Please prove your minor premiss in its new form, *faveas probare minorem subsumptam* (i.e., your subsumed minor proposition, or your minor premiss under the treatment to which it has been subjected.)

And is met by the objector:—

> I will prove my minor premiss in its new form: Blind acts are predetermined by secondary causes—but, human acts are blind—therefore they are predetermined by secondary causes.

Theology has been left for psychology, predestination for the unconscious drives of the organism. Beneath the bare terms of the syllogism, the defender marks the strong line of thought; that when all is said and done, we act as we are and cannot help ourselves[1]; if you probe human acts to their root, behind the appearance of rational motives, you come to darkness; ultimately acts do not spring from reason; from what, therefore, but from some blind and greedy force? As before, he repeats the whole argument, and then takes it premiss by premiss:—

> As for the major premiss—blind acts are predetermined by secondary causes—I distinguish: totally blind acts, I concede; partially blind acts, I deny.
>
> As for the minor premiss—human acts are blind—I counterdistinguish in the same sense; are partially blind, I grant you; are totally blind, I deny.
>
> As for the conclusion—human acts are predetermined by secondary causes—I deny it therefore and that it follows and will explain my distinction.

Let us pause again. The actual words of a distinction are often little more than labels for the direction of the following explana-

---

[1] *Disputations*, VI *de Malo*, 1.

tion. Sometimes they are expressive in themselves, and recognized as such. Thus the distinction between foreground and background, between what is significant, special, to the point, and what is included, common, and coincidental. Most distinctions are variations of a few standard forms: materially and formally, *materialiter et formaliter*,[1] express the dualism of matter and form that by analogy runs throughout the system of St Thomas; this probably is the most frequently used of all distinctions: essentially and incidentally, *per se et per accidens*[2] runs it close; and with them we may group absolutely and relatively, totally and partially, *simpliciter et secundum quid*.[3] The etiquette of distinction affords a breathing space; it is a conventional way of finishing with the apparatus of the argument and of coming to the answer[4]; if it is treated as an end in itself, the scholastic system is made to appear a chaff-cutting machine.

But to return to our disputation on freewill. The distinction applied to the second formal objection is the occasion for an important delimitation of the field. It admits that the will is surrounded by necessity, but affirms that there is an element within its activity that cannot be explained by these surroundings.[5] As in the reply to the first objection, the defender has distinguished the middle term of the argument; that is the classical treatment for

---

[1] Disputations, *de Anima*, 2.

[2] *Summa Theologica*, 1a: XLIX: 1.   [3] *Ibid.*, 1a–2ae: LXVI: 3.

[4] There is a legend among the English Dominicans of one of their members engaged in a solemn disputation in a foreign college: faced with a cumbersome objection, he drew the genial distinction: *in sensu Pickwickiano, concedo*; *paraphanaliter, nego*. Nor did his opponent and the academic officials in front of him demur, but waited interestedly for his explanation of the terms of his distinction. History does not relate whether the objection was the last of the series, in which case the objector would have been spared the necessity of following it up.

[5] The thomist doctrine of freewill does not hold that a free act is so creative as to spring from nowhere; it is not a bolt from the blue; a declaration of complete autonomy. It is grounded in the natural and biological impulses of the organism fundamentally unconscious or blind; and it can be admitted without detriment to the limited doctrine of freewill that these urges are conditioned and even predetermined by environment, that is by secondary causes. (*Summa Theologica*, 1a: XIX: 10.) But against this necessary background and within these necessary drives, inborn and acquired, there still remains a patch where a psychological adult can make up his mind. Even in morbid cases, as when a man has an irresistible craving for drink let us say, we are still left to enquire why he chooses beer instead of brandy.

exposition. The objector, if he is to keep the debate to human acts, should then take up the minor premiss in its new form and seek to prove that human acts are totally blind. But for the sake of enlarging on the nature of freewill we will make our defender adopt the less symmetrical yet admissible design of distinguishing not the middle term, but the minor term, namely human acts. As Aristotle says, a science expands, not by the interposition of new middle terms, but by the apposition of fresh extreme terms.[1] Accordingly he will despatch the second objection as follows:—

As for the major premiss—blind acts are predetermined— I grant that, or, I let it pass, *transeat*.

As for the minor premiss—human acts are blind—I distinguish: human acts as natural desires, I admit; as elicited desires, I deny.

As for the conclusion—human acts are predetermined—I distinguish it in the same sense: as natural desires, I grant, as elicited desires, I deny.

And I will explain my distinction.

There is a technical distinction of moment: a natural desire, *appetitus naturalis*, lies behind every conscious desire, *appetitus elicitus*,[2] which is the immediate principle of a voluntary act, *voluntarium*.[3] It matters little whether the special elements of volun-

[1] *Posterior Analytics*, I: 12: 78a.
[2] *Summa Theologica*, 1a: LXXX: 1. 1a–2ae: VIII: 1. A natural desire or appetite is the blind tendency of a thing, substance and accidents included, to a goal; its natural gravitation, *pondus naturae*, in which, as such, there is no recognition of the operating purpose. It is the inclination of every potentiality to its proper actuality, more general and more profound than the articulations of intelligence; stone to fall, plant to light, animal instinct to the conservation of the individual and of the species. Such drives are present in every human act; we have an unconscious motion to the satisfaction of our needs, antecedent to deliberation and choice. Such appetites cannot be unwilled or fundamentally modified. But based on them there are specialized and conscious appetites, called elicited appetites, which operate through the knowledge of what we want.
[3] *Summa Theologica*, 1a–2ae: VI: 1, 2. Every natural motion, that is every activity from within, towards an object that is known, is termed a voluntary act, *voluntarium*. This consequently in its widest sense applies to operations from the sensitive appetite, in animals as well as in men, though in the strict and special sense reserved to acts that proceed from the will, since only then is there a recognition of purpose as such.

tariness are developed from within the stream of natural desires, or whether they are launched on it from elsewhere: the origins of the act may be necessitated by blind forces, but the precise direction and the special consciousness of choice remain to be accounted for.

The objector, however, still has plenty of fight; he takes up the distinction, and retorts with the third formal objection:—

Elicited desires are predetermined; and therefore the difficulty remains.[1]

And I will prove my conclusion in its new form: Responses to sense stimuli are predetermined—but, elicited desires are responses to sense stimuli—and therefore they are predetermined.

He has moved from the psychology of the unconscious to a mechanist and behaviorist doctrine which teaches, in brief, that given certain material factors the human organism will necessarily react in a certain way, with a reflex action that can be resolved in terms of muscles and nerves, and these in their turn can be reduced to the terms of physics and chemistry. Or the objector may not mean to give his argument such a thorough paced materialist meaning, but be content to affirm that sense objects emotionally coloured are sufficient determinants of the human act.

The defender, after repeating the syllogism, takes it step by step:—

With respect to the major premiss—responses to sense stimuli are predetermined—I let that pass, *transeat*.

He could contest it and, appealing to the psychological evidence of poise and indeterminacy present in animal actions, refuse to allow that sensation and emotions are reducible to the mechanics of the situation; but he has another distinction in mind, and one at a time is enough.

With respect to the minor premiss—elicited desires are

---

[1] For the sake of brevity we shall henceforward leave out the repetitions demanded by the etiquette of scholastic disputation, and also such terms that have served their purpose, though they remain implicit in the argument. In full form the objector should say: Human acts considered as elicited desires are predetermined by secondary causes. But to repeat all this would be unnecessarily redundant.

responses to sense stimuli—I distinguish: elicited sensitive desires, I concede; elicited rational desires, I deny.

With respect to the conclusion—elicited desires are pre-determined—I apply the same distinction.

The distinction has again limited the field of discussion. The psychological determinancy of sense reactions has been granted for purposes of argument, and the attention is fixed on the nature of the effect that follows rational perception. If there be freedom it is nowhere else but there.

Three formal objections were considered enough in ordinary debate. Let us press on, however, for the thesis demands more qualification and the objector is still primed. He could pick up the minor premiss and argue with some force that rational desires in fact are responses to sense stimuli. But let us suppose that he takes the modified conclusion, and, after the due exchanges, argues:—

The proper end predetermines an act—but, rational desire has a proper end, namely the Good—therefore it is pre-determined.

He has become more platonic and metaphysical and has left the efficient causes of human acts for the final cause, he has moved from impulsion to attraction. Such a shift of ground is allowable, though it lacks the compactness of keeping to the distinction of the middle term and arguing on the modified form of the minor premiss.

In reply, the defender will draw the distinction between the elements of wish and choice in human desire. To speak in general and ultimate terms, the will is not free to choose the end prefixed to its stirring; if it acts at all, then the desire for goodness and happiness is the necessary core of the motion.[1] By this relation-ship to the end, every act of the will contracts a streak of necessity. Here is the period of wishing and fundamental willing, *velle* and *volitio finis*. But what particular good will be accepted as embody-ing a share of this general goodness, and what means will be adopted? Here is the element of choice, *electio mediorum*.[2] Freedom is not the absolute power of making a universe, or indeed of con-

---

[1] *Summa Theologica*, 1a: LXXXII: 2. 1a–2ae: VIII: 1, 2, 3.
[2] *Ibid.*, 1a–2ae: XIII: 3.

ducting one individual life just as we fancy, but a capacity to recognize necessity and yet make up our own minds with respect to certain means that are but contingently related to the universal end. Were there no such means, in other words, were everything in our environment urgently involved with perfectly apprehended infinite goodness, the will would not be in a position to exercise its freedom. The defender explains that complete autonomy is no part of his thesis, which claims no more than that within the limits set by an imperfectly appreciated goodness, a man must come to his own decisions, since the world will not do this for him.

But, the objector urges, in a fifth formal objection:—

> The inevitable acceptance of the stronger of two alternatives is predetermined—but choice, in fact, is that inevitable acceptance of the stronger of two alternatives—and therefore it is predetermined.

The powerful doctrine of psychological determinism toughens the argument. Is it not true that when faced by two alternatives we invariably select the more attractive? Obviously this does not mean the more immediately pleasant, for there is much evidence against an easy-going hedonism; but when all is said and done, and allowing for altruism and the apparently disinterested performance of duty, are we really unlike Buridan's donkey, which always takes the nearest and juiciest carrot?

And now the defender comes to the heart of the debate, which hitherto, despite much useful exposition, has been largely a process of elimination. He agrees that there comes a moment when the very act of choice becomes necessitated, but insists that there still remains a previous period of uncertainty and balance, *indifferentia*. Yet before entering on the delicate analysis of the stages in the development of a typical human act[1] a preliminary distinction must be drawn. Granting, for the present, that choice will be of the stronger of two alternatives once the will is supposed to be in action, we may yet enquire, but is it bound to act at all? Accordingly the defender distinguishes the minor term of the argument, namely *choice*:—

---

[1] *Summa Theologica*, 1a-2ae: VIII–XVII. In these questions a human act is subjected to prolonged analysis, its parts isolated and separately examined. Twelve different periods are taken.

as implying the freedom to act or not to act; and
as implying the freedom to act in such a direction.

The former is called freedom *quantum ad exercitium actus*, freedom as regards the unloosing of the act, and is also known as the
libertas contradictionis, because the issue lies between acting or not
acting, which are contradictories; the latter is called freedom
quantum ad specificationem actus, freedom as regards the kind of act,
also known as the *libertas contrarietatis*, because the issue lies
between acting for this or for that object, which are supposed to
be contraries, such as roundabouts or swings.[1]

Human freedom is sufficiently demonstrated when it is proved
that the will can withhold activity in the initial stages of choice
and is not compelled by its immediate environment to choose at
all. This minimum of freedom is sufficient to prove the thesis; a
little is enough. Nevertheless, the defender will probably seek to
show the reasons for allowing more freedom than that: the subject
is psychological, he will say, and to be judged by psychological
phenomena and data, and here the impact of the consciousness of
freedom is at least as strong as the apprehension of necessity, and
therefore not legitimately to be suppressed; the banner of freedom,
'torn, but flying,' as in *Childe Harold*, 'streams like the thunder-
storm against the wind.' Let us suppose that the choice lies
between two courses of action: what, the defender will ask, makes
one of these contraries stronger than the other? He will grant that
at a certain moment the stronger will prevail; but what if the
mind and will together have contributed to make it the stronger?
He may go on to show that this is indeed the case, and that psychological determinism is truly a statement of what happens, but no
explanation of why it happens. The discussion has now engaged
the real point of the problem of human freedom though we cannot
prolong the analysis, but must return to the logical treatment of
the minor premiss of the fifth formal objection:—

> Choice is the acceptance of the stronger of two alternatives,
> I distinguish: choice, meaning liberty of contradiction, I deny;
> choice, meaning liberty of contrariness, I subdistinguish; the
> self-determined stronger, I grant, the predetermined stronger,
> I deny.

[1] *Summa Theologica*, 1a–2ae: X: 2. 1a–2ae: IX: 1.

Let us suppose that the objector now makes his final throw. Strictly speaking, he should now, in his sixth formal objection, attempt to prove that the liberty of contradiction is necessitated by factors outside the control of the will. But instead he contests the relevance of the distinction and affirms that it is of the essence of liberty to lie between two contrary alternatives. Perhaps with his tongue in his cheek he appeals to religious philosophy, employing an *argumentum ad hominem* calculated to touch other personal convictions:—

> Good and evil are contrary alternatives—but human freedom is essentially the power of choosing between right and wrong—and therefore it is essentially the power of choosing between contrary alternatives.

In reply, the defender will probably distinguish between freedom as a specific notion and as a coupled notion. To freedom as a specific notion the danger of choosing evil does not enter, and the nature of freewill can be considered without reference to morality, as in the case of God's creative acts[1]; considered as a coupled notion, that is as placed in a world where moral evil exists, it may be allowed that the power of doing wrong is implied. Freedom contracts this sense in homiletics and in an historical appreciation of the way we behave. It may be an essential note in a romantic philosophy of will, but it is incidental to the thomist conception. The conditions for freedom are found when the issue lies between acting or not acting, with no obligation either way: and granted that the will is going to act, then the alternatives may both be good, with no stigma attaching to that which, in the abstract, might be considered the lesser of the two. This is an important doctrine, not least for ascetical moral theory; to scrupulous consciences the best in the abstract can turn out in practice to be the enemy of the good. God himself is not bound to make the best of all possible worlds[2]; he is free, but he cannot sin: there are many moral choices for the human will which are not fraught with evil. That liberty is the antithesis of obedience may have been the persuasion at a period when the conventional patterns were inimical to the play of personality, and individual cases had to be protected against the codes.

---

[1] *Summa Theologica*, 1a: XIX: 2, 3, 5. [2] *Ibid.*, 1a: XXV: 6.

Chapter XXXIII
PARENTHESIS AND INFORMAL OBJECTIONS

THE formal debate need not be protracted; enough has been exposed of the tracery. It will have been noticed how the six formal objections are joined together, and how the successive distinctions serve to define the point at issue. Not until the fifth objection was the fundamental problem reached, but the opening rounds served to place the question in its proper setting. In a true dialectical debate, aiming at agreement, the attitude of the defender is expository rather than polemical; the manners are not those of a couple of wrangling pedants; the effect will be at least to prepare the ground for disciplined thought.[1]

---

[1] The successive operations that have cleared and determined the concept of human freedom may be set out in schematic form.

free act

	1st distinction
unforced and spontaneous act, called by the scholastics *libertas a coactione,* freedom from coercion; which includes all natural activity, and especially vital activity, all intrinsic drives, all motion from within, the *naturale,*	in contrast to the artificial and the violent, *artificiale et violentum*
	2nd distinction
conscious or voluntary act, motion from from within with knowledge of the object, the *voluntarium,* the act of the elicited appetite, *appetitus elicitus,* sometimes called the *appetitus animalis,*	in contrast to the unconscious cravings of the organism, the acts of the natural appetite, *appetitus naturalis.*
	3rd distinction
at the level of intelligence, or the act of the will, the appetite for a good proposed by the reason, *voluntas,* and *appetitus rationalis;*	at the level of sensation, such an act, though both spontaneous and through knowledge, is not sufficiently indifferent with regard to its immediate physical environment to be termed free; *appetitus sensitivus.*

The formal objections having been dealt with, the question is then thrown open to a more free and easy style of opposition and interrogation; all comers are welcome, after the appointed objector has produced three objections not in set form, *objectiones extra formam*. Closely knit arguments and finished syllogisms are not demanded,[1] a loping and ranging manner is encouraged, dialectical prudence can be thrown to the winds, and a keen and imaginative disputant will sometimes succeed in rattling a defender who has given a good account of himself in the formal debate. These concluding stages, then, are a release, not only of spirits, but also of evidence after what may have been the over-restraint of a punctilious logic. As we have noted several times already, the scholastics were not imprisoned in their methods: equity, which is the peak of justice, is unconventional,[2] and virtue is sometimes gamesome[3]; so also for the reason to have its fling is a condition of health.

To keep to the subject we have chosen for disputation, the objector will develop, perhaps at great length, three arguments against human freewill, not necessarily connected with one another. First, he may have a mind to invoke the so-called law of the conservation of energy: were our actions free, would this not mean that we would be able to produce more energy than is in the pool? Now this is a scientific scandal. Secondly, he might recast the same argument in more profound and philosophical terms by

	4th distinction
deliberate act or choice, *electio,* the mind and will are confronted with means to ends, particular goods which are not immediately bound up with immediately and completely apprehended necessary good, and therefore do not evoke an inevitable response; *liberum arbitrium* and *actus humanus,* sometimes called *boulesis*;	non-deliberate act of the will preceding choice, volition of the end, the necessary object of will, *velle* and *volitio finis,* sometimes called *voluntas* and *thelesis.*

	5th distinction
indifference as regards acting or not acting, *quoad exercitium,* or *libertas contradictionis*;	as regards acting for this or that object, *quoad specificationem,* or *libertas contrarietatis.*

good or good	right or wrong

[1] *de Fallaciis,* Ch. 1.
[2] *Summa Theologica,* 2a–2ae: CXX: 2.
[3] *Ibid.,* 2a–2ae: CLXVIII: 4.

objecting that the doctrine of freewill entails the cosmic irresponsibility of positing actions without a sufficient reason; for after pondering one is obliged to say that a sufficient reason is a necessary reason, which a free act, supposedly indeterminate in its cause, must lack. Thirdly, he may go to medical psychology and show that a man is a mass of compulsions, and not least when he thinks he is acting with civilized deliberation.

The defender should know the art of seizing the salient point, and disentangling the middle term. Then having answered the difficulties, and the questions that may be addressed to him, he comes to a stop. He receives the criticisms of his masters and steps down from the rostrum, with no more modesty and relief than the writer feels in finishing this book.

INDEX

CUM APPROBATIONE SUPERIORUM

NIHIL OBSTAT:
Canon G. D. Smith, S.Th.D., Ph.D.
Censor deputatus.

IMPRIMATUR:
E. Morrogh Bernard
Vic. Gen.

Westmonasterii,
die 21a Junii, 1948.